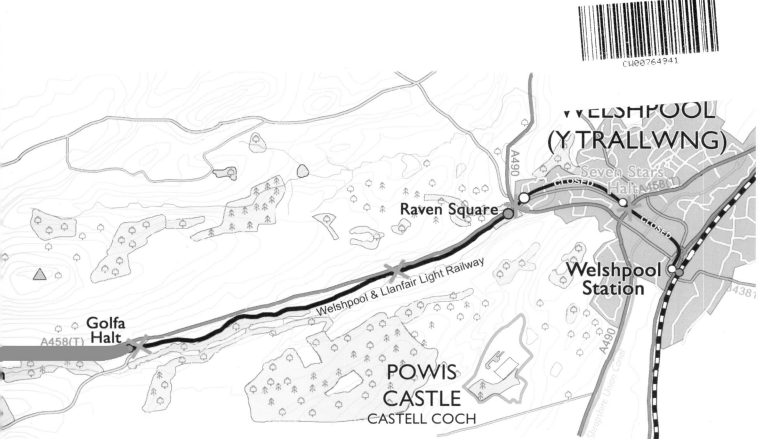

WELSHPOOL (Y TRALLWNG)

Seven Stars Halt *CLOSED*

Raven Square

Welshpool Station

Welshpool & Llanfair Light Railway

Golfa Halt

A458(T)

POWIS CASTLE
CASTELL COCH

Shropshire Union Canal

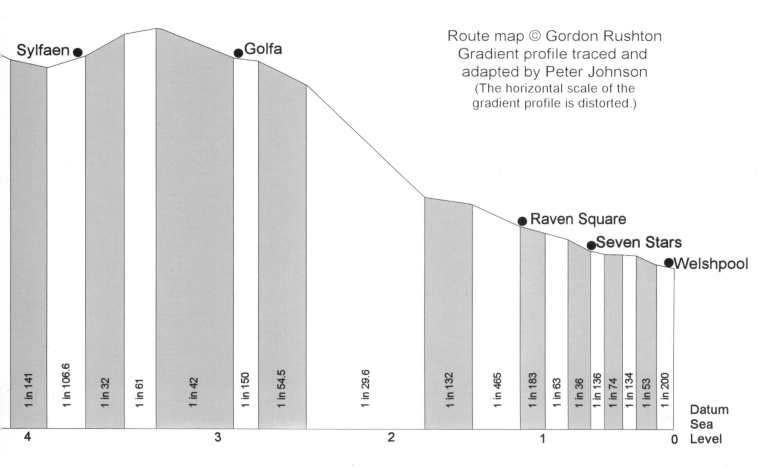

Route map © Gordon Rushton
Gradient profile traced and
adapted by Peter Johnson
(The horizontal scale of the
gradient profile is distorted.)

Sylfaen   Golfa

Raven Square

Seven Stars

Welshpool

| 1 in 141 | 1 in 106.6 | 1 in 32 | 1 in 61 | 1 in 42 | 1 in 150 | 1 in 54.5 | 1 in 29.6 | 1 in 132 | 1 in 465 | 1 in 183 | 1 in 63 | 1 in 36 | 1 in 136 | 1 in 74 | 1 in 134 | 1 in 53 | 1 in 200 |

Datum Sea Level

4   3   2   1   0

THE WELSHPOOL & LLANFAIR LIGHT RAILWAY
THE STORY OF A WELSH RURAL BYWAY

Front Cover: The first of the Welshpool & Llanfair Light Railway's original Beyer, Peacock locomotives, 0-6-0T *The Earl*, with a train of Hungarian and Austrian carriages at Heniarth.

Half-title page: The restoration of regular services to Welshpool on 16 May 1982 was a proud day for the preservation company. Hunslet 2-6-2T No 85 and Kerr, Stuart 0-4-2T *Joan* hauled the train. (J.W.T. House)

Title Page: Beyer, Peacock 0-6-0T *Countess* climbs the Golfa bank with the train of recreated Pickering carriages in 2017.

Endpapers: Map by Gordon Rushton

THE WELSHPOOL &
LLANFAIR LIGHT RAILWAY

THE STORY OF A WELSH RURAL BYWAY

PETER JOHNSON

PEN & SWORD
TRANSPORT

AN IMPRINT OF PEN & SWORD BOOKS LTD.
YORKSHIRE – PHILADELPHIA

Crown copyright is reserved for illustrations sourced from the National Archives, the Parliamentary Archives, and the Ordnance Survey.

Welsh place names

Apart from Welshpool, the communities served by the light railway did not suffer from the imposition of English versions of their names. The Earls of Powis, and their castle, retain the archaic form of their name, whereas the present administrative county of Powys is spelled thus.

First published in Great Britain in 2020 by
Pen and Sword Transport
An imprint of
Pen & Sword Books Ltd
Yorkshire - Philadelphia

Copyright © Peter Johnson, 2020

ISBN 978 1 52674 477 7

The right of Peter Johnson to be identified as Author of this work has been asserted by him in accordance with the Copyright, Designs and Patents Act 1988.

A CIP catalogue record for this book is available from the British Library.

Typeset in Palatino 11/13 by Aura Technology and Software Services, India

Printed and bound in India by Replika Press Pvt. Ltd.

Pen & Sword Books Ltd incorporates the Imprints of Pen & Sword Books Archaeology, Atlas, Aviation, Battleground, Discovery, Family History, History, Maritime, Military, Naval, Politics, Railways, Select, Transport, True Crime, Fiction, Frontline Books, Leo Cooper, Praetorian Press, Seaforth Publishing, Wharncliffe and White Owl.

For a complete list of Pen & Sword titles please contact

PEN & SWORD BOOKS LIMITED
47 Church Street, Barnsley, South Yorkshire, S70 2AS, England
E-mail: enquiries@pen-and-sword.co.uk
Website: www.pen-and-sword.co.uk

or

PEN AND SWORD BOOKS
1950 Lawrence Rd, Havertown, PA 19083, USA
E-mail: Uspen-and-sword@casematepublishers.com
Website: www.penandswordbooks.com

CONTENTS

INTRODUCTION

On 2 June 2019 the *London Gazette* announced that the Welshpool & Llanfair Light Railway had been honoured with the Queen's Award for Voluntary Service.

Although the citation stated that the award was for 'Operating an eight-mile steam railway to demonstrate how it served its rural Mid-Wales community from Edwardian times,' it also brought home the scale of the achievement since 1962, when the Welshpool & Llanfair Light Railway Preservation Company took over a neglected railway from British Railways and with minimal resources, grit and determination, overcame numerous obstacles to become one of the leading tourist attractions in the former county of Montgomery in northern Powys.

The railway is unusual among Welsh narrow-gauge lines in having been built to serve agriculture rather than mineral extraction. And while its route westwards out of Welshpool has features as challenging as any of its contemporaries, its location in lush agricultural scenery lacks their impact. Its significance as a narrow-gauge light railway, the first built using powers awarded by the 1896 Light Railways Act, is often overlooked.

Since the 1860s several attempts had been made to secure rail communication between Welshpool and its outlier, Llanfair Caereinion, nine miles away but the Treasury and local authority grants and loans enabled by the 1896 Act were essential to overcome the difficulty of securing sufficient funding.

With finance from these sources and a small contribution from shareholders, it never fulfilled its promoters' ambitions regarding profits and payments of dividends and interest but, remarkably perhaps, the investors never turned against it or threatened to close it down.

There was enough business for the railway to pay its way, just, but nothing to spare. Rules imposed to secure the Treasury's support calling for the railway to be operated by an existing company, the Cambrian Railways in this case, in order to contain operating costs meant that there was no one on the ground to promote the railway's cause and find new business.

The grouping saw both the Cambrian and the railway absorbed into the Great Western Railway, which maintained narrow gauge services to the agricultural community after it withdrew passenger services in 1930.

Operation of a narrow-gauge steam railway running a goods-only service by the nationalised British Railways from 1948, and the increased availability of motor transport, attracted the attention of enthusiasts keen to photograph the line. There was even a fare, 2s 6d, for a ride in the brake van. Several excursions run for enthusiast societies with passengers travelling in open wagons proved popular.

However, talk of closure was in the air and it was clear that this anomaly in the national rail network did not have much time left, encouraging enthusiasts to explore means of taking it over to run with volunteer support, following the examples of the Talyllyn and Festiniog Railways further north. No plans had been put in place before the last train ran in November 1956.

In the face of opposition from the town council regarding continued use of the route through the town and the highways authority concerning the Raven Square level crossing, terms for taking over the line between Raven Square and Llanfair Caereinion by a volunteer-supported company were not agreed until 1962, operation under new management being launched on the 60th anniversary of the railway's opening to passengers in 1963.

Development from nascent heritage railway to leading tourist attraction status has not been easy. The Banwy river bridge sustained serious damage soon after services were started. Funding was limited and facilities were minimal but eventually the business grew and became sustainable.

Additional locomotives and carriages obtained from overseas gave the line a distinctive character. The mortgage for the railway's purchase was redeemed and services to Welshpool resumed, albeit only as far as Raven Square. Gradually the railway developed all the facilities that

it needed, and needs, as a self-contained tourist railway.

The railway's centenary in 2003 was celebrated with panache, accompanied by a lottery-supported development that included reboilering the two original locomotives. With an eye on its heritage, members were generous in their support of the creation of a vintage train that saw replicas of the original passenger carriages constructed.

In its twenty-first century guise as a heritage railway attracting tourists to Montgomeryshire the Welshpool & Llanfair Light Railway is repaying the confidence of its nineteenth century promoters and the local authorities, not forgetting the Treasury, that invested in its construction.

Countess stands at Llanfair on 14 September 2019, when the Queen's Award for Voluntary Service was presented to the railway.

ACKNOWLEDGMENTS

This book has its origins in the chapter about the railway published in *An Illustrated History of the Great Western Narrow Gauge* (Oxford Publishing, 2011), now out of print, which was based on the files of the Board of Trade, the Light Railway Commissioners, the Ministry of Transport, the British Transport Commission, the original Welshpool & Llanfair Light Railway, the Cambrian Railways and the Great Western Railway held at the National Archives, Kew. This has been greatly expanded by the addition of material

The ceremonial spade and wheelbarrow presented to Lord Clive at the 1st sod ceremony on 30 May 1902 is displayed in Welshpool's Powysland Museum.

extracted from newspapers digitised at the National Library of Wales, Welsh Newspapers Online (newspapers.library.wales), the British Newspaper Archive (britishnewspaperarchive.co.uk) and the digital archives of the *Times* and the *Guardian*. I also referred to the Cambrian Railways' directors' minutes and officers' reports to the board, a file created by the Ministry of Transport's Cardiff-based divisional road engineer and one dealing with the 1963 light railway order, all held at the National Archives. Various newsletters and journals published by the preservation company have been useful too. Genealogical material was obtained from ancestry.co.uk.

Michael Bishop, Ralph Cartwright, John Scott Morgan and Dave Waldren (Cutting Edge Images) kindly contributed photographs from their collections. Unfortunately the identities of many of the photographers are unknown, but their names are given where possible. Unattributed photographs were either taken by me or are from my collection. Some images have been chosen for their historic interest. Crown Copyright is reserved in images derived from Ordnance Survey mapping.

Many thanks once more to my friend Gordon Rushton for providing the map reproduced on the endpapers.

I have visited the railway many times over the years and have always appreciated the warm welcome I received from its staff, employees and volunteers, which has often included coffee and cake. My thanks to all.

Responsibility for any errors or omissions remain with me.

Peter Johnson
Leicester
January 2020

CHAPTER 1

THE FIRST PROPOSALS

Located to the north of a line across the centre of Wales, on the border with England, the former county of Montgomery acted as a gateway into Mid-Wales. Development of transport links was hampered by mountains rising to 2,730ft, Cadair Berwyn, although the Severn and Vrnwy valleys to the east are particularly fertile.

The Montgomeryshire Canal reached Welshpool, the county's second largest town, from Llanymynech in 1796 and was extended to Garthmyl in 1797 and to Newtown, the largest town, in 1819. The first railway, the Oswestry & Newtown, was opened to Welshpool in 1860 and extended to Newtown in 1861. In 1864 the ONR became a constituent of the Cambrian Railways.

Until 1889 local government affairs were managed by unions controlled by the landed gentry. Welshpool was in the Forden Union and Llanfair Caereinion in the Llanfyllin, the border between them passing close to Castle Caereinion. County-wide administration was passed to the newly formed county council, with an increased electorate and based in Welshpool, in 1889, local affairs being handled by urban and rural district councils. Local government reorganisation saw the county absorbed into the new county of Powys and the urban and rural councils amalgamated into larger district councils in 1974.

Nine miles from the market town of Welshpool, Llanfair Caereinion is a village at the centre of a rural agricultural community that grew around the junctions of the local road network and a crossing of the Afon Banwy, which by a somewhat circuitous route is a tributary of the Afon Vrynwy and then the Severn. It is around 400ft above sea level, surrounded by hills rising to 1,141ft at Rhos Fawr to the south east, but more usually around 600ft. A fire in the eighteenth century destroyed the half-timbered houses in the centre of the village. The name is usually shortened to Llanfair.

Agriculture was the mainstay of economic activity in the locality yet, despite maintaining a static population in 1841 and 1851, labourers leaving in search of work thereafter saw the parish decline to 1,839 by 1901. A hundred years later, the population was 200 fewer. Life was obviously hard for some of those who stayed behind. In December 1900, the *Border Counties Advertiser* reported that Mrs Howell of Craigydon, Aberdovey, had sent parcels of winter clothing for distribution amongst the parish's poor.

Originally known simply as Pool, Y Trawllwng in Welsh, Welshpool developed from the twelfth century, located at a point around 300ft above sea level, close to the western bank of the navigable River Severn and some four miles from the English border. The pool refers to a lake on the Powis estate, close to but out of sight of the present railway, at Glyn Golfa, its dark appearance causing it to be named Llyn Dû, black lake or pool.

The General Post Office instigated the town's change of name in 1835, to distinguish it from Poole in Dorset. Sometimes rendered Welch Pool, the town was still referred to as Pool by some into the twentieth century.

Its economy was typical of that required to sustain the town and its surrounding locality. The only manufactory was flannel, with six makers listed in an 1858 directory. To the west of the town the Powis estate was the largest and most influential landowner; the area became known as Powysland. To

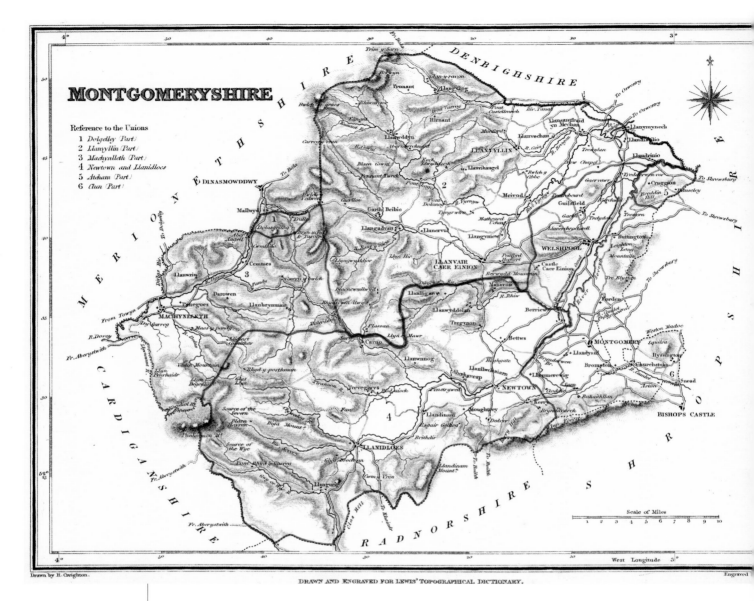

Montgomeryshire showing the union boundaries in 1833. (R. Creighton/Lewis' Topographical Dictionary)

the southeast, the broad Severn Valley is ideally suited to agriculture. Elsewhere farming life is harder, with ground reaching around 600ft above sea level to the northwest with Y Golfa dominant at 1,118ft two miles to the west. Until 1881, Welshpool parish was expanding, with its population peaking at 4,988. Decline into the twentieth century was eventually countered by revival and expansion, the population reaching 6,269 by 2001.

Like the village, the town also developed around a road network, with two routes from England meeting others from the west and the hinterland. As noted, transportation was improved by

the arrival of the canal in 1797 and the railway in 1860. By 1864 it was possible to take a train from Welshpool eastwards to Shrewsbury and westwards to Aberystwyth.

Welshpool's first railway had been built to serve the canal, delivering stone from the Stondart (or Standard) quarry on the north-western edge of the town. The railway, which is little documented, followed the present Brook Street, crossing Church Street to reach the canal, the last section appropriated by the light railway in due course. It appears to have been built around 1818 and had been abandoned by 1854. Excavations for a water main in 1939

VIEW IN GLYN GOLFA, GOLFA STATION, WELSHPOOL

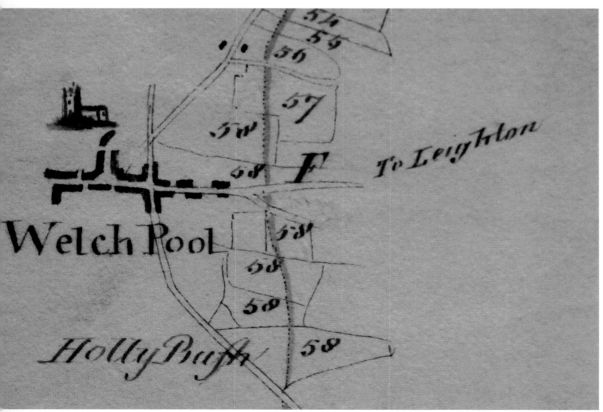

Looking towards Welshpool, Glyn Golfa showing the railway soon after it was built, Llyn Dû, the black pool below giving Welshpool its name. In the 1870s the town council had adopted the pool as the town's water supply and in 1893 enlarged the facility by damming the valley at its eastern end. (Dainty Series)

The extent of Welshpool in 1824, from the deposited plan for the Newtown Canal. (Parliamentary Archives)

The toll house on the Llanfair road, just outside Welshpool. Cadw, the Welsh Heritage agency, gave the building a Grade II listing in 1981. The railway runs to the left of the fence on the left of the picture. The road was reckoned to be the most expensive to maintain in Montgomeryshire.

uncovered a section of railway in situ two feet below the then current road level but the excavation was too small to determine the gauge. Stone sleepers and iron rails and chairs were recovered however, and deposited with museums.

In the nineteenth century, the road between town and village was a poorly maintained turnpike. By no means direct, it was two miles longer than a line drawn between them, and costly to maintain; it was said to be the most expensive road in the county. The way to obtaining a railway to unite them turned out to be as rocky as the road.

There were no less than four attempts to obtain a railway between Welshpool and Llanfair, a process that took some forty years. There were also three attempts to make a railway to Llanfair via the Meifod valley.

The first Welshpool/Llanfair scheme originated in Llanfair in June 1862, no doubt inspired by seeing the benefits brought by the Oswestry & Newtown

Railway, which passed to the south, as well as the poor state of the main road. The *Shrewsbury Chronicle* (6 June 1862) reported a meeting of 'several influential and respectable gentlemen' held 'during the week' which resolved to hold a public meeting about a railway.

That meeting was held on 27 June, when those gathered were presented with a 'rough survey' made by Messrs Piercy. Working with his brother Robert, Benjamin Piercy was not only the Oswestry & Newtown Railway's engineer but that of most of the constituents of the Cambrian Railways. The Llanfair survey had already been submitted to the 3rd Earl of Powis, who had objected to its routing through the 'Blackpool dingle', saying that it would destroy one of the most beautiful parts of his park. The meeting therefore resolved to ask Piercy to amend the route. A deputation would meet his lordship when he had done so.

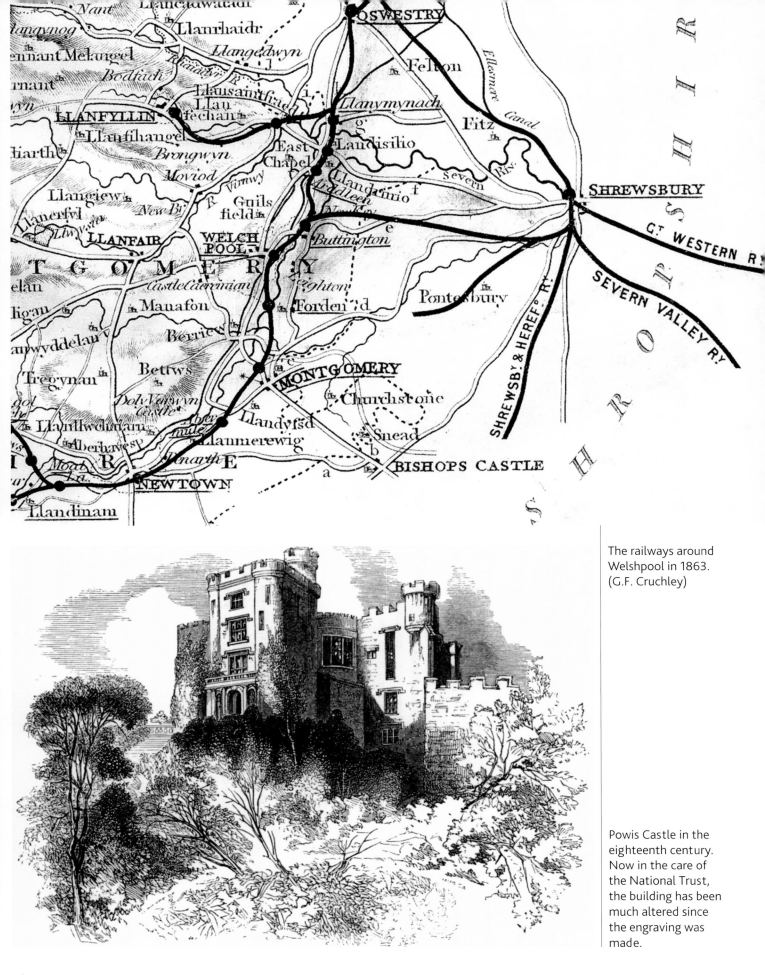

The railways around Welshpool in 1863. (G.F. Cruchley)

Powis Castle in the eighteenth century. Now in the care of the National Trust, the building has been much altered since the engraving was made.

Abraham Howell, the solicitor, was mayor of Welshpool in 1862.

Three weeks later an auctioneer promoting the sale of a farm at Llangadfan described it as being 'within a convenient distance of the turnpike-road from Welshpool to Aberystwyth, and is distant seven miles from Llanfair, to which place a railway is projected,' optimism which turned out to be unfounded.

The promoters met again, at the Goat Inn, Llanfair, on 29 August 1862. The deputation had met the earl and he had approved the route from Welshpool via Trefnant, Castle Caereinion and Brynhelan, entering Llanfair on the town side of the river Banwy, although it was 1½ miles longer. The meeting looked for guidance from Abraham Howell, mayor of Welshpool, a solicitor with railway experience; he had worked on the promotion of the Oswestry & Newtown Railway and the other associated lines.

He said that in his experience railways connecting small towns with almost barren country between paid the best, as did those with poor prospects, because they were well and economically managed. The survey made by Messrs Piercy, without charge, would cost little to build. The line was ten miles two chains long. There was an embankment with easy gradients five furlongs long at Welshpool to carry the line over the road and the canal, a steeper embankment near Dysserth, to the south of Powis Castle, and only 'trifling' obstructions beyond Dolarddyn; that these would include a gully that eventually required a three-arch viaduct escaped his audience.

At a third meeting on 26 August its chairman, Enoch Pugh, the vicar of Llanfair, said that the railway would be achieved for the benefit of shopkeepers, farmers and others by adopting the proverb 'God helps those who help themselves.' He had been at Aberdyfi and Tywyn and seen the railway under construction there. In comparison the Llanfair railway would be easy to build. Llanfair was growing, he said, five or seven houses had been built in the past twelve months.

The Piercys were otherwise engaged but Howell had the confidence to say that the line would need £50,000 capital to build. A Major Williams did not attract any support for the notion that the railway would be better routed to Newtown rather than Welshpool. Ultimately it was agreed that a committee should consult with landowners to get their agreement.

Presumably this was done but no reports of activities relating to the proposal can be found during 1863 and 1864, then on 25 November 1864 notice of intent to deposit a bill for the Llanfair Railway was published in the *London Gazette*.

The route was described as starting from a junction with the Cambrian Railways, three furlongs southwest of the Cambrian Railways' Welshpool station, following a route close to the unclassified road, passing Powis Castle and turning towards Castle Caereinion near Trefnant Hall. Passing to the east and north of Castle Caereinion it picked up the route of the later railway at Dolarddyn, but instead of crossing the Banwy it kept to the south of the river to

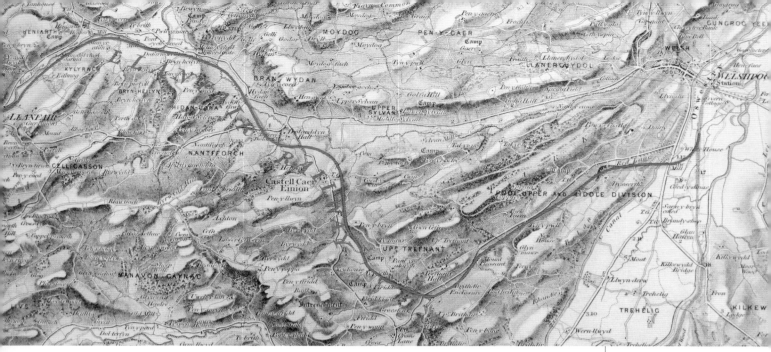

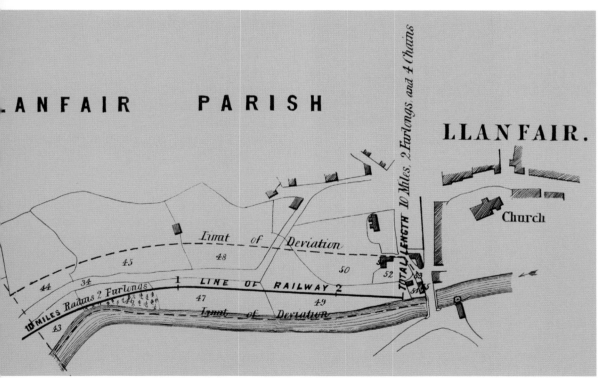

terminate near the Llanfair bridge, 10¼ miles distance. The alignment was almost on a continuous gradient towards Llanfair Caereinion, the easiest gradients where it diverged from the Cambrian, 1 in 256, and two short level sections. The engineer was George Owen, working with Charles Mickleburgh, Montgomery land agent and surveyor.

Born in Tunbridge Wells in 1829, Owen played a significant role in the development of Welsh railways and became the Cambrian Railways' engineer. Like Benjamin Piercy, he had been apprenticed to Mickleburgh and each had married one of his daughters.

The railway's gauge was not mentioned in the Parliamentary papers, nor at any of the meetings held in 1862, but at a meeting held in Llanfair on 31 December 1865 the chairman, Pugh again, explained that while he and the promoters were in favour of the 'ordinary gauge' it was feared that a line so constructed would not pay so it had been

George Owen, the Llanfair Railway's engineer. As the Cambrian Railways' engineer he was involved in the early stages of planning the light railway.

decided to adopt the narrower gauge of 2ft 3ins, as used on the Corris Railway and adopted by the Talyllyn Railway, although he did not say that. The estimated cost of such a line was £30,000, half the amount of a similar standard gauge line.

He continued that it had been estimated that the traffic of the line from Llanfair to Welshpool would be 25,000 tons, at 1d. per ton per mile, and that the passenger traffic would amount in the year to 16,800 persons, at 2d. per mile, which would give a return of something like £3,500 per annum, or £7 per mile per week. Less would not pay. Five per cent on £35,000 capital would cover all expenditure, including the rolling stock. Notwithstanding the disadvantages of the narrower gauge, they had to consider whether it would not be better to have it than to have no railway at all. Should the line be found to justify additional expenditure at any future time, it could be easily converted into the broader gauge.

Howell explained that he had consulted with the contractor David Davies, whose estimates for various railway projects he had found to be extremely accurate, over the costs of the Llanfair proposal. He calculated at £33,000, including rolling stock, would be sufficient. He, Howell, had a copy of Captain H.W. Tyler's, the government railway inspector's, report on the safety of narrow gauge railways as related to the Festiniog Railway, which had started carrying passengers the year before.

Robert Davies Pryce, of Cyfronydd, described the likely economic impact of a railway. Carriage of coal from Welshpool cost 5s 6d to 6s per ton. The best price he could get for haulage in connection with his new house was 5s per ton. A railway would charge about 1d per ton per mile, less than 1s in total. Pryce owned the Braich Goch slate quarry in Corris and had objected to the Corris Railway carrying passengers, claiming that slate traffic should be the railway's priority. A director of the Cambrian Railways from 1864 until his death in 1891, he was chairman from 1884 until 1886. On 1 January 1883 he was a passenger on the train that ran into a landslip at Friog, killing its driver and fireman when the locomotive fell down the cliff.

The reason for abandoning the proposal is unknown but the Shrewsbury & North Wales Railway stepped into the gap with an application for what it called the Meifod Valley Extension Railway, a standard gauge line from a junction with the Potteries, Shrewsbury & North Wales Railway near Llanymynech to Llanfair, promoted in December 1865. Such a line would have given access to Oswestry and its market, but it failed during the Parliamentary process.

The prospect of a railway to Llanfair was revived in 1872, a meeting held in the Cross Foxes Inn at Llanfair on 26 October favouring another route via the Meifod valley that connected with the Cambrian Railways at Four Crosses. The one speaker who supported a route to Welshpool did not get much of a hearing and 'abruptly resumed his seat.' R.D. Pryce, who chaired the meeting, said that the previous proposal was dormant.

George Owen spoke on the subject of the gauge. He had attended the Fairlie

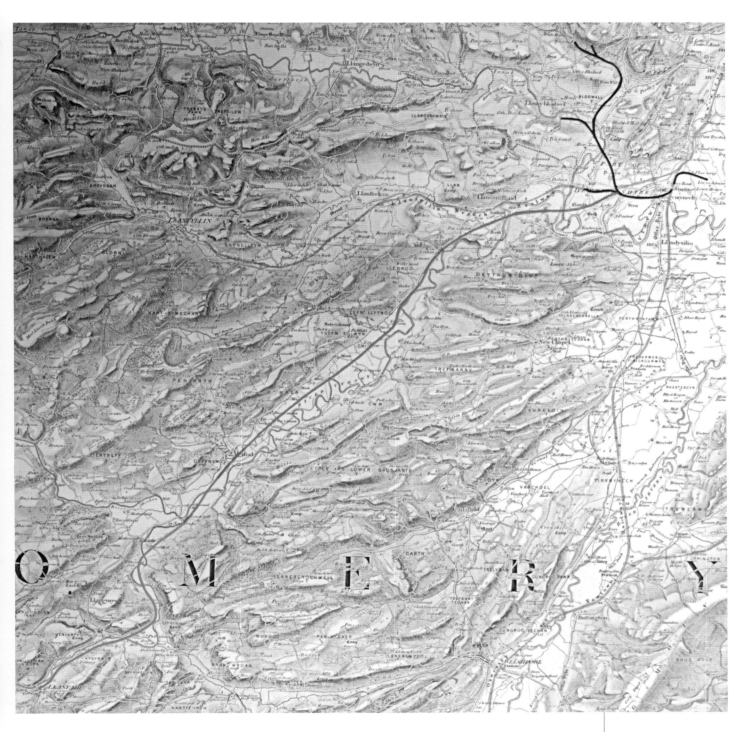

locomotive trials on the Festiniog Railway in 1870 and recommended a ride in the 'boat' carriage to remove any doubts about the safety of narrow gauge, although he preferred 2ft 3in or 2ft 6in to the FR's 2ft if narrow gauge was to be adopted.

On 30 November another meeting considered the option of connecting with the Cambrian at Llansantffraid to avoid the cost of bridging the canal and the main road at Four Crosses. The objection to this option was that the junction would face Welshpool, preventing the operation of through trains from Oswestry. R.D. Pryce, the chairman, also told the meeting that standard gauge would be preferable to narrow gauge

The deposited plan for the Shrewsbury & North Wales Railway's proposed Meifod Valley extension railway to Llanfair, 1866. (Parliamentary Archives)

because the railway company would have to buy the rolling stock if the latter was adopted, whereas standard gauge stock could be hired from the Cambrian Railways.

Nevertheless, the meeting supported the concept of a railway while leaving the question of its junction and gauge open to the directors to decide when the level of financial support had been determined. After another meeting, on 27 May 1873, this scheme also went into limbo with nothing more said about it.

Work on the second scheme for a railway to Welshpool started on 24 November 1874, when a meeting was held at the Cann Office Hotel. The *Cambrian News* report (27 November 1874) was headlined 'Welshpool & Llanfair Railway'. Although the list of those attending is quite short, they do seem to be different from those who led the previous schemes.

The initiative appears to have been taken by a George Slater, a land agent from Northwich, Cheshire, who owned property in Llanfair. He had attended the meeting on 26 October 1872 and had been one of fifty appointed to the provisional committee. This was not the first railway that he had been involved with, for he had been active in the promotion of, and a director of, the Cheshire Midland Railway, which ran between Altrincham and Northwich, 12½ miles. Opened in 1862/3 and absorbed into the Cheshire Lines Committee's group of railways in 1867, Slater had contributed to its Parliamentary deposit and had been a director.

He said that he hoped the Welsh would take a leading role in the construction of the railway and that Englishmen like himself, with property on both sides of the border, were prepared to help. He forecast that Welshpool to Llanfair would only be the first stage and that the railway would eventually be extended to Dinas Mawddwy. Sixty letters seeking support had attracted fifty promises in favour and offers of £10,000 to invest in the proposed £40,000 capital. He ended his speech with doggerel verse that incorporated the names of all the pubs in Llanfair, saying there was plenty of accommodation for railway users.

A brief comment in the *Wrexham & Denbighshire Advertiser* (5 December 1874) said that the scheme was being promoted by an 'influential committee' of fifteen landowners. Slater led several meetings during 1875, continuing to obtain commitments to subscribe for shares. Undertaking to defray the preliminary expenses himself, no survey would be commissioned until it was established that the railway could be funded.

The provisional committee was chaired by R.D. Pryce, who led a deputation to see the Earl of Powis on 9 September 1875, securing the promise of a £4,000 investment.

Added to existing promises of £16,000 from around Llanfair it was time to see what support there was in Welshpool.

A meeting held at the town hall on 4 October 1875 was chaired by Abraham Howell, who urged support. If a railway from Llanfair did not come to Welshpool, he said, the town would suffer.

At some point the promoters decided that the costs of promoting an Act of Parliament could be avoided if they were able to secure the landowners' agreement for the purchase of their property and established a limited liability company to build and operate the railway, a strategy that had been used by the Festiniog & Blaenau Railway in 1868 and the Van Railway in 1871. Accordingly, articles of association were produced and presented to a meeting at the Cross Foxes Inn, Llanfair, on 28 January 1876.

Slater described how he had written to three railway companies to see if any of them would be willing to work the line when built but none of them had made a firm commitment. The Cambrian directors had resolved, on 29 October 1875, to tell him that they received the proposal favourably and promised to give every assistance. The others were the Great Western Railway and the London & North Western Railway.

The chairman, Edwin Hilton, a retired Manchester silk merchant and a director of the Manchester & County Bank who owned Glynhiriaeth, a property 1½ miles from the centre of Llanfair, suggested that they might get a better response when the company was registered and shares allotted, Slater replied that as they stood he could not sign the articles, unhappy that they appeared to give those who had agreed to take shares the option of withdrawing, negating the effort he had put in to obtaining their support.

Slater also proposed that as there were landowners who objected to the railway and whose property could not be avoided, the idea of registering a limited liability company could be abandoned in favour of promoting a special Act of Parliament.

As is often the way of these things, a committee was appointed. On 19 February the *Wrexham & Denbighshire Advertiser* declared, 'The Welshpool and Llanfair Railway scheme is likely to fall through.'

The paper's scepticism was initially misplaced, the *London Gazette* published on 26 November 1876 containing an advertisement announcing the intent to deposit a Bill for the Welshpool & Llanfair Railway. No reports concerning the railway have been found in the period February-November 1876.

The route was quite similar to that of the 1864 proposal but with a separate line parallel to the Cambrian, as well as a junction, and its own terminus at Welshpool, passing to the west of Castle Caereinion, and on the approach to Llanfair Caereinion crossing the river to terminate in the field to be used by the light railway for that purpose, 400 yards from Llanfair bridge. The road by the Llanfair Caereinion terminus was intended to be diverted in what appears to be a quite unnecessary manner. The total length was just short of 10½ miles. The gradients were easier than on the 1864 scheme, with several level sections, but the steepest was still 1 in 41 near Powis Castle. The engineers were Powell & Swettenham of Newtown.

The Welshpool & Llanfair Railway's 1877 route. The detached section is the coach road from Pontsycoed to Mathrafal that the railway also sought powers to build. (Parliamentary Archives)

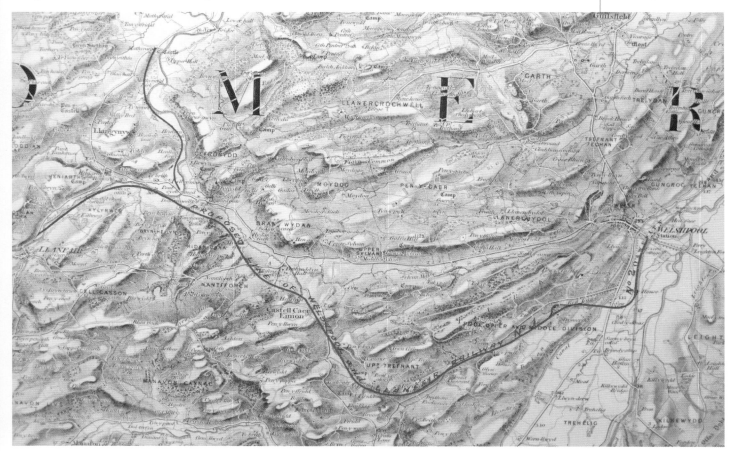

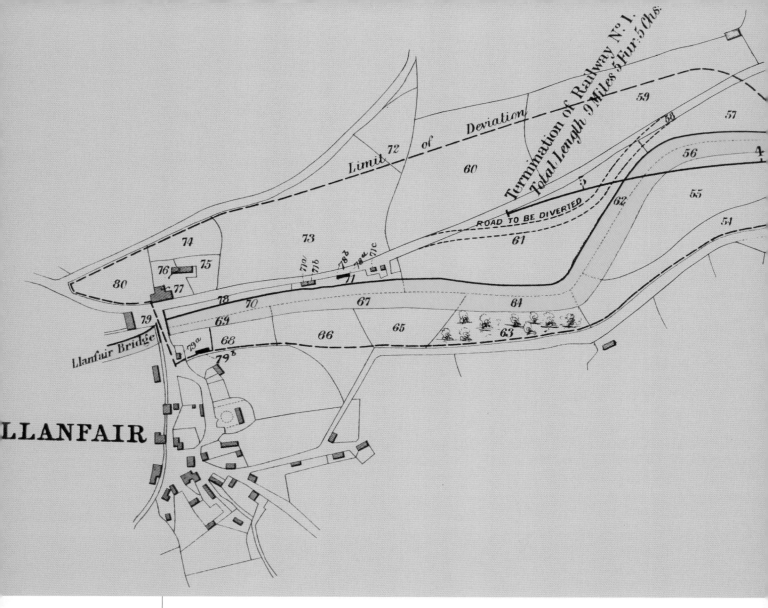

The map contains the following labels:

Limit 72 of Deviation

Termination of Railway No. 1.
Total Length 9 Miles 5 Fur. 5 Chs.

ROAD TO BE DIVERTED

74 73 60 59 58 57 56 55 54
80 76 75 77 70a 70b 71e 71d 71c 61 62
79 78 70 71 67 64
69 68 66 65 63
79a 79s

Llanfair Bridge

LLANFAIR

The Welshpool &
Llanfair Railway's
proposed terminus
in Llanfair.
(Parliamentary
Archives)

Llanfair residents met on 28 November, complaining about the location of the station, resolving to support the railway if the terminus were brought nearer or into the town.

At a meeting in Llanfair to approve the Bill on 9 December, William Norman Swettenham, one of the engineers, said that he was certain that the railway could be built for £40,000 inclusive of promotional expenses, land, rolling stock and stations. Standard gauge, it would be classified as a light railway, he said. The 1868 Regulation of Railways Act empowered the Board of Trade to issue a licence authorising the construction and operation of a railway as a light railway providing axle loads did not exceed eight tons and speed did not exceed 25mph. The Board of Trade's reluctance to relax the requirements of the 1845 Regulation of Railways Act meant that it was a little used facility.

Recalling the scheme in 1896, Abraham Howell, the solicitor, claimed that David Davies, the contractor who had built the Llanidloes & Newtown Railway and who later made a fortune developing Barry docks, had been over the proposed route and estimated its cost at £40,000.

Concerning the location of Llanfair station, the meeting was told that locating closer to the town would cost about £200. It was suggested that if Llanfair residents subscribed £1,000, they could have the station where they wanted it; at the date of

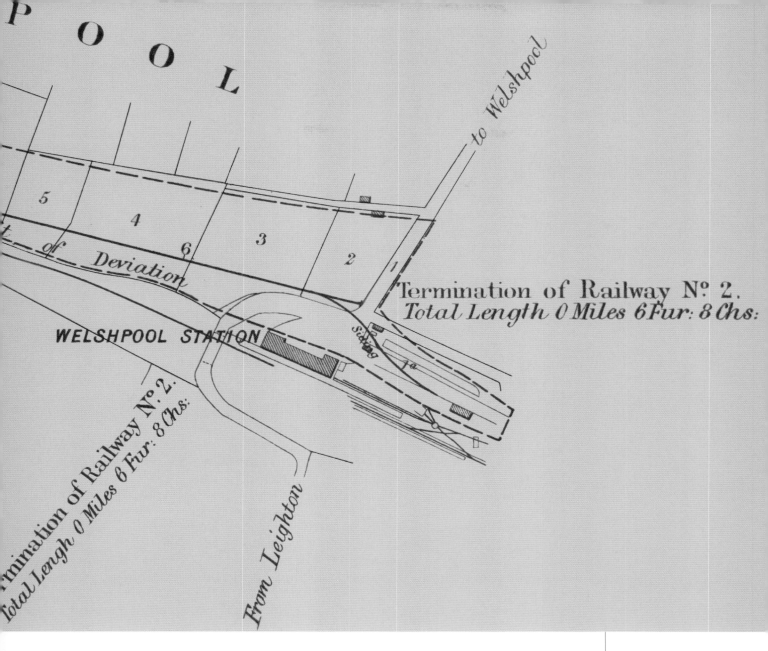

POOL

5

4

6

3

2

1

of Deviation

WELSHPOOL STATION

Termination of Railway Nº 2.
Total Length 0 Miles 6 Fur: 8 Chs:

to Welshpool

siding

Termination of Railway Nº 2. Total Length 0 Miles 6 Fur: 8 Chs:

From Leighton

the meeting they had promised to subscribe £550. Leaving this in abeyance, the meeting gave its approval to the Bill.

By the time they met at the Cross Foxes on 27 January the promotors had agreed terms with the Cambrian. Railway No 2, the independent line into Welshpool, would be withdrawn in return for the Cambrian withdrawing its objection. The Cambrian would work the line for 65% of receipts for the first two years, for 70% for the following three years and for 65% for the next three years, or for 60% in perpetuity, or at cost price. The Llanfair company would pay £250 for the use of Welshpool station. It would also make

the junction with the Cambrian and make a double line between it and the station if required by the Board of Trade. The Cambrian would subscribe £2,000 to pay for the heavier rails needed to take its locos and the toll for the use of the line between the junction and the station by the Llanfair Company, three-quarters of a mile, would be as for two miles. The shareholders wished to revisit the subject of the station rent, the mileage charge and the cost of the second track.

Despite some shareholders being doubtful of the scheme's ability to raise its capital and therefore concerned about the wisdom of proceeding with the Bill,

The Welshpool & Llanfair Railway's terminus in Welshpool would have been quite close to the site of the light railway's terminus. (Parliamentary Archives)

it passed through Parliament unopposed and received the royal assent on 10 August 1877, church bells being rung in Welshpool to celebrate.

The capital was set at £39,000 with power to borrow an additional £13,000. The promoters were named as Ralph Dickinson Gough, Owen Jones, Richard Owen and Frederick Bromley Jones; they and one other to be nominated would be the first directors. An unusual mitigating measure, although not described as such, was an obligation to contribute not more than £2,000 for a carriage road from the road at Pontsycoed, near Cyfronydd, to Mathrafal Castle, no money to be paid over until responsibility for maintaining the road had been accepted by the Llanfyllin highway board. The station rent and the charge for using the junction line were not mentioned.

The first ordinary meeting, required to bring the Welshpool & Llanfair Railway Company into existence and to be held within eight months of the royal assent, was not held until 16 March 1878. R.D. Gough, a Staffordshire solicitor, took the chair. He, R.D. Pryce, E. Hilton, and F.B. Jones, a Llanfair landowner, were elected permanent directors. George Slater was appointed one of the auditors.

Another meeting, on 14 June, was intended to provide shareholders with a progress report but ended by approving a motion that required the directors to investigate the requirements for adopting a narrow gauge because the shares currently subscribed were insufficient to move forward. R.D. Pryce, as chairman, listed the benefits: the smaller area of land required; fewer and smaller earthworks; sharper curves and steeper gradients; timber bridges; permanent way at half the cost and lower working expenses. There would be a limit on the weight of engines and the speed at which they could travel but the biggest disadvantage, he said, was the transhipment of goods and minerals as passengers transhipped themselves. He also thought that 'The novelty of a miniature line would be peculiarly attractive to tourists in a beautiful and picturesque part of Wales, such as their line would traverse.'

On 5 July the shareholders learned that the Board of Trade was prepared to issue a certificate authorising the railway to be built and operated as a light railway but it would not approve a change of gauge from that sanctioned by Parliament. The Earl of Powis was willing to support a change and would still invest £4,000 providing the other 'chief supporters' did likewise, but David Davies, the contractor, was against the move, claiming that a narrow gauge line would be of no use for lime, timber or live stock. Nevertheless, the shareholders resolved that unless sufficient subscriptions could be obtained in support of the railway as authorised by 1 November 1879 'the necessary steps be taken for making a narrow gauge line.'

The *Cambrian News* report of a meeting held on 8 November refers to an earlier meeting, for which no report has been found, where the guarantors of the Parliamentary deposit resolved that the railway should be built from Welshpool as far as Pontsycoed, the river bridge on the main road at Cyfronydd, 7½ miles, which could be achieved with the capital already promised, in anticipation that starting work would attract more subscriptions, or, if the shareholders did not agree, that powers should be sought to abandon the undertaking.

At the 8 November meeting shareholders were told that the scheme had attracted subscriptions totalling £18,010 of the £35,700 required. The directors were under pressure because the compulsory purchase powers expired in nine months and any application for fresh powers had to be deposited within weeks. Discussion about the Pontsycoed proposal, with talk of subscribers withdrawing if the railway did not connect Welshpool to Llanfair, eventually led to a resolution in its support.

In the event, the scheme stagnated for two years, before the directors moved on two fronts, depositing a straightforward Bill for abandonment and one for an extension of time and change of gauge in November 1881. A report in *Eddowes's Journal* (23 November 1881) said that the narrow gauge proposal required £34,000 capital, including rolling stock, and that no liability would be incurred until £22,500 was subscribed. W.N. Swettenham signed the plans.

Only the abandonment bill was pursued, assent being given on 19 June 1882. The company's inability to raise capital was cited as the reason for its failure. Local newspapers did not comment on the Act or the withdrawal of the narrow-gauge proposal. In 1896 Abraham Howell, the solicitor, claimed to have possession of a subscriptions list which totalled only £12,000.

George Slater, whose idea it had been, had attended all the reported meetings. In accordance with his preference for the company to be run from Wales and not from outside he had not taken any position with it. He died at Woodford Hall, Winsford, Cheshire, on 6 September 1894, aged 82.

The background to the third Welshpool/ Llanfair scheme, also called the Welshpool & Llanfair Railway, is unknown. Only the *Wellington Journal* said anything about it, and that was a month after the notice of intention to deposit a Bill had been published in the *London Gazette* on 23 November 1886.

Engineers Simpson, Davies & Hurst produced a route similar to the earlier schemes, with an independent line into Welshpool and no junction with the Cambrian, passing to the east of Castle Caereinion before picking up an alignment close to that later adopted by the light railway, crossing the river at Heniarth and terminating at the later station site, 340 yards from the Llanfair bridge, a distance of 10 miles 2 furlongs 8 chains. This time the gradient near Powis Castle was slightly easier, at 1 in 68 and 1 in 58, but it then steepened to 1 in 40 for nearly a mile. There was a summit for nearly a mile near Dolarddyn before the line fell to the terminus. (Appendix 2)

Before proceeding to obtain powers of abandonment, the Welshpool & Llanfair Railway produced this plan for an independent route into Welshpool. (Parliamentary Archives)

The route of the 1887 Welshpool & Llanfair Railway proposal. (Parliamentary Archives)

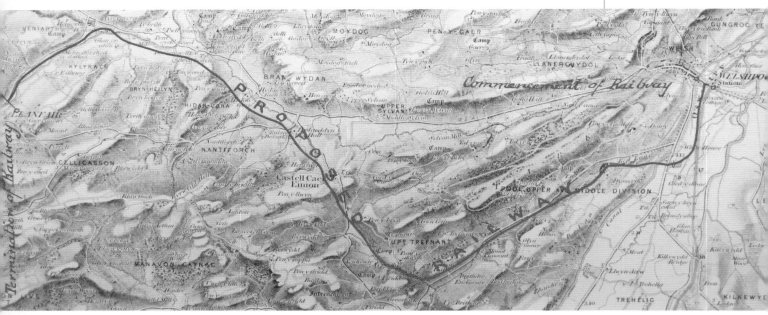

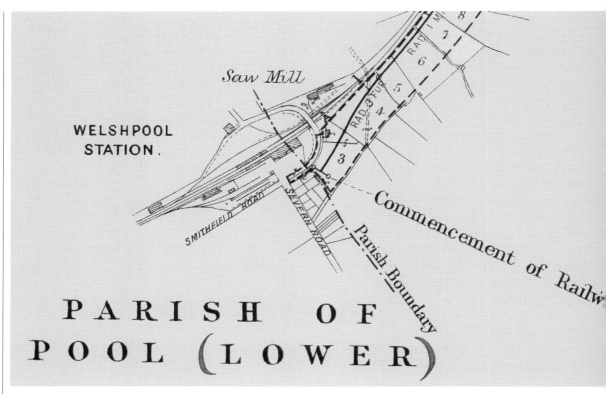

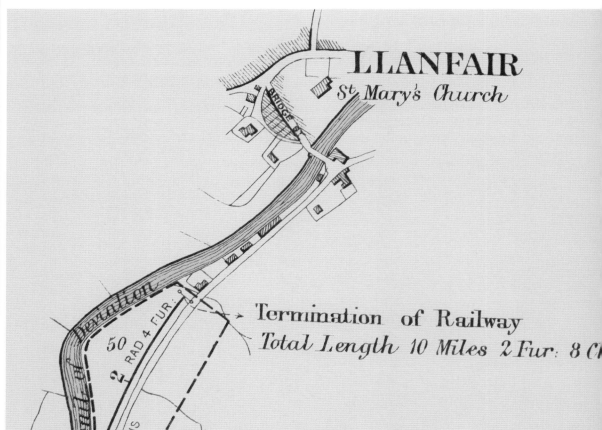

Gaining assent on 23 August 1887, the Welshpool & Llanfair Railway Act authorised a 3ft gauge railway. The promoters were William Page, John Greenbank and John Wilmer Ransome; with two others to be nominated, they were the first directors. The capital requirements were the same as for the 1877 scheme. A contractor from Yorkshire, Greenbank was a director of the Brazil Great Southern Railway. Ransome was a civil engineer from Ipswich, Suffolk. Both were based in London. Page has not been identified. No explanation has been found for them promoting the railway; they probably saw it as an investment opportunity.

Reporting on the Bill, mistakenly saying that it had been enacted, the *Cambrian News* (27 May 1887) had presciently commented: 'It is to be hoped the next we hear of the Llanfair Railway will not be of a Bill to abandon the undertaking.'

Held in London on 8 February 1888, the first general meeting was not reported. J.W. Alison had called the meeting, signing the notice as 'Secretary (pro tem)'; the secretary of the Corris Railway Company, he made the first of several connections between the two railways, albeit that one of them was not built. Public meetings for the Llanfair line were held at Llanfair's national school and Welshpool's town hall on 1 June. Speaking for the railway, Sir Pryce Pryce-Jones, a Newtown merchant who had been appointed a director, said that although it was a scheme promoted by 'gentlemen at a distance' it deserved and required local support to bring it to fruition.

Representing the engineers, William Hurst said that the locality was suited to a 3ft gauge railway. It was intended to have the best rolling stock and engines that could be made and there would be five stations. A good proportion of the existing traffic on the main road should be diverted onto the railway, he implied. £21,000 capital had already been promised, leaving £30,000 to raise.

At Llanfair, Pryce-Jones had read out a letter on behalf of R.D. Pryce, Cyfronydd, saying that although he did not wish to participate in public meetings he would

Sir Pryce Pryce-Jones, figurehead of the 1887 Welshpool & Llanfair Railway scheme.

Robert Davies Pryce of Cyfronydd was buried with his wife in St Garmon's churchyard at Castle Caereinion.

give 'reasonable' facility for carrying out the project. In addition to Pryce-Jones and John Greenbank, the only promoter to remain involved, the directors were Oliver Wethered, who in 1891 was living on his own means, and James Fraser, an accountant and director of the Corris Railway Company.

A prospectus was published in the *Standard* on 18 July 1888. The solicitor was Hugh Charles Godfray, who became a Corris Railway Company director in 1892, and the secretary (pro tem) was George Fraser, one of James Fraser's sons.

Figures were given to demonstrate that the railway's cost per mile and its estimated income were reasonable compared with others and that the net revenue would be sufficient to pay debenture interest and 6% dividend on the ordinary shares. A 'responsible', but unnamed, contractor had contracted to construct the railway, supply all rolling stock and signalling and telegraph equipment, purchase land, to build stations and to defray all preliminary expenses. The landowners had agreed to sell their land at its agricultural value and to accept payment in shares.

The table shows the cost of constructing and equipping comparable railways given in the prospectus. In referring to the Manx railways the promoters were practising a mild deceit, for there were two English 3ft gauge lines, the Ravenglass & Eskdale Railway in Cumbria and the Southwold Railway in Suffolk, which had cost £4,571 and £6,625 per mile respectively, but including them in the table, particularly the Ravenglass line, would have taken the shine off their comparisons.

	Gauge ft. in.	Cost of Construction, Equipment, and other charges per mile
Festiniog	1 11½	£10,542
North Wales Narrow Gauge	1 11½	10,215
Isle of Man	3 0	9,490
Manx Northern	3 0	7,550
Welshpool and Llanfair	3 0	4,930
Average cost per mile of all Railways in the United Kingdom – as per Board of Trade Returns for 1886		£42,646

A typical Isle of Man Railways mixed train. This 3ft gauge railway was well equipped, well-funded and profitable. The locomotive, Beyer, Peacock 2-4-0T No 9 *Douglas*, was built in 1896.

WHIT MONDAY.
ON THE R.&.E.RY

The Ravenglass &
Eskdale Railway was
one of two English
3ft gauge railways.
It was underfunded,
poorly equipped and
unprofitable. The
picture shows one
of the railway's two
locomotives with
its three passenger
carriages, one of
them home-made,
four wagons adapted
to carry passengers
on busy days, and its
brake van.

Commenting on 21 July, the *Wellington Journal* said that the prospectus was modestly and unpretentiously worded, and 'there seems no reason why the expectations of the promoters should not be fully realised,' but before long it would be disabused of this notion.

On 23 April 1890 the *Oswestry Advertiser* reported that Joseph Richards Dix, the manager of the Corris Railway, had been appointed engineer and that he had 'prepared a scheme for making the line on exceptionally economical principles' that the directors had approved. The remarkable thing about this appointment is that Dix had no qualifications as an engineer. How his scheme varied from the authorised scheme is unknown. Work would start as soon as another £10,000 had been raised, the paper declared. A correspondent to the *County Times*

published on 18 January 1896 said that the original engineers had abandoned the railway in favour of a more lucrative scheme in Egypt.

Support was obviously not forthcoming, for on 17 November 1891 the *Montgomeryshire Express* announced that the promoters had decided to apply for powers to abandon the undertaking. Saying that this would be a calamity, the paper's wish that another attempt would be made to increase subscriptions was not fulfilled. Indeed, Godfray, the solicitor, had signed the notice of intention to deposit a Bill the day before the newspaper was published. It passed through Parliament without objection and the Welshpool and Llanfair Railway (Abandonment) Act received the royal assent on 20 May 1892. Once again, the inability to raise capital was given as the cause.

ROLLING STOCK 1903-1956

The Earl at Llanfair. The maker's plate is attached to the smokebox, and the owner's plate, which indicates that the loco belongs to the light railway company, to the cabside.

The Countess, also at Llanfair.

The GWR did not take long to proclaim its ownership of the railway, applying a simple livery and renumbering the locomotives and stock. With its GWR branding applied, *The Earl* is seen being coaled alongside the Smithfield siding.

Pre-war photographs of both locomotives together are uncommon. Here *The Earl* appears to have pulled out *Countess* for the photograph. The locos retain their original boilers but *The Earl* is missing its steam heating connecting pipe. (H.W. Whitworth)

A portrait of *The Earl* showing all the features altered by the GWR: steam heating, chimney, boiler top-feed, safety valve cover and cab roof whistles.

The Earl outside the shed at Welshpool circa 1950, before its nameplates were removed.

Countess seen running round the Birmingham Locomotive Club's special train on 9 July 1949. The letter 'W' painted below the number plate designates the loco's allocation to the western region of British Railways.

The Oswestry shedplate and the location of *Countess*'s nameplate are clearly visible in this 1951 view.

With the railway's closure approaching, in March 1956 Oswestry works returned *The Earl* for its last period in traffic with its paintwork smartened and its numberplates highlighted in white.

One of the railway's forty goods wagons at Llanfair soon after the GWR took control. Originally No 32, No 71687 was one of six rebuilt as sheep wagons in 1930.

The brake vans retained GWR livery until the railway closed. A number of changes were made over the years, the chief of them being enclosing the verandah they had been built with. No 8755, seen here, was No 1 when built. Both vehicles survive in the preservation company's ownership. To No 8755's right is one of the railway's four goods vans, No 100663, originally No 3. It was condemned in 1956. The preservation company bought two of the others.

A portrait of van No 100665, originally No 5.

No 38089 was one of two cattle vans built by the GWR for use on the Vale of Rheidol Railway in 1923 and transferred, regauged, to Welshpool in 1937. In 1960 British Railways sold it to the Festiniog Railway which converted it to carry stores. Falling out of use, it was sold to the Vale of Rheidol Railway in 2014 and restored to its original condition in 2017. The preservation company bought the other van, No 38088.

In 1911 six goods wagons were adapted to carry sheep and in 1930 the GWR modified six more to be capable of carrying cattle or sheep. No 71699 was created in this form in 1937. As none of them survive, the preservation company converted a Royal Navy armaments depot wagon to represent one.

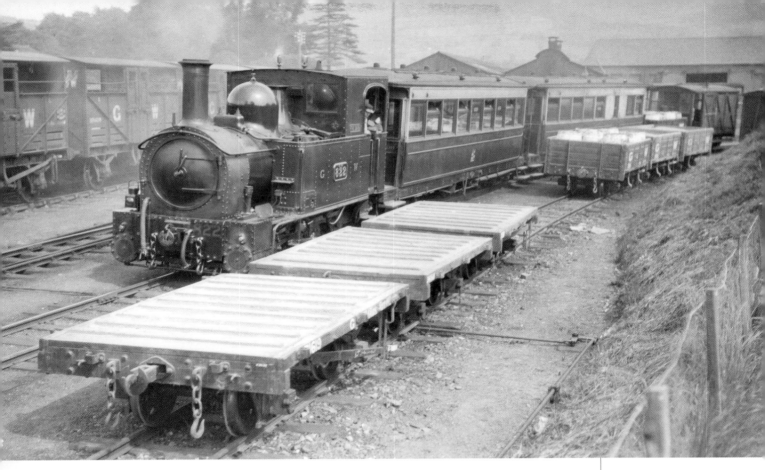

Three of the 1930 sheep/cattle wagon conversions stabled at Welshpool without their superstructures soon after they had been converted.

The Pickering bolster wagons after they had been re-liveried in 1924.

The GWR built six bolster wagons with steel underframes in 1924. One of the two survivors is seen in this view of *The Earl* at Heniarth on 24 August 1948. (H.C. Casserley)

In 1946 the Pickering bolsters and four of the GWR variety were converted to be goods wagons, their short (4ft) wheelbases distinguishing them from the original wagon stock (5ft 6in).

CHAPTER 2

THE LIGHT RAILWAY ORDER

I n the 1890s agriculture in Britain was considered to be in depression. In 1895 the agent of Sir Watkin Wynn, a major North Wales landowner, told a royal commission on agriculture, appointed in 1894, that it was mainly attributable to foreign competition and preferential rates for its transport, by rail, to major centres. The price of wool had fallen from 1s per pound in 1880 to 6½d per pound in 1894. The price of butter had fallen considerably, also affected by the availability of margarine. Foreign meat was sold as home-grown and food produced 'for the masses' was adulterated. A dry and hot summer in 1893, he did not call it a drought, had not only made cattle and horses unsaleable but had damaged pasture land in a way that would take years to recover. The reduction in working hours from 14 or 15 to 12 or 10 per day and competition in areas with extractive industries, he cited Caernarfonshire slate, also reduced the labour force.

The commission did not report until 1897 and the only comments made to it regarding railways concerned rates. The government, however, came under pressure to support agriculture by improving access to 'remote areas' by means of 'light railways', railways that were cheaper to authorise, cheaper to construct and cheaper to operate.

Legislation to address this issue had been attempted twice. 1864's Railways Construction Facilities Act provided that where no compulsory purchase powers were required the Board of Trade could issue a draft certificate for approval by Parliament, but its requirement to have the consent of all landowners and other affected parties and no opposition from any railway or canal company meant that no use was made of it. Its 1870 amendment

giving objectors the right to address Parliament merely increased its prospective cost to applicants.

Powers for light railways were contained within the Regulation of Railways Act, 1868, as mentioned in Chapter One, but little use was made of them. The agricultural issue in Ireland was addressed by the Light Railways Act, enacted in Westminster in 1890, but the remainder of the United Kingdom had to wait until 1896 to obtain similar powers.

There were many letters to newspapers deprecating the red tape and expense imposed on 'ordinary' railways by the Board of Trade, some contrasting the UK with the continent were there were, it was said, light railways in abundance. Among the letters, a writer to *The Times* (7 November 1894) said that his friend had been killed because he had tried to board a moving train, not by the height of the platform, adding that 'until we are allowed low-priced works, cheap fencing, abolition of unnecessary staff, and some respite from the circumlocution department, we shall never get light railways in England.'

The Times took the credit for setting the ball rolling, with a series of articles published in March 1894. Later in the year a 'voluntary committee' was established in the House of Commons and in November a light railways conference was appointed under the auspices of the Board of Trade, meeting for the first time on 6 December. It obtained the views of county councils as to whether there should be light railways under an improved system of procedure and regulations, the desirability of state and local aid to private enterprise and 'the mode of construction of light railways, as to gauge, etc.' and made recommendations to the government.

Concurrently, the royal commission on agriculture took evidence on the subject in July 1894 and in February 1895. On the latter occasion the newly-elected MP for Montgomeryshire, Arthur Charles Humphreys-Owen, said that powers should be given to county councils to promote light railways, as already existed for borough councils in respect of tramways, adding that in Montgomeryshire there were two valleys eminently suitable for being worked by cheap railways. One ran from Welshpool to Llanfair and the other from a point on the Cambrian Railways to Llangynog. Humphreys-Owen was also a director of the Cambrian Railways.

A Bill was introduced in the House of Commons in April 1895, but progress was brought to an end by a general election on 12 August. The conference was resumed on 28 November, with representatives from 'county and parochial associations' attending. There were some who held that the state should not be involved and one county had responded that whatever was done 'they must not obstruct for hunting', but the meeting resolved to urge the government to introduce legislation authorising light railways with an improved system of procedure and regulations, and adding state and local aid to private enterprise.

A second Bill was introduced in February 1896. Speaking in its support, the president of the Board of Trade, Charles Thompson Ritchie, said that the proposal was not a panacea for agricultural depression but by reducing costs and bringing consumers and producers closer together it would do something to mitigate the issue. The government, he said, accepted that light railways would not be made without some aid, both from the localities and the state; the absence of financial support had been a criticism of the 1895 Bill.

He had been to France and Belgium to see how things were done there. In France so-called light railways were really secondary railways, built to complement major trunk routes, whereas in Belgium light railways were steam tramways, mainly based on the use of public roads with occasional use of cross-country routes. There were few signals, hardly any stations, and simple branches served particular farms and industries. One thousand miles had been built over ten years. Funded by the state, provinces, communes and outside subscribers, the returns had been satisfactory.

He favoured the Belgian system, and wondered how it could be applied to Britain. Hitherto, the main difficulties had been the reluctance of Parliament to devolve the power to authorise compulsory purchase and the expense of meeting the Board of Trade's requirements for public safety. He hoped that Parliament would release its grip on the approvals process and that landowners would be content with a 'simply organised enquiry' without insisting on appeals to the legislature. With regard to safety, the public must decide, if it wanted light railways, to exercise a certain amount of caution and not insist on the elaborate precautions necessary on trunk lines.

While the Bill traversed the Parliamentary process, the Auto-Car Club arranged a demonstration of 'motor carriages' at the Imperial Institute. Among the oil motors, noted the *Daily Telegraph* (2 May 1896), there were some, 'by no means the least successful,' powered by electricity, and one powered by steam. At the dinner which followed, the prevailing view of the speakers was that the auto-car would render light railways unnecessary, as delivery companies welcomed it and commercial houses were anxious to be free to employ horseless vehicles, which were destined to be every man's own railway and pleasure carriage. In time this came to pass but it took more than 100 years for electric vehicles to achieve prominence in the market.

During the Bill's committee stage in June a member complaining about the lack of a definition of the term 'light railway' was told that as localities varied, attempting a broad definition 'would greatly embarrass the working of the Bill.' Those who called for all railways to be 4ft 8½in gauge appear to have been ignored.

The royal assent was given on 14 August 1896. The Locomotives on Highways Act was enacted at the same time, exempting 'light (road) locomotives' from certain provisions while imposing restrictions regarding weight, traction and other matters. Two very different Acts with very different purposes but one would have a great influence on the outcome of the other.

The Light Railways Act comprised twenty-nine clauses and three schedules. Briefly, it established the Light Railway Commission and charged it with facilitating the construction and working of light railways. Applications for orders could be made by any council through which the proposed railway was to pass, by any individual, corporation or company independently or jointly.

Councils could contribute to a railway's capital either by loan or by shares, in which case the Treasury could lend an amount not exceeding a quarter of the total amount required or the amount being advanced by the council, providing that at least half of the amount required was share capital and at least half of that had been subscribed and paid up by persons other than local authorities. If the Board of Agriculture or the Board of Trade certified that a light railway would benefit agriculture or the development or maintenance of a specified industry, the Treasury could also make a special advance not exceeding half of the amount required, either by a free grant or a loan or a combination of both, provided that the land required had been provided without charge. The Treasury was allocated £1 million to disburse on light railways, of which not more than a quarter could be by free grants. Local authorities could fund their contributions by borrowing.

Any order made by the commissioners had to be submitted to the Board of Trade for confirmation and once confirmed would have effect as if enacted by Parliament and treated as evidence that the requirements of the Act had been complied

with. The Board of Trade decided that the cost of making an application should be £50, an amount that remained unchanged until the legislation was replaced in 1992. Significantly, orders could include powers to take land compulsorily without recourse to Parliament.

Reporting of the Bill's progress had attracted much interest in areas that thought they might benefit from the legislation. In Llanfair, Charles Evan Humphreys, the local GP, had been the first to speak locally in favour of a light railway, addressing the parish council on the subject in November 1895. Its fairs were three times larger than those of nearby towns, he said, but the market had gone because there was no railway. Lime was in demand by farmers, but transport costs made it expensive. Traders and farmers would both benefit from a railway, he added, concluding that although the council had no power to make a railway it could agitate for one.

A committee appointed by the council had resolved 'That the Parish Councils of Garthbeibio, Llangadfan, Llanerfyl, Llangyniew, Meifod, Llansantffraid, Llanllugan, Llanwyddelan, Manafon, and Castle Caereinion be invited … to further the object of getting a light railway to Llanfair, and … to petition the County Council … with a view of getting that body to urge upon the Government the importance of introducing a Light Railway Bill and passing it into law as early as possible.' The list of councils, which between them surrounded Llanfair, demonstrated that at this stage the committee was expressing no preference for the route to be adopted, whether towards Oswestry or Newtown or to Welshpool.

This seemed to change after a comment about the councils made at the Montgomeryshire County Council meeting on 20 December, assuming that it was accurately reported, produced an angry letter to the *County Times* published on 28 December. 'A Burgess' seems to have misunderstood a point made generally as

Llanfair Caereinion, River Scene, No. 2

The Banwy at Llanfair Caereinion, looking eastwards. The railway terminus was established on the north bank beyond the built-up area.

being one made specifically, alleging that it proved that Llanfair was campaigning to divert its traffic from Welshpool to Oswestry to the detriment of the former. It was the 'bounden duty,' he said, of Welshpool and the other affected councils to frustrate the Llanfair committee as there was only one outlet for Llanfair and that was Welshpool.

Dr Humphreys replied to say that Welshpool people should have supported the 1887 scheme and that no deliberate attempt was being made to ruin Welshpool but self-preservation was the first law of nature and in Llanfair they would consider their own interests and welfare before those of Welshpool.

The correspondence continued until July, with several other readers joining in, mostly using pseudonyms. Humphreys argued that by taking a railway from Llanfair to the Cambrian line at Four Crosses an extensive and fertile area would be opened up as well as providing easy access to Oswestry and its market, and Liverpool and Manchester. There was already a telegraph along the route, there were no engineering difficulties, only a few

bridges, and lime, stone and coal would be cheaper at Llanfair than if routed via Welshpool. He also noted that most of the route ran along the river Vyrnwy its water power being an advantage when steam power was replaced in the near future, he claimed, by electricity.

It would take several years for the issue to be resolved but on 16 May an editorial in the *County Times* commented that 'it is almost certain that if the idea should ever take practical effect the scheme which will be adopted will be the one connecting Llanfair with Welshpool.'

A joint committee of the Llanfair and Meifod councils had previously resolved to find out if the land owners affected would cooperate, and if the Cambrian and London & North Western Railways would be willing to construct a light railway.

At Llanfair's meeting on 12 May, a privately produced and anonymous handbill was circulated, calling for residents to reserve judgment until they had heard 'both sides of the question'. The Meifod route would access Oswestry (23 miles), the north-west and Scotland. There were, it said, four options for

Oswestry cattle market, circa 1912. Its popularity may be judged by the existence of several commercial postcards of it. (J. Valentine)

a Welshpool route, two via Castle Caereinion, one via Dolarddyn, Golfa, Welshpool (Raven) thence via Guilsfield to Pool Quay, which also gave a 23-mile route to Oswestry, and one via Dolarddyn, Golfa, Llanerchydol and through Welshpool town. With connections to the Cambrian, LNWR and GWR, they would give access to London, Birmingham and the Midlands, Shrewsbury, Newtown, and the Severn Valley; to Aberystwyth and the coast and South Wales.

When Welshpool town council met two days later, Abraham Howell, the solicitor, said that he thought that Llanfair inhabitants were playing off one route against the other, to get either Meifod or Welshpool residents to pay for the railway. The council appointed a committee to watch the town's interests.

Apart from noting some highlights, there are too many arguments and counter-arguments to go into all of the meetings, letters and editorials the issue generated. The key issues were set out in the *Montgomeryshire Express* on 19 May, an issue that also included an editorial, a letter and reports of meetings in Llanfair, Meifod and Welshpool.

Llanfair traders thought that a railway to Welshpool would lose them business. Goods obtained from Manchester, source of most provisions, would cost more if routed via Welshpool. A 4lb loaf that cost 3½d to 4d at Newtown cost 5d to 6d at Llanfair.

Oswestry, the farmers claimed, had the best market in North Wales. Llanfair's market was damaged because hucksters (peddlers) bartered goods in Llanfair and profited by selling them in Oswestry. Cattle dealers bought in Llanfair and sold in Oswestry. Newtown, which had a good market, was too far away.

The case for Welshpool was that it was central to Newtown, Shrewsbury and Oswestry, it had good accommodation and good communications. Dealers visited Llanfair via the town and exported their purchases the same way. Oswestry was not a natural centre for Llanfair. Llanfair farmers might go to Shrewsbury butter market but very rarely went to Oswestry.

Supporters of the Meifod route argued that it would be convenient for coal obtained from Ruabon, but the district's coal was obtained from Hanwood, near Shrewsbury. Similar arguments were made for the destination of timber. It was almost

High Street, Welshpool

26630 (JV)

as if Oswestry was being promoted as a solution to a problem that did not exist, particularly as Meifod was already within easy reach of the Llanfyllin branch.

Another issue mentioned was that the Welshpool route passed through several council areas with insufficient impact on any one of them to enthuse them in the idea of raising a rate to pay for it.

Finally, the feature discussed the prospects of tourism in the Meifod valley, which the author contrasted favourably with the Vale of Llangollen, the Mawddach estuary, Dinas Mawddwy, Beddgelert, Aberglaslyn, Snowdon and the Conwy valley.

In August John Edmund Thomas (1841-1900), a surveyor and consulting engineer from Ruabon and working in Wrexham, was appointed to make a survey of the Meifod route. He was to adopt the cheapest possible route. The *Montgomeryshire Express* (11 August 1896) reported that he had already started work. The committee sent 'collectors' around the area to solicit donations to cover preliminary expenses, including Thomas's fee. The same issue reported that in Newtown consideration

was being given to making a railway from that place to Llanfair, a notion that was not treated with much respect when it had been raised in Llanfair in May.

Thomas presented the results of his survey to a committee meeting held in Meifod on 20 August. His route started 35 chains north of Arddleen station and kept to the south of the Vyrnwy and Banwy rivers. Standard gauge, its length was 13 miles 57 chains, its steepest gradient 1 in 80, its sharpest curve 10 chains radius. He estimated that it could be built for £36,141, including charges, land and stations at Arddleen, Sarney, Trefnanney, Meifod, Newbridge, Pontsycoed, and Llanfair. He proposed using 45lb rail for trains running at 25mph. He thought that it could be worked for 50% of its projected revenue.

Criticised about the route going through 'certain good fields', Thomas pointed out that he had been commissioned to find the cheapest and best route. The committee decided to submit an application for an order to the Light Railway Commissioners.

In Welshpool on 3 September the town council was told that although engineers

had been appointed and the LNWR, GWR and Cambrian railways approached, its report on a Llanfair railway was incomplete. The council's apparent inaction, criticised in the *Montgomery County Times* (*County Times* henceforward) on 29 August, prompted 'Erfyl Lad' to suggest that if the Meifod route was built then Welshpool could build a railway to meet it at Pontsycoed and divert the Llanfair traffic back to Welshpool.

Later in the month Oswestry town council voted to allocate £80 to be donated towards the preliminary expenses for the Llanfair and Tanat valley railway schemes as the town would benefit from them.

A deputation of Meifod promoters visited C.S. Denniss, the Cambrian's manager, and George Owen, its engineer, on 17 September, hoping to secure their company's agreement to build and operate their railway. As three-quarters of Llanfair's merchandise reached Welshpool by canal, they claimed, worth £800-£1,000 a year to the canal, having the railway would divert it all to rail, to the Cambrian's benefit. Another source would be the Welshpool–Llanfair goods traffic by road, estimated to be 27,000 tons and 57,000 passengers annually.

Shorthand notes of the meeting were filed with Denniss's board papers. Perhaps not unnaturally, the deputation not only promoted its own scheme but attempted to cast doubt on the feasibility of any Welshpool scheme. Denniss told the deputation to get the assent and support of

Broniarth hill and Penylan Hall. The Llanfair & Meifod Valley Light Railway would have run along the far bank of the river.

Charles Sherwood Denniss, the Cambrian Railways' general manager from 1895 to 1910.

the affected landowners and that he would put the proposal to his board.

When Montgomeryshire County Council met the next day, its chairman, the MP A.C. Humphreys-Owen, recommended that the council should not favour either scheme but let the Light Railway Commissioners decide. After another presentation from the Meifod promoters the council resolved to 'be willing to give favourable consideration to a proposal for granting financial aid to the proposed light railway to Llanfair, after the scheme had been considered by the Light Railways Commissioners.'

Not everyone was enthused by the notion that light railways were the solution for the area. Edward Parke, an architect living and working in Newtown, wrote four letters to newspapers on the subject during 1896. On 22 September he told the *County Times* that railways were only profitable in populous areas and the Cambrian had never paid its original shareholders a penny in thirty years. To imagine, he continued, that a railway to Llanfair would pay, when the Cambrian did not was expecting too much. Good agricultural land would be taken out of production to build it. Cannot steam power be used on the road between Welshpool and Llanfair, he asked. If there was such an urgent demand for additional capacity, then surely the demand would have been met. He closed by making a point that would attract more interest. If the Meifod route were made it would be partially paid for by Montgomeryshire ratepayers, thereby subsidising a Shropshire market.

On 26 September the Cambrian's traffic and works committee, meeting at Euston, decided to tell the Meifod promoters that for economy of working through traffic and public convenience the adoption of standard gauge was recommended but that the company had no funds available for subscription.

Denniss's 24 November report to his board dealing with Meifod conditions also included his opinion that 'the alternative scheme from Llanfair to Welshpool should be judiciously discouraged, if not opposed, as it would inevitably drain traffic from your Llanfyllin

branch and intermediate stations and connect with the North Western Company at Welshpool, thus depriving your company of a considerable amount of revenue.' Regarding the Meifod proposal, he recommended saying that the company was prepared to enter into an agreement to construct and work it providing it was sanctioned by the Light Railway Commissioners and the necessary capital was raised.

Welshpool town council had met to consider its committee's report on a railway to Llanfair on 20 October. Bearing in mind that previous schemes had failed because they had been unable to raise the necessary capital, the committee had appointed Moorsom and Ward, civil engineers with offices in Manchester and Welshpool, to devise a route that took into account cheapness of construction and the usefulness of such a railway, how to make it pay and be of advantage to the county at large.

Lewis Henry Moorsom (1836-1914) was Manchester-based, a member of the Institution of Civil Engineers who had been engineer of the LNWR/GWR joint lines around Shrewsbury since 1866. Another Mancunian, Frederick Darwent Ward (1866-1935) lived in Welshpool and was the Powis estate's architect and surveyor. He was the active partner on the Llanfair scheme although Moorsom attended several meetings.

The committee had decided that the gauge should be 2ft 6in because less weight of materials would be required, 'quicker' curves and steeper gradients could be adopted, embankments and cuttings would be cheaper and less land would be required. The chief objection would be the cost of transhipment but not everything would need to be transhipped. Even with standard gauge some goods needed to be transhipped at junctions.

Moorsom and Ward's route was described as starting at the Cambrian station, following the council's Smithfield siding and the Lledan brook before crossing the canal, where sidings would be located, by a swing bridge then following the brook and vicarage grounds before crossing Church

Street on the level and then continuing along a new street to be created by demolishing some properties. It would then follow the 'back road' to Raven Square and then take the Llanfair road to Park (New) Drive, then past the black mill before re-joining the main road at Sylfaen, at which point it would follow the road to Llanfair, except for short diversions to avoid steep gradients.

They estimated construction at £21,000, including equipment, telephones, locomotives, rolling stock, transhipping machinery and buildings at Welshpool and Llanfair. With £4,000 needed for land, the total was £25,000.

A table showed the impact on the length of journeys likely to be made by Llanfair residents using the two proposed railways:

promoters expected the Cambrian to work their line, including the provision of rolling stock, for 50% of the gross income, their expectation must be very sanguine, the paper commented.

The Meifod route could not rely on attracting all the Llanfair traffic as a proportion of it would still be routed to Welshpool. The promoters would have to show that roadside traffic on their greater mileage would exceed the loss of the Welshpool traffic. It would be reasonable to assume that the income would equal that of the direct route, and not far wrong to estimate that expenses on both lines would be the same. Making these assumptions, the paper was 'forced' to the following conclusions:

	Llanfair & Welshpool Railway	Llanfair & Meifod Railway
Length to construct	9 miles	14 miles
Llanfair to Welshpool	9 miles	20¼ miles
Llanfair to Oswestry	24 miles	22½ miles
Llanfair to Newtown	22 miles	33¼ miles
Llanfair to Shrewsbury via Buttington	28 miles	37 miles

Figures were given to show that revenue would be enough to pay 4% on capital. The council decided to accept the route and to obtain the support of affected landowners and authorities. It also voted 'a sum towards the expenses incurred in preparing the plans'. The *County Times* concluded its report: 'Energetic action is to be taken to carry out the proposed scheme.'

The paper published a detailed analysis of the two schemes on 31 October, pointing out that the Meifod estimate did not include the cost of rolling stock, which the promoters expected the Cambrian to provide. Against anticipated earnings of £6 a mile on both lines, the Meifod promoters thought that their standard gauge line would cost £3 per mile to run, compared with the £4 per mile forecast for the narrow gauge line. If the Meifod

Estimated income by either route £2,808

Working expenses of the Welshpool line (nine miles) £1,872 – Profit £936

Working expenses of the Meifod line (14 miles) £2,912 – Deficit £104

If the Meifod expenses really were only £3 per mile then the Welshpool line's expenses should be less as it would be narrow gauge and intended to own its own locos, which would give the Meifod line £624 profit, less than 2% on capital, while Welshpool line profit would be £1,404, more than 6%.

The Meifod route might have better prospects than the paper could assume, it concluded, but public confidence would not be established by reticence and reserve. The Welshpool scheme, on the other hand, was cut and dried, and if it was a question of investing in one or the other then it was obvious which one a capitalist would support.

After a notice published in the *Border Counties Advertiser* on 26 November 1896, an application for the Meifod scheme was submitted on 10 December. The railway was described simply as 'a Railway 13 miles 7 furlongs 7.50 chains in length commencing at Arddleen on the line of the Cambrian Railways in the Parish of Llandrinio and terminating in the Town of Llanfair Caereinion both in the County of Montgomery.' The capital required was £42,000 and J.E. Thomas signed the estimate for £41,343 6s 3d. The draft order included a table of the land required:

The deposited plan for the Llanfair & Meifod Valley Light Railway. (National Archives)

Parish	Quantity A. R. P.	Purpose
In the parish of Llandrinio	9 1 0	Construction of railway and station at Arddleen
In the parish of Guilsfield	13 2 0	Ditto and station at Meifod
In the parish of Meifod	31 2 16	Ditto including stations at Sarney, Trefnanney and Newbridge
In the parish of Castle Caereinion	8 0 0	Ditto including station at Pontsycoed
In the parish of Llangyniew	0 0 3	Construction of railway
In the parish of Llanfair	15 5 18	Ditton including station at Llanfair
	78 1 24	

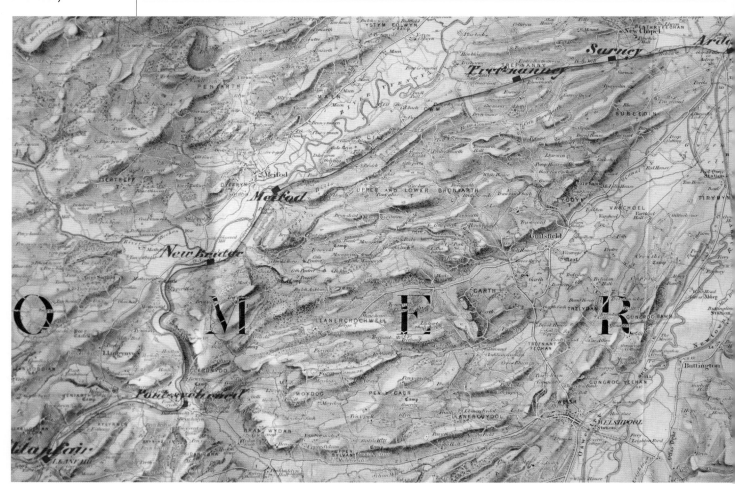

Oswestry Urban District Council sought, and obtained, approval for powers to be included in the order authorising it to make an advance to the scheme despite the proposed railway not passing though the district and being in a different county.

W. Forrester Addie, Welshpool's mayor, called a public meeting in the town hall to 'consider the desirability of promoting a light railway from Welshpool to Llanfair' on 3 December 1896. All ratepayers were invited.

Introducing Moorsom and Ward's scheme, Addie explained how the council's committee had led to it and said that there were two points that the audience should consider. Was it in the interest of the borough to promote such a railway and should the borough contribute to its cost, as authorised by the Light Railways Act. The *County Times* (5 December) devoted over 5,000 words to its report of the meeting.

Two resolutions put to the meeting, that it was desirable that steps should be taken, without delay, to promote a railway to Llanfair and that the meeting approved the steps already taken by the council and that the council took such action as necessary to promote the line and to contribute financially. Both were carried unanimously.

The *County Times* (2 January 1897) congratulated the council on the way it had handled the matter, placing it before the public in such a way as to secure whole-hearted support. The council had been criticised for its apparent lack of interest and action but ratepayers and landowners were now united in support of the enterprise.

Meanwhile, the local councils had been dealing with the Meifod application. In December Llandrinio and Pontrobert parishes gave their support, Llangyniew agreed to the diversion of a footpath near Pontsycoed and the county council appointed a committee to deal with its response to the proposed level crossings. The mayor of Oswestry called a meeting to be held on 1 February 1897 to consider the steps to be taken to support the proposal.

Advertisement for the first public meeting called in support of the light railway published in the *Montgomery County Times*.

Even before the route was decided the railway concept intruded into Llanfair's cultural consciousness. On 9 January 1897 a dinner held at the Goat Hotel to mark the completion of a landowner's half-yearly rent audit was followed by several songs being sung, 'including "The Llanfair Railway," by Pryce Davies, which caused roars of laughter', reported the *County Times* (16 January).

A committee, comprising eighty-seven persons, councillors, landowners and others, was formed on 28 January and a more manageable executive committee of twenty was appointed a week later.

Advertisement for a meeting called by the mayor of Oswestry in support of the Llanfair & Meifod Light Railway published in the *Montgomery County Times*.

In reports of this committee's activities it was called the general committee. The town council voted £200 towards the preliminary expenses the next day, the *County Times* (30 January) noting that this sum would cost the ratepayers 1d in £1.

On 6 February its report of a meeting promoting the Meifod scheme in Oswestry prompted the *County Times* to cast doubts on claims made by Dr Humphreys, commenting on his assertion that the railway would access a district of 160 square miles. Look at a map, it said, and ask how this could be done without impinging on the Cambrian's main line on one side and the Llanfyllin branch on the other. Did he expect people in Welshpool to travel to Arddleen via Llanfair, instead of the existing direct route, it asked? Did he not think that the Cambrian Railways' shareholders would be concerned about the prospective loss of revenue?

The town council's light railway committee met on 8 and 11 February. On the first occasion it appointed Moorsom and Ward as engineers and G.D. Harrison as solicitor. On the second it decided to adopt 'the Golfa route' and asked the engineers to report on the relative cost of narrow and standard gauge in construction and working. The reference to 'the Golfa route' suggests that there were variants, but no plans survive from this period. It was, of course, a variant of the route rejected by the 3rd Earl of Powis in 1862 because it would destroy one of the most beautiful parts of his park.

A sub-committee was appointed to go over the route with the engineers to determine if a route 'avoiding the line being carried along the roads' could be found, to avoid the 'the probable hostility that may be expected from the county council should the railway be carried here and there along the turnpike road.'

The report, submitted on 25 February 1897, was 'very favourable' to the narrow gauge, reported the *County Times* (27 February). The committee accepted the recommendation that the route should 'be kept off the road after passing Raven Square' and that the route shown on the plans be adopted 'until the Independent chapel at Cyfronydd is reached ... that the route be diverted to the south side of the Banwy river and kept as near to the river as possible until the mill opposite Eithinog is neared. There ... the line should cross the river on the westerly side, but close to the mill, and that thence it should be kept as close to the northern side of the river up to Llanfair. ... the railway should terminate in the field adjoining the last cottage on the left-hand side of the road before getting into Llanfair and that there the terminal depot should be located.' A proposal to move the river crossing to a point 'about 15 chains below Heniarth mill' was accepted.

In the town, the sub-committee's recommendation that the line be diverted around the back of the Montgomery Militia's armoury, re-joining the proposed route to Smithfield at Seven Stars, was also accepted. This amendment probably reduced the number of houses requiring demolition.

Considering the engineers' comparative estimates on the cost of standard gauge and 2ft 6in gauge lines, the latter was adopted with a proviso that a statement be issued explaining the reasoning behind the decision. Capital of £26,000 was expected to be sufficient to build and equip the railway.

Finally, the committee resolved to ask the Welshpool members to bring the matter before the county council and to ask the town council to pass a resolution to fix the amount it would subscribe to the share capital. It also agreed that Moorsom and Ward were to be paid £75 to cover their expenses up to and including the order.

Although they could not contribute financially, the Welshpool promoters sent deputations to the local councils to obtain their support: Llanfair on 4 March, Guilsfield 8 March, Forden 10 March, Llanfyllin 18 March.

The deputation could not always attend meetings when expected or required. When it failed to attend Llangyniew parish council on 2 March the council immediately passed a resolution in favour of the Meifod scheme but when it failed to attend Llanfair parish council on 13 March, because the council had given the promoters insufficient notice of its preferred date, the promoters sending a telegram saying that they could not attend, council's response was more blunt, resolving 'That this Council is disappointed not to receive the deputation from the promoters of the Welshpool and Llanfair Light Railway, and is of opinion that their non-attendance is a proof of the absence of a real and genuine interest on the part of the Welshpool people in any railway to Llanfair, and that the Council again pledges itself to support to the utmost of its power the scheme for bringing a line to Llanfair through the Meifod Valley.'

To address the public's concern on the issues of gauge and transhipment, the promoters secured the services of Everard Richard Calthrop, the engineer responsible for the 2ft 6in gauge Barsi Light Railway in India, a 21-mile-long line that was opened in 1897, who spoke on 'light railways and the advantage of the narrow gauge' at Welshpool town hall on 24 March. The offer of over 100 'lime-light pictures' no doubt contributed to the hall being packed. The *County Times*'s verbatim report was over 6,000 words.

Calthrop started his talk by saying that he had worked on the London & North Western Railway, the Great Western Railway and the Great Indian Peninsula Railway and would prefer to maintain the uniformity of gauge if the traffic justified it. If it did not, then there were three choices. The first was to guarantee a minimum return on capital and set rates to cover the deficiency. The second was to reduce capital costs to suit the revenue, which meant adopting narrow gauge. The third was to have no railway.

In addition to adopting narrow gauge, to reduce construction costs further Calthrop designed locomotives and rolling stock to have a common 5-ton axle loading, meaning that lighter rail could be used. The Leek & Manifold Railway, in Staffordshire,

The advertisement for Everard Richard Calthrop's presentation, illustrated by 'limelight pictures', on light railways organised by the mayor of Welshpool in support of the light railway published in the *Montgomery County Times*.

was built to his system in 1904 and did not require any track renewals during its 30-year existence. Extended in stages to 202 route miles, the Barsi Light Railway was converted to Indian broad gauge, 5ft 6in, between 2002 and 2008.

The lecture was well received and if the published report is an accurate representation of what Calthrop said then he had a good speaking style, but what the audience thought of being shown numerous photographs of Barsi rolling stock was not recorded.

Expenses of £4 2s 11d were incurred by the promoters to host the lecture. The next day Addie announced that he had arranged for Calthrop to assist the engineers in presenting the case to the light railway commissioners.

In an editorial on 3 April 1897 the *County Times* said that Calthrop had complimented F.D. Ward, the engineer, saying that he had never seen a preliminary survey better done or more carefully carried out. Ironically, the bulk of it was to be discarded.

Locomotives on the Barsi Light Railway. The one on the right was designed by E.R. Calthrop. Had funds allowed, a smaller version would have run on the light railway.

A train on the Leek & Manifold Light Railway, the only British line designed by E.R. Calthrop. Two 'transportation' wagons can be seen carrying standard gauge vehicles.

Coincidentally, on the same day that that issue of the paper was published Welshpool town council resolved to subscribe £8,000 to the proposed railway. Meeting specially to discuss railway matters, W.F. Addie, the mayor, said that it was intended to submit an application for a light railway order by 1 May.

The £8,000 would be borrowed at 3¼% interest from the government loans board for fifty years. The interest, £325 16s 8d, was the equivalent of a 2d rate, assuming no return from the railway. The investment would be 50% by loan and 50% in shares, the loan attracting not more than 3½% interest; the railway was expected to repay the £4,000 by instalments. If the railway earned enough to pay a 5¼% dividend, as forecast, then the council would profit from its borrowing.

Calthrop, Addie said, was advising Ward and approved of his route. If the line was built Ward and Calthrop would be joint engineers. It must have been at this point that Ward's original route, which followed the road from Sylfaen to Llanfair, except for short diversions to avoid gradients, was changed for the route in the application and constructed.

At its meeting on 6 April 1897, the county council voted to advance £6,000 to either of the Meifod or Welshpool schemes, whichever obtained an order from the Light Railway Commissioners, on the assumption that both lines would not make successful applications. During the debate one of the councillors said that he could not support the Meifod line, as the benefit would go to a Shropshire town.

The next day Forden Rural District Council agreed to support the Welshpool railway and one of the councillors gave notice of his intention to propose that the council give financial support to it too, a move that required a month's notice before it could be considered. When another councillor forecast that light railways would go out of fashion and be superseded by motor cars he was greeted by laughter and the clerk said that they, motor cars, would never get 'up through Castle

Caereinion'. The first turned out to be unusually perceptive and the second was just wrong.

With an estimate from Calthrop and Ward of £21,309 8s to hand (Appendix 3), notice of intention to apply to the Light Railway Commissioners for an order in respect of the Welshpool & Llanfair Light Railway was published in the *County Times* on 17 April.

The intended railway would, it said, commence near the Welshpool railway station, at the junction of Smithfield and Severn Roads, and terminate in the parish of Llanfair Caereinion at a point one furlong four chains north-east of the bridge over the river. It would run along the easterly side of Smithfield Road for 200ft and then proceed in a westerly direction, crossing the Shropshire Union Canal at the northern end of the aqueduct before following the course of the Lledan brook at the side of the vicarage grounds to Church Street, which it would cross, continuing to follow the brook before crossing Union Street and the Back Road near their junctions with Hall Street, taking in the property known as the 'Severn Stars'. It would then run at the back of the houses on Back Road and behind the armoury to Raven Square.

Crossing the main road opposite the Llanerchydol lodge, the line would run to the south of Llanfair Road, following it for three-quarters of a mile before crossing the Powis Castle drive, then leaving the road to pass north of Blackmill houses and Nantycaws, to a point opposite Sylfaen dairy farm, where it would take a south-westerly direction towards Castle Caereinion, passing Cwm Farm before crossing the roads from Sylfaen and Dolarddyn, then running north-westerly to cross the old Llanfair road near Dolarddyn farm house and then the Dolarddyn road near its junction with the Ty'n y Coed road, to reach the river Banwy. It would then follow the river until a point north-east of Heniarth mill, where it would be crossed, running between the river and the main road until the terminus was reached.

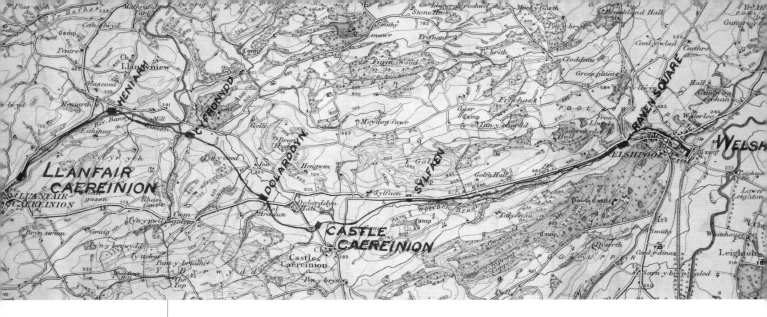

The deposited plan
for the Welshpool &
Llanfair Light Railway.
(National Archives)

A schedule of the land required was included and is reproduced below. The notice was signed by W.F. Addie, the mayor, on behalf of the promoters.

The deputation that should have visited Llanfair parish council on 13 March made it on 24 April but did not get a warm welcome and some councillors stayed away in protest at the cancelled meeting. After the deputation had made its presentation and answered questions, the council, after the deputation had left, unanimously passed a resolution expressing its dissatisfaction with the deputation's statement in support of the narrow gauge scheme, and pledged the Council to renewed support of the Meifod route!

The *County Times* (1 May) acknowledged the promoters' courtesy in attending the meeting when the council had made it clear that it favoured the Meifod scheme and was not interested in the Welshpool line.

Forden RDC voted in favour of making an advance to the railway on 5 May but the resolution failed to secure the required two-thirds majority required. The *County Times* (8 May) reckoned the voting had been subject to a procedural irregularity. The motion to advance £2,500 had attracted amendments to advance only £1,500 and to make no advance. The paper claimed that the amendments should have been voted on first, then the winner put against the original resolution. Instead the councillors were offered the choice of advance or no advance, which, carried by 8 to 6, failed the two-thirds test. The paper expected the council to review a decision achieved in a 'doubtful manner.'

The paper was proved right and when the council met on 2 June 1897 the clerk ruled that the resolution had been in contravention of standing orders. To set the matter right a motion to advance not more than £1,500 to the railway was proposed to

Parish	Quantity A. R. P.	Purpose
Parish of Pool	10 3 6	Construction of Railway and Station at Welshpool.
Parish of Castle Caereinion A. R. P. Urban 5 2 32 Rural 6 0 19	11 3 11	Construction of Railway.
Parish of Llangyniew	0 2 16	Ditto
Parish of Llanfair Caereinion	8 0 19	Construction of Railway and Station at Llanfair.
Acres	31 1 12	

be considered on 14 July. Another motion called for the original resolution to be rescinded.

The Meifod promoters must have thought that they were making good progress with the news that on 18 May the Board of Agriculture had certified that their scheme justified financial support from the state, but it was the last document placed in the Board of Trade's file dealing with their application.

At a meeting of the Welshpool promoters' general committee on 3 June, Addie explained that, taking into account the expected grants from the local authorities and the Treasury, the railway needed to raise £6,500 in shares. The Earl of Powis had offered to take £1,500 and Robert Charles Anwyl, the owner of property near Meifod who lived at Machynlleth, £300 with a promise of more if required. Others promised a total of £200 during the evening, leaving £4,500 to raise. Canvassers were appointed and Addie and his colleagues set off on a tour of the area to solicit subscriptions.

The Light Railway Commissioners arrived at Llanfair to start their enquiry into the Meifod and Welshpool railways on 3 August 1897. Starting at 3.30pm, they announced that the Meifod application would be dealt with first because it had been the first received.

The first witness was J.E. Thomas, the engineer. Although he said that he had 'large experience' in constructing railways and had been chief assistant engineer on the Liverpool–Wrexham line and on the Hereford & Brecon Railway, he was poorly prepared and did not know much about the area through which his proposed railway was to run. He denied that the Meifod line ran parallel to the Llanfyllin branch until the Welshpool engineers produced a map that showed that between Arddleen and Meifod it did. He was unaware that trains only stopped at Arddleen twice a week as it had been superseded by Four Crosses. His claim that the distance between Llanfair and Oswestry was twelve miles was greeted with laughter.

Questioning revealed that the areas served by the proposed stations were sparsely populated. Meifod, half-a-mile from its proposed station, was the largest community, with 400 inhabitants. There was only one bridge over the Vyrnwy to give access from the north bank of the river to the railway.

Dr Humphreys claimed that in Llanfair opinion was unanimously in favour of the scheme. There had been no meeting promoting the Welshpool scheme in Llanfair and none of the Welshpool promoters lived in Llanfair and paid rates there. His claim that most cattle and produce from Llanfair was routed through the Meifod valley to Oswestry got him into a spat with the Welshpool scheme's barrister until he admitted that it went through Welshpool. It also took some effort to get him to admit that he did not know anyone in Llanfair who regarded Oswestry as his market town. Re-surveying the route had increased the estimate from £36,000 to £42,000. (Appendix 3)

At 8 pm the enquiry was adjourned to be resumed at 9 am the next day. The scheme's secretary gave evidence that there were thirty-one landowners affected by the railway. Nine dissented, twelve assented and ten had not expressed an opinion. Eight of the twelve who had assented had agreed to take payment for their land in shares. The nine who dissented were all large landowners.

John Jehu, a Llanfair miller and corn merchant, said that he paid 6s per ton for the 500 tons of goods that he received from Welshpool every year. Farmers sold poultry to hucksters who took three cartloads a week to Oswestry. The farmers themselves did their business at Welshpool. Llanfair trade came through Welshpool but was not with Welshpool. Although the county court, the assizes and quarter sessions were all held in Welshpool and Oswestry had little connection with Welsh counties he still considered the Meifod scheme to be the better line.

Landowners complained that the line was the wrong side of the river for them to make use of. Adding more bridges would not help unless new roads were made to access them. The £30 an acre estimated for land purchase was too low, and they would not sell except by compulsion. One tenant had threatened to give up his farm if the railway divided his fields, saying that it would be unworkable.

An agreement had been reached with the Shropshire Union Canal but the Cambrian objected to the installation of a siding at the canal, saying that it would deprive the company of a considerable amount of revenue. The question of the canal interchange, desired by railway and canal but objected to by the Cambrian, was to become an issue with the Welshpool railway too.

Commenting on the Meifod case, the Welshpool barrister contended that the landowners were not giving sufficient support to justify the award of a Treasury free grant. He also commented on the evidence presented by the technical witnesses, Thomas the engineer, Denniss, the Cambrian's manager, and George Owen, the Cambrian's engineer, remarking on the unpreparedness of their plans.

For the Welshpool scheme, W.F. Addie explained that he was the chief agent of the Powis Castle estates and a member of the Surveyors' Institute. He produced a plan showing the district that he thought would benefit from the railway, amounting to 81,280 acres, omitting land within a three-mile radius of existing railways, and a rateable value of £38,000.

Deciding to give his support to the railway, he had been guided by ten reasons:

(1) At Llanfair large and important fairs were held, and Llanfair was a convenient centre for holding them for the disposal of the stock (mainly store stock) of the district.
(2) Welshpool was geographically the natural outlet for the produce of the district to be served.
(3) Welshpool had better railway facilities than could be given by the proposed Meifod line, joining the Cambrian at Arddleen, as at Welshpool producers had the advantage of three competitive railways and would be enabled to place, at a cheaper rate, more direct, and in less time, the products of the district in the hands of the consumers, and those wanting to purchase what was produced and bred in this portion of the county.
(4) In his opinion Oswestry would not be so good a market for the main product of the district (store stock) as Welshpool, as Oswestry was, so far as he knew, a fat stock market.
(5) In consequence of the building improvements being made by Lord Powis upon his Llymystyn estates, Lord Powis has been obliged to undertake the haulage of the materials himself, a distance of twenty miles, involving a considerable outlay per annum. The railway would be of great advantage for this work. The Meifod line would be of no use to Lord Powis.
(6) The narrow gauge, best suited to the district, could be constructed at much less cost to the ratepayers, would be more likely to prove a financial success, and less likely to involve the ratepayers in any additional burden.
(7) Taking all into consideration, that there would be no advantage to be gained by the proposed broad gauge line, which would cost nearly double the sum of the narrow gauge line, transhipment now being an easy matter.
(8) A narrow gauge line could be cheaply and easily constructed to Llanerfyl or Garthbeibio; it was the promoters' intention to proceed with this extension, and Lord Powis had promised to aid it financially.
(9) Such an extension would almost emancipate the people of this district, and would bring about a revolution in the improvement of the land by the application of manures, cheap transit of feeding stuff, other materials, the use of which was almost entirely prohibited.

(10) In addition to Llanfair, Welshpool market was the one mainly used by people between Welshpool and Llanfair. Welshpool markets were the best for the products of these districts.

Addie added that Lord Powis's main tenants were all in favour of the proposed line and Lord Powis desired him to say that he had no antipathy to the proposed Meifod line, that he would be glad to see it constructed, but in view of the fact that two lines could not be a financial success, he had had to consider which line would be likely to render the most benefit to his property, as well as the district generally, and in deciding to support and aid financially the Welshpool and Llanfair line he had been guided by these considerations.

E.R. Calthrop said that they would begin with two six-coupled engines and the carriages would have a centre gangway. There would be two wagons and two cattle wagons, each capable of carrying sixteen beasts. There would be 'transportation cars' on which standard gauge wagons could be carried. He had heard the Meifod evidence and thought the estimate too low. He had been over that route and would be sorry to be a contractor working to those estimates. The steepest gradient was a distance of a mile at 1 in 30.

A single sheet from what must have been Calthrop's specification survives at the National Archives (RAIL1057/613). It covers his thoughts on the rolling stock requirement in more detail. It states that it was intended to order two six-coupled tank locomotives capable of hauling 40 tons up a gradient of 1 in 30 initially, then, if traffic required it, a locomotive 'of the Barsi type', capable of taking 80 tons up the 1-in-30 gradients, would be used on market days and when traffic was heavier. One carriage 40ft long by 7ft 6in would be provided, capable of carrying 60 passengers. It would have end doors, a central gangway and be 'of the tramway type.' 'A similar car of shorter length will also be provided.' The wagon stock would comprise two low-sided wagons 24ft long by 7ft wide fitted with loose ends and bolsters, capable of carrying goods or timber; two cattle wagons 30ft long, capacity 12 to 16 beasts; two transportation cars 22ft long to carry standard gauge wagons without transhipment of contents, and four small high-sided four-wheel goods wagons. A five-ton travelling crane would also be required.

The last witness was J.R. Dix, the Corris Railway's manager, and engineer of the Welshpool & Llanfair Railway from 1890 until it was abandoned in 1892. He gave evidence that his railway paid its way, was sufficient for the district, and the inconvenience of transhipment was outweighed by the benefits of the narrow gauge. The commissioners brought the proceedings to a close, saying that they reserved their position.

For their appearances at the enquiry, Calthrop was paid £30 1s 8d in fees and expenses and Dix £11 9s. On 9/10 August one of the commissioners inspected the routes of four proposed light railways in the area, the two Llanfair schemes and two targeting Llangynog, in the Tanat valley, one from Llanfyllin and one from a junction with the Cambrian Railways at Porthywaen.

In September 1897 the commissioners decided to recommend to the Board of Trade that the Welshpool order should be made and that the Meifod order should not be made. In their annual report the commissioners said that they had decided in favour the narrow gauge line from on the basis that Llanfair should be directly connected with Welshpool, its nearest market town. But Welshpool and Llanfair would still have to wait several years to get their light railway.

The promoters met at Welshpool town hall on 28 September 1897. Congratulating them on getting the order, Addie explained some time would elapse before they received the formal sanction, because the Board of Trade was dealing with the rush of applications that had followed the 1896 Act. In the meantime, he thought they should take 'vigorous steps' to demonstrate to Welshpool and Llanfair that they intended to build the railway and that the application had not merely been a ruse to stop the Meifod route being built. In the first place they should approach the three railway companies and the canal company to see how far they would help. The engineers should settle on the line in order that landowners could be approached and it could be established who was supportive and who objected.

On 29 January 1898 the Light Railway Commissioners sent Welshpool town council a certificate authorising the payment of £453 14s expenses incurred in making the light railway order application. After some discussion led by councillors who had forgotten that it had been approved twice before, it was passed for payment in February.

An offer of a £7,500 Treasury loan made in February 1898 was rejected because the promoters could not comply with the terms under which it was made, section 4 of the Light Railways Act, probably the requirement that half of the capital required was to be share capital and that half of that should be subscribed by persons other than local authorities. If that is so, it demonstrates unwillingness on the part of the promoters to contribute to the capital in any substantial amount themselves.

Section 5 of the Light Railways Act allowed for a free Treasury grant to be made if, inter alia, the railway was constructed and operated by an existing railway company. In October 1897, a fruitless approach to the GWR and LNWR as operators of the Shrewsbury–Welshpool joint line had been made. After rejecting the section 4 grant the promoters turned to the Cambrian.

The appointment of directors was the headline business when the promoters' general committee met on 10 March 1898. Addie said that having obtained approval for the order the committee's work was done but the order could not be made before directors had been appointed. It would be the directors' responsibility to

negotiate with the Cambrian Railways if that company was chosen to build and operate the railway and to find more share capital. As the company was still not incorporated the directors had their activities recorded in the committee's minute book.

With the number of directors in the draft order set at seven it was proposed that two of them would be nominated by the town council in recognition of the council's support. The Light Railway Commission's approval would be sought to increase the number to eight if the county council sought representation. The five appointed by the committee were: Lord Powis; Athelstane Robert Pryce, who had inherited Cyfronydd Hall from his father in 1891; R.C. Anwyl, Dr John Gill and John Cooke Hilton. Pryce and Hilton were the sons of men who had been involved in the 1877 Welshpool & Llanfair Railway proposal. Gill was a GP living in Welshpool.

The town council met on 19 March. Although it had not been formally requested to appoint directors, it responded to the reports about the committee meeting. A councillor thought that as the council was putting more money into the railway than the county council, and had paid the preliminary expenses, it should have three directors instead of two. Addie and William A. Rogers were elected to the available positions and David Jones, Addie's successor as mayor, was nominated if a third directorship could be obtained. Rogers had been mayor in 1883-6 and 1891-2 and was a farmer and draper. Jones was a grocer, farmer and milk seller.

The *County Times* (2 April) complained that as its status as a supplier of loan capital, the equivalent of a mortgagee or debenture holder, the county council had no right to a directorship, unlike the town council, which was investing in share capital.

There was no more reported activity until 27 August when the *County Times* noted that Sir Watkin Williams-Wynn's agent had been commissioned to report on the line's benefit to agriculture by the

Board of Agriculture. In fact the board's certificate to the effect that the railway would benefit agriculture in the district had been issued on 26 August 1898, achieving a requirement of Section 5 of the 1896 Act to qualify for a free grant.

On 4 September 1898, Denniss advised the directors that the Cambrian was prepared to enter into an agreement to construct and operate the railway provided the necessary capital was subscribed. Slowly, the pieces were coming together.

In an editorial on 10 December 1898, the *County Times* suggested that because its readers had heard nothing about the railway recently, they might have thought that it had collapsed. The paper had obviously been fed information, because it went on to suggest that there would soon be an announcement on the subject and that government departments moved very deliberately. The directors, it said, were still working hard to complete the enterprise.

Sure enough, on 19 December 1898 the Treasury announced that it would make a £7,000 free grant to the railway, requiring that no more than £3,000 should be paid for the land, that the promoters should raise £21,000 locally and that the Cambrian should enter into an agreement to work the line for 99 years.

The Earl of Powis and other landowners had offered land for about five miles of the route free of charge. However, in Welshpool, urban property was required from owners who would gain no direct benefit from the railway and who would want paying its commercial value. Until the company knew precisely what land it needed and was able to treat for it, the cost could not be estimated. The matter was settled with an undertaking, communicated on 10 March 1899, that if the land cost more than £3,000 additional capital would be raised to meet the excess.

On 10 January 1899 the directors resolved to approach the Cambrian's engineer, George Owen, and find out what his charges would be to oversee the construction, and to ask Calthrop if he would act as consulting engineer.

Before making a recommendation about the railway to his directors, C.S. Denniss decided that he, Alfred Jones Collin, the Cambrian's engineer, Addie, and Winnall, the solicitor, should visit the Lynton & Barnstaple Railway in Devon. With a 20-mile route across Exmoor, this best-equipped of English narrow gauge railways had been opened in 1898.

Denniss had read about it in the *Railway Magazine* and thought that a visit would be worthwhile before any decisions were taken about equipment. On 4 January 1899 he had asked the Lynton line for facilities, including a special train. He was offered accommodation on a timetabled train from Barnstaple to Lynton and back to Blackmoor, then a trolley down the gradient to Chelfham where a train would meet the party to return it to Barnstaple. All stations except Wooda [sic] Bay could be visited. The visit took place on 13 February, travelling from Welshpool the previous day, and back the day after. Denniss also requested free passes from the GWR for the journey.

Addie called a public meeting at the town hall to promote the need for new subscribers on 27 January 1899. In a heartfelt speech, David Jones, the new mayor, said that if they wanted the railway to happen Welshpool had to get behind it or someone else would build one to the town's disadvantage. Apart from Lord Powis, the town had only subscribed £400 to the capital. There were men who had made fortunes in the town who were standing aloof from it. Llanfair people had been criticised for committing only £700 to the Meifod line yet with three times the wealth Welshpool had subscribed barely half that. He hoped that the £2,500 outstanding balance would be considerably reduced by the end of the meeting.

Addie said that he thought the mayor had been a little harsh on the town, which had agreed to contribute £8,000 without dissent and had paid the preliminary expenses. So every ratepayer was already invested in the scheme but there were those who had spare capital and he hoped that they

LIST OF SUBSCRIBERS.

The following is a list of subscribers to Share Capital, including £300 subscribed on the day of meeting.

	£
The Right Hon the Earl of Powis	1,500
Sir Watkin Williams-Wynn, Bart	500
Captain A R Pryce	500
Mr H R E Harrison	500
Mr J C Hilton	400
Mr R C Anwyl	300
Mr J M Howell	200
Mr W A Rogers	100
Mr J Jehu	100
Mr Richard Owen, Cann Office	100
Executors of the late Mr E O Jones	100
Mr David Jones (Mayor)	50
Messrs J & M Morris	50
Mr Edward Wyke	50
Mr Thomas Evans, Berriew Street	50
Colonel Pryce-Jones, M.P.	35
Mr William Morris, Broad Street	25
Mr W Forrester Addie	25
Mr Robert Owen, Broad Street	20
Mr D Rowlands	20
Mr Edward Hughes	20
Mr David Lloyd	20
Mr David Jones, Moelddolwen	20
Mr Howell Howells, Coedtalog	20
Mr Humphreys, Berriew Street	20
Mr Charles T Pugh, Berriew Street	20
Mr H Payne	20
Mr J F Francis	20
Mr A E Bond	20
Mr John Eddowes	10
Mr James James, Cross Lane, Cann Office	10
Mr Ellis Jones, Neuaddwen	10
Mr Thomas S Pryce	10
Mr E E Jones, Post Office, Castle Caereinion	5
	£4,850

would respond. Another £300 was subscribed by the close of the meeting, taking the total to £4,850. Another £300 was subscribed during a meeting at Llanfair on 17 February and £100 at Llangadfan on 19 April.

Another landmark on the road to making the railway was achieved in February 1899, when the Light Railway Commissioners sent the order to the Board of Trade for confirmation. Objections had to be submitted before 18 March. Llanfyllin Board of Guardians objected to the clause freeing the railway's land from being assessed for rates at a higher value than the land occupied had been previously assessed for a period of ten years. The council was informed that the clause was a condition upon which the free grant depended. The county council made representations about several clauses but no changes were made.

Just as the directors thought that they had done all that was required for the order to be made, in April 1899 the Cambrian produced a shock. Its solicitor had noticed that the draft order included clauses obliging the company to make a siding to the Shropshire Union Railways & Canal Company (SURC) wharf at Welshpool. The position was not serious, the solicitor told his directors, and the connection was at Welshpool so traffic arising on the light railway would be carried the maximum distance before it was transferred to the canal, but the Cambrian would still suffer. It would not enter into an agreement unless the clauses were removed, it declared.

The directors were embarrassed. They had agreed to the clauses to secure the withdrawal of the canal company's objections to the order. They had been included in the draft orders that had been approved by the Cambrian and it could not be expected to ask the canal company to agree to their withdrawal. Meeting the promoters at Oswestry on 2 May, Denniss implied that they were at fault for not drawing attention to the clauses, which, considering his company employed a solicitor whose job it was to examine Bills and the like to look for clauses that might affects its interests, was somewhat disingenuous. The Cambrian still wanted to make an agreement and would 'assist the promoters in inducing the Board of Trade to strike out these clauses.'

Two days later, the committee resolved that before asking for the clauses to be removed it would ask the canal if it was prepared to construct and work the line. Maybe the directors were unaware that it was leased by the LNWR, which had already indicated its lack of interest in their railway. Despite a three-page impassioned appeal from the railway's solicitors sent on 2 June, the Cambrian stood its ground. The Light Railway Commissioners called all parties to a meeting in London on 11 July and the Cambrian got its way, the 'objectionable clauses' being removed. The canal was given an opportunity to appeal against the decision but took no further action. Strangely, in November 1901, the Cambrian approved a siding being located near the canal for the benefit of the Powis estate. 'It is not intended to give the canal company facilities for traffic, in violation of the agreement already arrived at,' Addie wrote to Denniss on 20 June.

The hiatus made scant impression in the local press. Brief editorials in the *County Times* (29 April and 29 July) and a letter in the same paper (17 June) expressed concern that the railway might be dropped.

The writer's concern was unfounded, and the Welshpool & Llanfair Light Railway Order was made on 8 September 1899, comprising 95 clauses and two schedules. The authorised railway was 9 miles 1 furlong 1.50 chains long, and 2ft 6in gauge. Instead of taking a route to the south-west of the main line station like the earlier schemes, the railway started from a point in Smithfield Road, opposite the station, taking a sinuous route through the town with some street running and partially astride the Lledan brook before passing the Standard quarry and reaching open countryside at Raven Square. Here it ran to the south of the turnpike, making the best of the contours as only a narrow gauge railway can, passing to the north of Castle Caereinion and then picking up the previously proposed route near Dolarddyn. Three years were allowed for its construction. The company was not required to fence the railway where it ran along the road in Welshpool. There could be up to five directors plus one appointed by the county council, and three by the corporation.

The first directors were the 4th Earl of Powis, A.R. Pryce, R.C. Anwyl, and

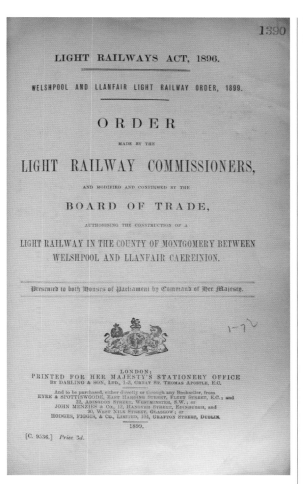

The 1899 light railway order.

J.C. Hilton, all landowners; Powis had succeeded to the title in 1891. The capital was set at £6,000 in addition to any treasury grants or shares subscribed by the local authorities or loans made by them. In setting the rates that could be charged, the commissioners incorporated the Cambrian's, except for the carriage of goods and minerals, where they allowed an increase of 25%, saying that the traffic would not be worthwhile at the Cambrian's rates.

ROLLING STOCK 1960-2019

The Countess and *The Earl* crossing Raven Square on 6 October 1962. The former had just been returned from its sojourn, and overhaul, at Oswestry works and the latter had steamed from Llanfair to fetch it.

On 3 June 2002 *Countess* and *The Earl* were posed together in public for the first time since the completion of their lottery-funded overhauls. They have been turned out in appropriate liveries to match their restoration to GWR condition.

Countess made an appearance at the Warley model railway show, held annually at the National Exhibition Centre, on 25/6 November 2002.

The first locomotive to run under preservation company auspices was this 16/20hp Ruston & Hornsby diesel, built in 1934 for an ironstone company in Lincolnshire. Donated to the railway in 1961 and named *Raven*, it was useful in the early days, especially after its weight was increased by half a ton in 1967. Of limited use as the railway acquired more and heavier stock, it was sold in 1974.

The Hibberd 'Planet' *Upnor Castle* had been built for the Admiralty's Lodge Hill & Upnor Railway in Kent in 1954. The preservation company bought it in 1962 but its short wheelbase made it rough riding, so it was sold to the Ffestiniog Railway in 1968.

Nutty was a chain-driven vertical boiler locomotive built by Sentinel Ltd in Shrewsbury for the London Brick Company in 1929. Originally 2ft 11in gauge, it was loaned to the railway by the Narrow Gauge Railway Museum Trust in 1964 and regauged at Llanfair, finding use on the easy gradients to Heniarth while the Banwy bridge was being repaired in 1965. By 1967 it was regarded as the 'works train reserve engine'. The circumstances of this photograph at Castle Caereinion are unknown. The loco was returned to its owner in 1971. (John Neville)

Monarch, an 0-4-4-0T articulated loco, was built for Bowaters United Kingdom Pulp & Paper Mills Ltd, Sittingbourne, Kent, by W.B. Bagnall in Stafford in 1953. A member funded its purchase by the railway in 1966 and it was photographed soon after arrival. After an overhaul, which included replacing the spark-arrester chimney with one of traditional appearance, it entered service in 1963. Withdrawn in 1978 for repairs and fitting the vacuum brakes necessary before it could work passenger trains down the Golfa bank, it was later set aside and in 1992 it was sold to two Ffestiniog Railway members who moved it to the FR.

At the FR, *Monarch* was dismantled as the first stage towards regauging but it was donated to the Festiniog Railway Trust as a kit of parts when its owners' priorities changed. Regret that the loco had been sold and no use made of it led to a group of company members, named 'Monarchists', to raise funds to buy it and donate it back to the company. It was delivered to Raven Square in January 2003. Reassembled and restored cosmetically by the Monarchists, *Monarch* is displayed to the public on operating days. (2 September 2017)

Upnor Castle was replaced a six-wheeled Baguley-Drewry obtained from the Broughton Moor munitions depot, Cumbria, in February 1968. Like *Upnor Castle*, it had started its working life, in 1949, at the Lodge Hill & Upnor Railway, which led to it being named *Chattenden* at Llanfair. Dated 29 June 1968, the photograph shows it in its original condition.

To enable it to work passenger trains when required, *Chattenden* was equipped with vacuum brakes. Its cab doors were plated up and a new access made to the rear. When photographed in 1986, its wheels had been removed to be re-tyred. The caravan in the background was used as a tea-bar.

The smallest steam locomotive on the railway, the Barclay 0-4-0T *Dougal* was built for Glasgow Corporation's Provan gas works in 1946. Owned by two members who subsequently gave it to the railway, it arrived at Llanfair in 1969. It was photographed there during an overhaul which was completed in 1975. *Dougal*, named after the *Magic Roundabout* character, is steamed on gala days and special occasions but at the time of writing its boiler requires replacement.

This six-wheeled 100hp Fowler diesel, built in 1951, was acquired from a South Wales cement works in 1969 and named *Wynnstay* after a Llanfair pub frequented by the volunteers. It proved to be unsuitable for the railway, however, and was sold for further use at the Zoological Society of London's Whipsnade Zoo railway in 1972.

Seen with *Countess*, Franco-Belge 0-8-0T 669 01 *Sir Drefaldwyn* was the first steam loco to haul passenger trains on the railway after the original Beyer, Peacocks.

Sir Drefaldwyn crossing Cwm Lane as it leaves Golfa station in the late 1990s. The lights originally mounted on the tanks have been replaced by a single lamp in front of the chimney. Out of service since 2000, the loco is being overhauled at the time of writing.

This Hunslet 50hp flameproof mines loco was delivered to the West Dean, Wiltshire, armaments depot in 1941. Acquired in 1971, it was named *Ferret*. When photographed in 1986 it had recently had its spark-arresting chimney changed for the straight one seen here. The brake van had been obtained from the naval armaments' depot at Trecwn, Pembrokeshire, in 1973.

After several years out of service, *Ferret* returned to operations in 2004, painted and lettered as if owned by the GWR. After it had been used to rescue *Countess* it was seen carrying a board that read '823 Support Engine.' The railway owns another locomotive of this type, obtained in 1992. Named *Scooby/Scwbi*, it has been fitted with a larger cab.

Joan is an 0-6-2T built by Kerr, Stuart in Stoke on Trent for export to the Antigua Sugar Corporation in 1927. Seen out of use by a holidaying member it was acquired in 1971 and entered service after being modified to suit its new home in 1977. The photograph was taken at Raven Square in 1984.

From 1989 until 1991 *Joan* ran in this blue livery before being withdrawn to await boiler repairs. It then spent several years on display with a collecting box. (31 August 1993)

Joan's day came in 2005, when work started on a thorough overhaul that included fitting new tanks and boiler. Designed to burn coal instead of bagasse, the smaller firebox increased the space in the loco's cab, making it more suitable for use on driver experiences. Coal bunker capacity was increased too. The overhaul was completed in 2011. *Joan* was photographed at Raven Square on 5 April 2015.

A line-up of black engines in October 1975. Leading the queue is ex-Sierra Leone Government Railway Hunslet 2-6-2T No 85 which had arrived at Llanfair with four carriages in August. Built in 1954, it was one of the last two steam locomotives built for the SLGR, which had been abandoned.

Following an extensive overhaul, No 85 entered service in a simple green livery at Easter 1979. The photograph was taken on 21 August 1981.

In 1992 No 85 was repainted in North Staffordshire Railway Indian red livery, as seen at Golfa on 30 December 1997. The train was a special run for staff and volunteers of several Welsh narrow gauge railways. The headboard was said to refer to the railway's varied gradients, 'over the hump in a sea of sand'.

In a livery applied in 2003, lined midnight blue, No 85 was captured crossing New Drive on 5 September 2004.

With its boiler certificate set to expire in 2010, No 85 appeared at the 2009 gala with two restored Sierra Leone carriages and painted in SLGR black livery. On its last day in service, 9 April 2010, it was photographed climbing the Golfa bank. From 2011 the loco was displayed at the national Railway Museum's Shildon outpost for five years. In 2017 the railway obtained a Heritage Lottery Fund grant of £22,800 to fund a tour back to Llanfair, via the Armley Industrial Museum, Leeds; Hull, twin town of Freetown, Sierra Leone's capital; the London Museum of Water & Steam, Kew Bridge; Tyseley Locomotive Works; Ironbridge Gorge Museum; and the Shrewsbury steam rally. An unofficial fund has made a considerable contribution towards the cost of the new boiler that the locomotive needs.

Orion is a 2-6-2T built by Tubize in Belgium for the Jokioisten Railway, Finland, in 1948. Withdrawn needing firebox repairs in 1963, it was offered for sale as scrap when the JR closed in 1972. Bought by an English enthusiast, it was sold to the railway in 1983. Dismantling for restoration started in 1993 and it entered service named *Orion* in 2000.

Despite its size, *Orion* proved less than ideal for the railway, as it had been designed for running at high speeds over easy gradients, not slogging up steep hills. In 2006 the opportunity was taken to sell it to the operators of a preserved section of the Jokioisten Railway, its original home. It ran for the last time during the gala on 2/3 September, with its new owners participating in its operation before it was formally handed over.

This small Wickham personnel carrier was allocated to the railway when it was made in 1940. No longer used operationally, it occasionally appears during galas. It is seen here arriving at Cyfronydd in 1999.

As a step towards automating the railway's track renewals and maintenance this Plasser tamper was obtained from its South African maker in 1999. Built in 1986 for use in diamond mines it had seen very little use.

Built in Romania in 1955, Resita 0-8-0T No 764.423 was imported into the UK for a scheme that failed to get off the ground in 1994. Ten years later it was donated to the railway, which placed it in store. It was sold to a Romanian dealer in 2016 and restored to working order.

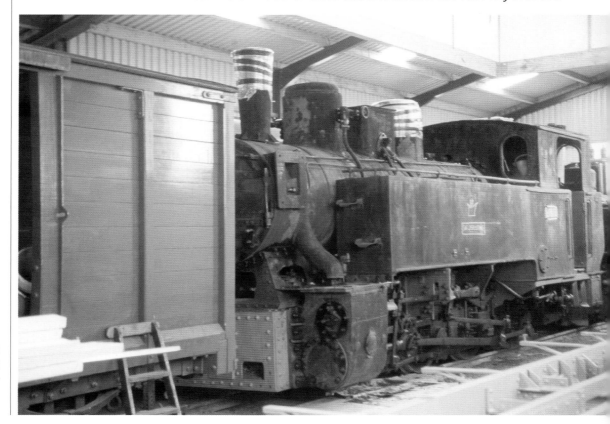

A diesel locomotive shortage in 2004 resulted in the hire of this 60hp Hunslet for a few months in 2004. It had been built for the Royal Navy's armaments depot at Dean Hill, Wiltshire, in 1965.

Built in Germany in 1979, this six-wheeled 235hp Diema diesel locomotive was obtained from the Taiwan Sugar Corporation in 2004 and is the most powerful diesel locomotive on the railway. Photographed at Raven Square on 26 June 2005, the loco retained its yellow and red livery when it was repainted.

To replace Tubize 2-6-2T *Orion* the railway bought Resita 0-8-0T No 764.425 from Romania in working order in 2007. It was photographed at Raven Square waiting for unloading to start on 20 June and entered service on 22 July. It had been built for a forestry railway in 1954. If it had been as satisfactory as hoped, then consideration would have been given to restoring 764.425.

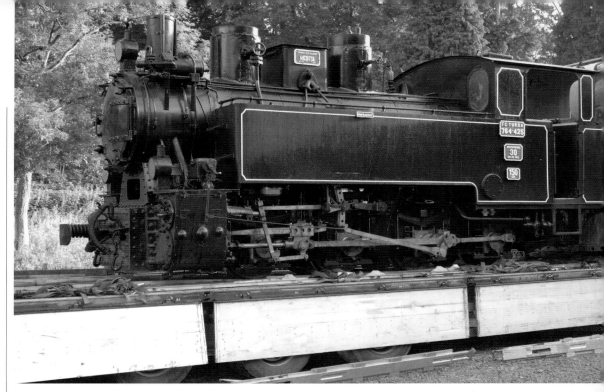

Unfortunately No 764.425 was not a success. It broke an axle in 2008, sustained a cracked boiler stay in 2010 and an axle crank failed in 2013. In the meantime, it had been fitted with a new cab, chimney, blastpipe and smokebox door, the condition represented by this 1 September 2012 photograph. Crew said that it was very strong and capable of pulling any load the railway required, but after the second major failure there was no confidence in it. Both Nos 764.425 and 764.423 were sold back to Romania in 2016 and found new homes in Romania and the Czech Republic. The railway decided that to fill the gap in its operating fleet it would return Franco Belge 0-8-0 *Sir Drefaldwyn* to service.

This ex-Ministry of Defence Baguley-Drewry railcar was delivered to the railway for trials and evaluation by its owner on 21 May 2008. It is seen being demonstrated to members of the Ffestiniog Railway the next day. Its stripes instantly caused it to be known as 'the wasp'. The railway announced that it would keep the vehicle on 29 August.

This 230hp Diema diesel locomotive was imported from Taiwan in 2004. Usually confined to works trains, on 31 August 2013 it was seen hauling a passenger train over the B4385 level crossing at Castle Caereinion. At this date planning was in hand to modernise the crossing with lifting barriers.

CHAPTER 3

BUILDING THE RAILWAY

The directors met for the first time on 30 September 1899, when Lord Powis, R.C. Anwyl and J.C. Hilton were joined by W.F. Addie, David Jones and W.A. Rogers, the town council's appointees. Little business was conducted. Even with the order, it was going to be more than three years before trains ran to Llanfair.

A.J. Collin, who had replaced George Owen as the Cambrian's engineer, had offered to work for the company for 5½% of the contract price, which was accepted on 14 November 1899. The directors were not so happy, however, with his demand for £500 to be paid if the railway was abandoned after the plans had been made, but he refused to back down.

A prospectus for £10,000 share capital was issued with a deadline of 19 December 1899. With the £4,000 already agreed to be taken by the corporation, £9,077 had been subscribed by 29 January 1900. In December 1899 and January 1900, the investing authorities put in hand the actions necessary to borrow the money to advance to the railway. In Welshpool, one of the councillors got the subject of the town council's share deposits deferred so that those 'who were not in love with the scheme' could discuss it, even though the expenditure had already been agreed and the council's commitment to it inviolate. The transaction was confirmed on 17 February.

The first statutory ordinary meeting, which brought the Welshpool & Llanfair Light Railway Company into being, was held at the town hall on 1 March 1900. It was chaired by the Earl of Powis, who started by saying that they met on an auspicious occasion as news of the relief of Ladysmith had just been received, which he thought augured well for the success of their undertaking. Summarising the steps taken to secure the order since 1897 he added that he was pleased to announce that the £29,100 capital was secured, including £10,000 subscribed by shareholders.

Lord Powis, A.R. Pryce, R.C. Anwyl and J.C. Hilton were confirmed as directors. No substitute was offered for Dr John Gill who had died on 11 July 1899, aged 55, just after he had been nominated. A plaque was erected to his memory in St Mary's parish church in Welshpool.

The final business of the meeting was to approve the agreement made with the Cambrian for the use, working, maintenance and management of the undertaking for 99 years for 60% of the gross receipts. In June 1898 the promoters had tried to get the Cambrian to work the line for 55% of the receipts, offering a compromise of 57% but the Cambrian insisted on 60%. The agreement was sealed immediately.

A notice that the Cambrian and the new railway company intended to make the

Alfred Jones Collin, the Cambrian Railways' engineer.

PUBLIC NOTICES.

WELSHPOOL AND LLANFAIR LIGHT RAILWAY COMPANY.

NOTICE IS HEREBY GIVEN that the First (Statuary) Ordinary Meeting of the Shareholders of the Welshpool and Llanfair Light Railway Company will be held at the Town Hall, Welshpool, on Thursday, the 1st day of March next. at 12 o'clock (noon), for the Election of the Directors and Auditors and for the transaction of the General Business of the Company.

AND NOTICE IS HEREBY FURTHER GIVEN that immediately after the termination of the Business of such Meeting, a Special General Meeting of the Shareholders will be held at the same place for the purpose of sanctioning an Agreement between the Welshpool and Llanfair Light Railway Company and the Cambrian Railways Company for the construction and use, working, maintenance and management of the undertaking of the Welshpool and Llanfair Light Railway Company by the Cambrian Railways Company upon the terms therein mentioned.

Dated this 8th day of February, 1900,
JOHN EVANS,
Secretary.

The advertisement calling the first shareholders' general meeting and the following special meeting to approve the agreement with the light railway company and the Cambrian published in the *Montgomery County Times*.

The light railway company's seal. (National Archives)

THE CAMBRIAN RAILWAYS COMPANY
AND
THE WELSHPOOL AND LLANFAIR LIGHT RAILWAY COMPANY.

NOTICE IS HEREBY GIVEN, pursuant to the provisions of the Railways Clauses Act 1863, and the Railway and Canal Traffic Acts, 1873 and 1888, and the Light Railways Act, 1896, and the Welshpool and Llanfair Light Railway Order, 1899, that it is the intention of the Cambrian Railways Company and the Welshpool and Llanfair Light Railway Company to enter into an Agreement for the following purposes, viz.:—(amongst other things) The construction, maintenance, and management of a Light Railway, authorised by the said Order, commencing at Welshpool and terminating at Llanfair Caereinion, both in the County of Montgomery, for the use and working of such Railway and the conveyance of traffic thereon, and the regulation, collection, transmission, and delivery of such traffic; the fixing, collecting, and appointment of tolls, rates, and charges; the supply and maintenance of rolling stock and plant; the employment of officers and servants for the conveyance and conduct of traffic and the division and apportionment of revenue, tolls, and receipts derived from the working and management of the said Railway. And that any Company or person aggrieved by such agreement and desiring to object thereto may bring such objection before the Railway and Canal Commissioners by sending the same in writing addressed to the Registrar to the Railway and Canal Commissioners at their Office, at the Royal Courts of Justice, Strand, London, on or before the Eighth day of May, 1900, in which Office a copy of the Agreement can be seen.

Dated this Fifth day of April, 1900.
JOHN EVANS,
Secretary of the Welshpool and Llanfair Light Railway Company.

The advertisement giving members of the public an opportunity to object to the light railway company and the Cambrian making an agreement for the latter to build, maintain and operate the light railway published in the *Montgomery County Times*.

agreement was published in the *County Times* on 7 April. Any company or person aggrieved by such agreement was invited to submit their objection to the Railway and Canal Commissioners by 8 May. The agreements with the investing authorities were sealed on 23 April.

A.J. Collin was quick to work at setting out the line. On 5 May the *County Times* reported that the centre line was approaching Heniarth and the cross-sections had been established for three miles.

Payments agreed on 3 July 1900 were £250 to Collin for work carried out to date, and £9 17s 4d to Edward Jones, the town clerk. Jones had billed the company for 'perusing' the agreement between it and the town council and for negotiating the council's £500 loan enabling it to pay the deposit on its shares. There appeared to be no question about the payment, but it does appear to be rather strange.

The Treasury had written on 21 June, seeking assurances that if the cost of the land and property required by the company exceeded £4,100, the company could raise additional capital to cover it. The solicitor was instructed to give the assurance required.

With his survey completed, Collin's revised estimate of £32,480, submitted on 1 October 1900, was a setback. The directors decided to ask the Treasury for an additional grant of £7,500 and to make an application to amend the light railway order. Dated 20 November, the notice explained that the company wished to increase its capital, extend the time for land purchase and completion of works, to empower the local authorities to make further advances to the undertaking, and to permit the Cambrian to subscribe to the capital.

Including Collin's estimate, the directors produced a total estimate of expenses totalling £43,204 on 27 November 1900.

Construction including land			£32,480
Rolling stock			
	3 engines	£4,500	
	2 large bogie passenger coaches	£900	
	2 smaller 3rd class coaches	£400	
	40 goods wagons @ £25	£1,000	
	4 covered goods wagons	£150	
	12 covered cattle trucks	£1,000	
	Travelling crane	£150	
			£8,100
Expenses			
	Engineers	£1,624	
	Legal and other	£1,000	
			£2,624
Total			£43,204

On 5 December 1900 Collin suggested deferring calling for tenders until February 1901, when prices were likely to be more favourable, and obtaining estimates for rolling stock at the same time, otherwise delay might arise. In Welshpool, the line had to have grooved [tram] rail, so he needed to know the wheel profile to be used in order to complete the specification. Land plans could be completed in two weeks and the contract plans, if required, in about six weeks.

The rolling stock requirement was discussed when a team from Welshpool met Denniss and other Cambrian officers at Oswestry on 10 December 1900, producing a new list. Denniss urged that three locomotives should be purchased to provide cover in the event of a breakdown, but the directors said that no more than two could be afforded at that time. Herbert E. Jones, the Cambrian's locomotive superintendent, was authorised to obtain designs of suitable locomotives and other rolling stock.

Rolling stock	
2 locomotives @ £1,600 each	£3,200
2 large composite passenger coaches @ £450 each	£900
1 extra 3rd class coach for use on fair days &c	£200
40 goods wagons @ £25 each	£1,000
4 covered goods wagons @ £60 each	£240
2 covered cattle trucks @ £85 each	£170
Travelling crane	£150
10 timber trucks @ £25 each	£250
2 brake vans @ £120 each	£240
	£6,350

The Treasury agreed to an additional grant of £7,500 on 11 December 1900. One of the standard conditions for making it was that it would not be paid until the railway had been completed and inspected by the Board of Trade, which would aggravate the cash-flow position during construction. Reporting the grant on 15 December, the *County Times* attributed it to the efforts of the Earl of Powis. The paper also said that the increased costs of materials and labour arose from external sources and that the circumstances were very different when the estimates were made. Continued involvement in the Second Boer War probably contributed to inflation reaching 5.1% in 1900.

Collin had produced plans and specification by 25 January 1901, when a sub-committee of the directors met to consider them. He was asked to make further provision for unloading stock at Smithfield, to straighten the line at Seven Stars, and to locate Cyfronydd station in field No 83. The realignment at Seven Stars required the demolition of the malthouse as well as the public house of that name. Copies of the large-scale plans that identify the field numbers have not come to light. On 31 January, the directors instructed Collin to obtain tenders as soon as possible. They also agreed to pay H.E. Jones 150 guineas for his services in procuring the locomotives and rolling stock. He had recommended ordering the locomotives as soon as possible, saying that there was no hurry to order the rolling stock. He also advised against buying a travelling crane.

Herbert Jones, the Cambrian's locomotive engineer, was responsible for producing the specifications for the light railway's rolling stock.

The railway company secretaries, C.S. Dennis and John Evans, signed the notice calling for tenders on 18 February and the six submitted were considered on 20 March 1901. Most offered a 2½% discount and an allowance for old materials. The *Shrewsbury Chronicle* (29 March 1901) said that they were all within the limits of Collin's estimate.

Tenders for Welshpool & Llanfair Light Railway	
A. Braithwaite	£26,353 5s 10d
Holme & King Limited, Liverpool	£26,239
H. & M. Nowell, Leeds	£26,000
Cleveland Bridge Company	£33,212 12s 4d
W. Jones & Company, Manchester	£21,227 3s 10d
J. Strachan, Cardiff	£24,282 13s 2d

Holme & King had built the Snowdon Mountain Railway in 1895/6. Still based in Darlington, County Durham, the Cleveland Bridge Company trades internationally as Cleveland Bridge UK Ltd. John Strachan (born 1848) was a Scotsman from Brechin, in Angus. Before settling in Cardiff when he married, he had worked on railways, docks and water works in Scotland and England. In Wales he worked on the Cardiff and Caerphilly Railway, the Rhymney Railway, Roath and Bute docks and the GWR's new station buildings at Cardiff in 1894. In 1891 he gave his occupation to the census enumerator as 'contractor man'. Ten years later he said he was a railway contractor. He was assisted in the Welshpool contract by his son, also John (1877-1934).

Collin explained that he had kept some items out of the specification because it would be cheaper to let the work locally. Denniss was asked to inquire into the status of the lowest bidder while the sub-committee was to pursue the three lowest bids with a view to reaching agreement with one of them. The solicitor reported that the notices to treat with land owners had been served and claims were being made. Addie was appointed to act as the railway's valuer.

Non-tender items	
Permanent way materials	£5,790
Station buildings	£535
Engine shed and carriage shed	£310
Water supply at Welshpool and Llanfair	£70
Signalling and telegraph	£240
Sidings in Cambrian company's yard	£260
	£7,205

On 1 April 1901, the status of the lowest bidder was considered to be unsatisfactory leading to consideration of Strachan's bid. A statement was produced showing the company's resources and anticipated liabilities.

Contract – Strachan		£24,290	
Less 2½%	£506 5s		
Old materials	£7 6s 10d	£513 11s 10d	
			£23,776 8s 2d
Works not included in contract, estimate			£7,202 1s 3d
Land, say			£6,000
Rolling stock			£6,500
Expenses			£3,000
Interest on loans during construction			£650
(Nothing allowed for contingencies)			£47,128 9s 5d
Towards which the company has:			
Original capital			£29,100
Additional free grant		£7,500	
Additional loans already promised		£2,250	£9,750
			£38,850
Sum still to be obtained	£8,278 9s 5d		

The directors resolved that Strachan's tender be recommended to the Cambrian for acceptance, subject to Strachan taking £1,000 in ordinary shares in the company. Accepting the tender on 3 April, the Cambrian said that Strachan had agreed to take the shares. Passing on the decision, Denniss asked how the capital was going to be raised.

When the directors met on 18 April, the resolution calling on the Cambrian to enter into and complete the contract with Strachan was carried with one director voting against; the identity of the dissenter was not revealed. The *Montgomeryshire Echo* (13 April) pointed out that it was the first tender accepted for the construction of a light railway authorised under the Light Railways Act. It also anticipated the railway being opened for traffic early in 1903, if not earlier.

At the 18 April 1901 meeting, the directors accepted an offer to buy the rails made by William Bailey Hawkins, a Cambrian director. The offer was supported by Collin, who said that it would secure the lowest price. Guest, Keen & Company's bid to supply 800 tons of flat-bottom rail at £5 1s per ton and fishplates at £6 16s per ton was accepted for delivery in three monthly instalments from July.

Foreseeing cash-flow problems with the grant being paid in arrears, the directors sought interim payments but the Treasury's offer was to pay the first half when a sum equal to the total grant had been spent, and the remainder on production of the

Original rail still in use in 1999. It had been rolled at Guest, Keen & Company's Dowlais steel works in 1901.

Board of Trade certificate that the railway was complete and open for traffic. With commendable speed, the decision was circulated on 28 May 1901.

The directors' attention had turned to cutting the first sod. Viscount Clive, the Earl's son, was proposed subject to his parents giving approval, and on 10 May 1901 the date was set for 30 May, with 'Colonel Hutchins' field' the location. The company would supply a silver spade while the engineer and contractor were expected to supply a wheelbarrow. The spade cost £15 15s plus the cost of engraving it, £2 5s 9d.

The ceremony was a grand affair and Welshpool took a holiday despite it being a Thursday. There was a grandstand, flags and festoons, several bands, large crowds and speeches. The Powis family arrived in a carriage drawn by a pair of bays and preceded by an outrider. The countess's attire was fully described, as was her son's, it being his first public engagement.

Presented with the spade and barrow, Lord Clive, assisted by A.J. Collin, cut the initials 'W.L.L.R' in the turf. Afterwards, the company and guests repaired to the assembly room at the town hall where 200 sat down for lunch provided by the Earl. If all those listed in the *Border Counties Advertizer*'s extensive report had subscribed £10 to the railway's capital its finances would have been much healthier. Notwithstanding Strachan's participation in the event, he erected the grandstand, the agreement for him to build the railway was not submitted for sealing until 4 June.

An amended estimate had led to the issue of a second prospectus in May 1901, soliciting subscriptions for the £5,000 unissued share capital. Would-be subscribers were told that although the original £10,000 share capital had been fully subscribed, the high cost of labour and materials had delayed the start of construction. With a degree of prescience

Assisted by A.J. Collin, the Cambrian's engineer, the young Lord Clive wheels a barrow load of turf away from the spot where they had cut the initials 'W.L.L.R.' in the grass to symbolise the start of construction on 30 May 1901. His proud parents, the Countess and Earl of Powis, look on.

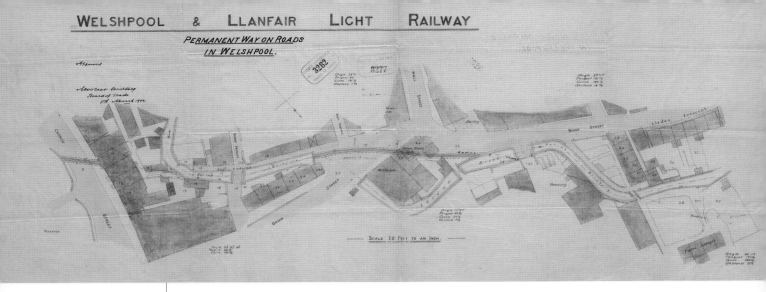

A.J. Collin's 1901 plan showing detail of the railway's route from Church Street in the Llanfair direction, illustrating how it was routed over the Lledan brook and through the site of the Seven Stars public house. (National Archives)

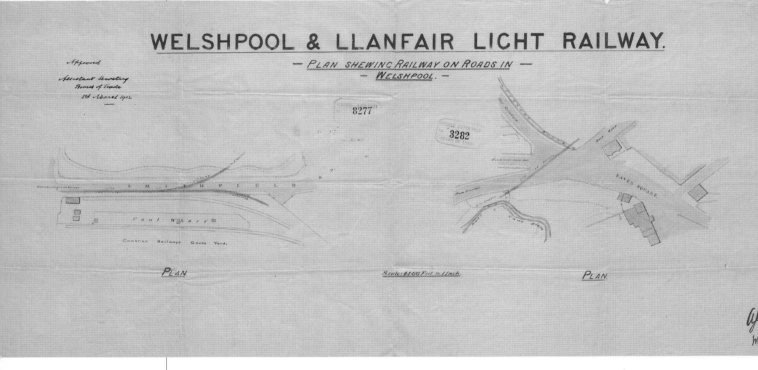

Detail of the railway's route at Smithfield Road and Raven Square. (National Archives)

untypical in such documents, Denniss's revenue forecast of £3,405 was only slightly in excess of what was to be achieved. (Appendix 5)

The location and nature of the road crossings in Welshpool had been sent to the Board of Trade by Collin on 31 May. The correspondence was protracted, expanded to include the town council and the county council, and accompanied within the Board of Trade by doubt as to whether the matter should be dealt with by its railway

department or its highways department. The crossings had been intended to be laid with 75lb grooved tram rail. On 21 November 1901 however, the railway informed the Board of Trade that rails of the desired profile, with a flangeway 1½in wide, were not made in any British mill. As the track concerned comprised only 300 yards out of nine miles of railway, it asked if approval would be given for ordinary rails to be used, with the formation between them filled with 'tarred macadam' instead

WELSHPOOL & LLANFAIR LIGHT RAILWAY.

— PERMANENT WAY FOR ROADS IN WELSHPOOL. —

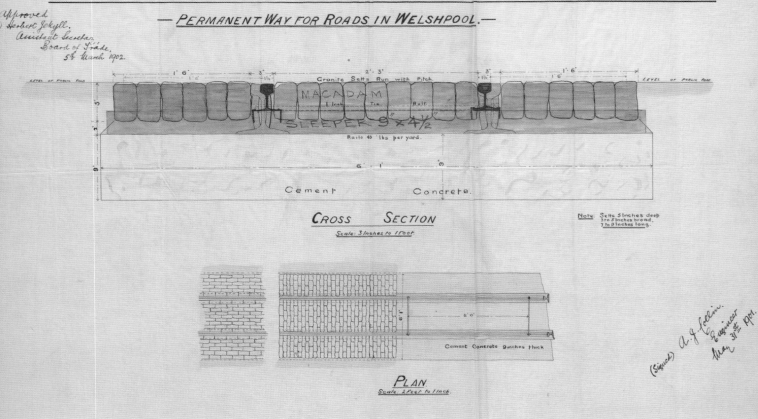

CROSS SECTION
Scale: 3 Inches to 1 Foot

PLAN
Scale 2 Feet to 1 Inch.

of sets so that the wheel flanges would form their own groove? The approval of the corporation and the county council, as the authorities concerned, was required before permission was given for the change, which followed on 5 March 1902.

Collin recommended that Beyer, Peacock & Company's tender to supply two locomotives at £1,630 each be accepted on 22 June 1901. If a third locomotive was ordered within six months this would reduce the price to £1,570 each. When the order was submitted to the Cambrian board for ratification on 2 July, Denniss sent a telegram to the company saying that his directors required a third loco to be procured, but a streak of rebellion appeared in Welshpool when it was read on 8 July; the matter was not on the agenda, so it was deferred until the next meeting. Following a meeting with Denniss, on 26 September the directors resolved to delay the matter. Eventually the Cambrian said that if the traffic warranted it, a third locomotive must be provided. Jones ordered two on 10 October.

Earlier, on 21 June 1901, the county council had agreed to increase its loan from £6,000 to £7,000. On 22 June a meeting was held in Llanfair to encourage subscriptions to fill the £3,000 capital shortfall. The meeting was said (*Merioneth County Times* 27 June) to be very enthusiastic but no new subscriptions were reported. A useful boost was reported by the *Montgomeryshire Echo* on 13 July however, in a report saying that David Davies, grandson of the contractor, had subscribed £1,000.

Construction had progressed during the summer, with the first certificate issued on 29 June. Collin submitted regular reports to the Cambrian directors but not, apparently, to the directors who were paying him for his work. On 2 July he had reported that some 6,000 yards of spoil had been removed at the Welshpool station site, that Strachan was at work on cuttings and embankments for about 1½ miles of the route, that the bridge over the canal had been started, and the repairs to the walls of the Lledan brook, over which the railway would run, were nearly finished.

The plan showing the proposed method of constructing the railway in the roads using grooved tram rail. (National Archives)

Beyer, Peacock's photograph of *The Countess*. The bell on the cab roof must have its origins in thought that the Welshpool road crossings should be treated as tramways, but it was removed before the loco entered service.

A train crossing the Montgomeryshire Canal bridge on 20 October 1956. The bridge now carries a footpath, the area to the left of the train occupied by a major supermarket. (H.F. Wheeller)

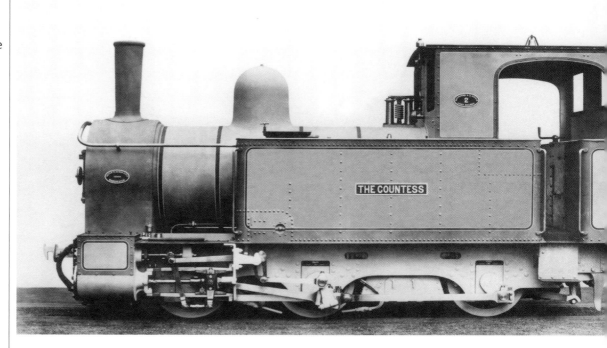

On 7 August he reported that the canal bridge masonry was nearly completed, the retaining wall at Rock Cottage, at the Standard quarry, two cattle creeps and a culvert were well advanced and the rebuilding at the tannery and most of the property alterations were completed. Earthworks for one mile were completed and in hand to two miles. Fencing was being put up as far as four miles and 3,000 sleepers were on site. In September some of the town councillors were unhappy about fencing, or the lack of it, in the town until it was pointed out that three of their number were directors and that would be where they would have to look if there were any problems.

The quality of stone being used at the Banwy bridge concerned the directors when they met on 29 August. They had been told that it was 'of a perishable nature' and wanted the Cambrian to check that it was satisfactory. They also wanted to hear from Collin on the subject. He reported, on 26 September, that he had given instructions for the work to be redone.

With no obvious sense of urgency, the amendment order was made on 22 September 1901. The capital was doubled to £12,000, the amount the investing authorities could subscribe was increased to £19,350 from £16,100, and the company could borrow on mortgage £1,000 per £3,000 of subscribed capital to a maximum of £4,000. No explanation is given in the surviving records for the lack of clauses authorising the extensions of time, but the matter was revisited by the directors.

With payments to Strachan and the property owners started, the directors were concerned that those who had promised capital support honoured their commitments. On several occasions the minutes recorded unpaid calls on shares and the apparent tardiness of some of the investing authorities in arranging the loans they needed to meet their obligations. Lord Powis even visited the public loan office to see if the authorities could be bypassed, but to no avail. The bank account was overdrawn by £1,135 19s

The 1901 amendment order.

10d on 26 September 1901, when £3,000 was received from the county council on account of its loan. £2,000 was received from the town council by 31 October. Against the outgoings there was a little income – £17 19s from the sale of timber, large chestnuts, from the former vicarage garden, in August 1901. (Appendix 7)

Of the land required, one small plot, ¾ acre, at Golfa was particularly troublesome, requiring more than two years of negotiations before agreement was reached over its use. It belonged to the Reverend G.R.G. Pughe, vicar of Mellor, Blackburn, who made it clear that he did not want to sell at any price; he had had a clause inserted in the 1899 order preventing access without his prior written approval. Once construction started he changed his attitude and an arrangement was made. The company paid £300 for the land and £59 2s 2d for his solicitor's fees.

The minutes contain a note to the effect that the protective clause was repealed, saving £800 in construction costs. As the clause was not mentioned in the amendment order the correct position must be that Pughe had agreed not to enforce it.

In September 1901 another problem site was the Seven Stars public house in Welshpool, which needed to be demolished. Addie valued it at £1,150 and had offered that amount, but the owner, Ann Dowthwaite, held out for £1,200. The company had already paid £50 as compensation for the tenant, although whether the tenant ever saw the money must be open to doubt as it had been paid to the owner. The company solicitor was instructed to reach an agreement with the owner's solicitor for £1,175, but it was still refused. On 31 October, the directors resolved that if the offer was not accepted in three days they would put it to arbitration. That did the trick and the building was demolished by January 1902.

Notwithstanding the dispute over the pub there seem to have been no objections to the properties that were demolished to make way for the railway; the demolition of the pub was accepted as a positive development, as it had projected into Brook Street.

The new vicarage boundary wall had been completed and the Standard quarry weigh house demolished, Collin reported on 3 October. Several cattle creeps had been started and some of them were ready for arching. The viaduct at Cyfronydd, a culvert at Castle Caereinion station site, and the river wall near Llanfair had been started.

Jones submitted a tender from R.Y. Pickering & Company for rolling stock on 31 October. Accepting the recommendation, the directors specified that delivery must be during 1902 or as arranged, and that payment would be made on delivery. Ordering the timber wagons was deferred for the time being.

2 composite cars	£690
1 3rd class	£235
40 goods wagons	£1,020
4 covered goods wagons	£260
2 cattle wagons	£104
2 goods brake vans	£168
	£2,477

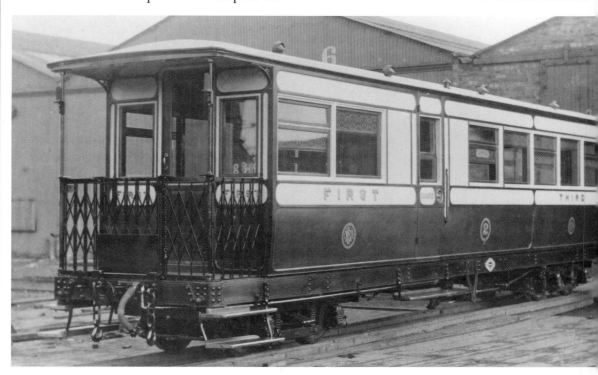

The second of the composite brake carriages at the maker's works.

The works photograph of goods brake van No 2, one of two. The preservation company acquired both of them.

Van No 4 awaits delivery to Wales. There were four of these, numbered 3-6. No 3 was condemned in 1956. The preservation company bought Nos 4 and 6 and one of them was damaged in the 1993 fire at Llanfair Caereinion.

Cattle truck No 8, one of two. Both were condemned in 1956. (John Scott Morgan collection)

Brynelin viaduct under construction. Cyfronydd Hall, R.D. Pryce's house, is visible between the trees in the upper centre distance. (Ralph Cartwright collection)

When Collin reported on 12 November, bad foundations had been encountered at the viaduct site. It had been necessary to excavate 8ft through soft blue clay before a good foundation of clay was encountered. The excavation had been filled with concrete to ground level. 70 tons of rail (600 yards) had been delivered.

THE INSCRIBED STONE ABOVE
ORIGINALLY INSTALLED
IN THE OPPOSITE PARAPET
WAS RE-FIXED IN ITS PRESENT POSITION
BY THE WELSHPOOL AND LLANFAIR
RAILWAY COMPANY
JANUARY 1902

UNION BRIDGE
BUILT FEB. 1817
ON THE HAPPY UNION OF THE
POWIS AND WYNNSTAY FAMILIES.
AND AT THE EXPENSE OF THE FUND
FOR THE EMPLOYMENT OF THE POOR.
UNDER THE DIRECTION OF THE ACTING
COMMITTEE OF WELSH POOL

David Jones having finished his term in office as mayor had left the council and the board. On 19 November his successor, Charles Shuker, who declared himself to be a political agent and secretary to the 1901 census-taker, was elected as a director to replace him.

The corporation expressed its disquiet about the Lledan brook, which had been culverted to accommodate the railway, on 25 November 1901. The councillors thought that the culvert would restrict the flow after heavy rain and subject the locality to flooding. Investigating, Collin agreed that the culvert was too small and suggested that it be removed and replaced by ironwork as on other parts of the brook. He produced a plan and estimated that it would cost £200 to replace. The culvert was actually a modification of Collin's original plans, implemented because it was cheaper. On 20 February 1902 he offered to bear the cost of the culvert if it was replaced. He had not mentioned the brook in his 9 December 1901 report although he did say that both it and the canal bridge steelwork were ready for inspection, adding that track laying had been started.

The tripartite agreement between the company, the Cambrian and the Treasury had been made on 7 October 1901 and was executed and exchanged on 12 November 1901. The agreement and the county council's financial commitment to the railway were the subject of a letter to the Board of Trade from the Manchester & Milford Railway on 20 January 1902. It was signed by James Rees, principal assistant to the general manager, who would be appointed to manage the Vale of Rheidol Railway a few weeks later. He was told to refer to the Treasury concerning the grant and to the light railway orders for details of the county council's contribution.

Christmas and New Year holidays had contributed to the lack of progress, Collin had reported on 13 January 1902, and 'bad weather had somewhat interfered with the progress of the earthworks.' Considering that the holidays would have accounted for three days at most the first remark does seem rather strange. The canal bridge and some of the Lledan brook steelwork had been erected and track laying was in progress.

These two stones are mounted in a dwarf wall over the culverted Lledan brook on the site of the Union bridge in Brook Street, Welshpool. The author is unaware of the existence of any photographs showing either of them in their original locations.

One of Strachan's locomotives on the Banwy bridge. (Ralph Cartwright collection)

Strachan had established his depot in the Standard quarry, near Raven Square. In January and April 1902, he advertised for an office boy, apply by letter only. So far as the local media was concerned, the workforce kept a low profile. Ralph Cartwright (see Bibliography) refers to an incidence of drunk and disorderly behaviour in Castle Caereinion in 1902 but no other similar reports have been found.

The Treasury was asked to release the first instalment of its grant on 14 January 1902. Seeking evidence from the Board of Trade that money had been properly spent, Major Edward Druitt was sent to make an inspection, reporting on 22 February. Accompanied by Collin and Addie, he had walked over part of the route and found half of the formation and half of the fencing were complete. About 1½ miles of track had been laid but not ballasted. The foundations of six of the seven piers

of the viaduct had been commenced. The abutments and piers for the bridge over the Banwy had been finished. He provided documentation that supported the company's claims about capital raised and expenditure.

The loans from the county council, £7,000, and Llanfyllin RDC, £2,600, had been received by the time the directors met on 23 January 1902. The £3,000 advanced by the county on account in September 1901 was reimbursed, along with interest of £16 11s 5d and costs of £51 12s 6d. Llanfyllin's solicitor's charge, £104 9s 8d, had been paid under protest; the threat of having the bill taxed and adjudicated was enough to have it reduced by £16.

Other matters dealt with included ordering dog spikes and fish bolts from Bayliss, Jones & Bayliss of Wolverhampton, a firm that became a part of Guest, Keen & Nettlefold in 1922, which cost a total of

£611 0s 5d in January and February. In March 1902 £225 14s was paid for points and crossings supplied by the Isca Foundry Company of Newport.

When Collin had reported on progress on 19 February some of his observations duplicated Druitt's. The weather had interfered with progress, stopping all masonry and concrete works, but earthworks had continued. One of the cuttings near Golfa was not quite complete. He expected Strachan to be in a position to lay three miles of temporary track within a few days. The bridge over the canal was completed except for painting and the Lledan brook steelwork was practically complete. Other work in the town would be nearly complete at the end of the month. Done without mishap and few complaints this section had been difficult to carry out. Consulting with Strachan, he thought that the railway would be ready for inspection in July or August.

The directors were concerned to learn, when they read Jones's report of 20 March, that not only had Beyer, Peacock not started building the locomotives, but that the drawings had not been finished and delivery could not be expected for another eight or nine months. In his report Jones said that this was because the locomotives were being specially designed. Lord Powis signed a letter to Beyer, Peacock urging the company to push forward with the locomotives as rapidly as possible. When a delivery date was not forthcoming, the directors decided to enquire of Bagnall & Company if a locomotive could be hired.

The company was £1,445 in credit with £3,000 due from the corporation and £7,250 from the Treasury when the directors met on 26 March. Collin was asked to give an estimate of the amount required to complete the railway not later than 23 April. On 22 May it became apparent that the company was £6,542 short of the

Navvies excavating a cutting on the Golfa bank. (Ralph Cartwright collection)

funds it required. Strachan's work was estimated to cost £850 more than his tender, because there had been more rock than anticipated and extra accommodation works had been required. Some savings were identified, the largest being to work the railway with one engine in steam to avoid the cost of signalling. The Treasury would be asked for a larger grant, the Cambrian would be asked to take up the shares authorised by the amendment order and the district would be canvassed to obtain more subscriptions. (Appendix 5)

Lord Powis wrote to the Treasury on the same day asking for a grant or loan of £3,000. He said that he and other landowners had given land valued at £2,400 and added that fastenings and sleepers had cost more than forecast. Land and property had cost £6,300 instead of the £2,950 estimated because of the difficulties in constructing a route through Welshpool and the need to take down several houses including a public house. The solicitor copied the letter to the Board of Trade seeking its support. Powis led a deputation to the Treasury on 11 June and on 21 June received notice that not only had he been successful but that the limitation on the amount permitted to be paid for land had been withdrawn.

Track laying, most of it ballasted, extended some 2½ miles, Collin reported on 13 May, and more rail had been delivered. The viaduct was being proceeded with and 47,000 cubic yards of spoil had been excavated.

Addie had met Denniss on 27 May and the latter had agreed to the line being worked with one engine in steam. The only saving on buildings that he agreed to was the elimination of the loco shed at Llanfair, but it would need to be reinstated if the traffic warranted a loco being stabled there. He was agreeable to a shelter not being provided at Welshpool, saving £40, provided one was located for local traffic at Severn Stars.

By July 10, Collin was able to report that all the cuttings were either finished or 'gulleted', presumably he meant the ground had been cut through, as far as the viaduct. One arch was 'practically turned' and the others were in progress. Between the viaduct and the Banwy bridge earthworks were in an advanced state. Track was laid for 6¼ miles and girders for the bridge delivered.

Without any comment or explanation, on 11 July 1902 the directors resolved to apply to the Board of Trade for an extension of time to complete the railway; six months from the date specified in the 1899 order, 8 September 1902. The application submitted on 14 July 1902 was not considered because it had not been properly advertised. The explanation given to the Board of Trade was that 'owing to the difficulties experienced in raising the capital . . . the directors were unable to proceed with the work until the spring of 1899.' The contract as let was due to be completed by 1 September and the track was expected to be completed by that date, but the station buildings and other works could not be completed by 8 September. No mention was made of having no locomotives with which to work a service. The formalities having been completed, the extension was approved on 6 September.

As the works approached completion, in July and August items dealt with by the directors had a tidying up air about them. Collin arranged for Cardiff-based J.B. Saunders to install the telegraph for £300, reduced from the £427 10s quoted. The £280 tender from the Clyde Structural Iron Company for the loco and carriage sheds at Welshpool was accepted. Easements were sought from the Cambrian for a water pipe and the tranship shed. Expenditure of up to £60 for a reserve water supply at Welshpool was deferred. Plots of surplus land were discussed. Plans for waiting sheds at Castle Caereinion, Cyfronydd and Heniarth, the tranship shed and goods sheds at Welshpool and Llanfair were approved. Those for the station buildings at the termini were approved subject to the addition of a verandah. T.F. Evans's offer to construct all the station buildings for £400 was accepted.

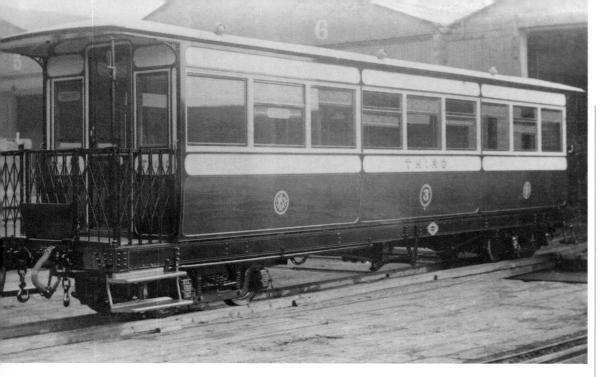

The 3rd class carriage, No 3, at Pickering's Wishaw factory.

The Banwy bridge girders were in position by 7 August, Collin reported. Rails had been laid as far as the bridge and would be continued as soon as the decking had been fixed. The viaduct and fencing were nearly completed.

Jones reported on 28 August that the first locomotive was finished but he had deferred delivery until there was covered accommodation available for it. The second loco would be finished in September and he expected the carriages and wagons to be available before the end of that month.

Beyer, Peacock was short of space and wanted the loco out of the way. It arrived at Welshpool on 2 September and was stabled on a temporary siding, covered by a tarpaulin, Jones holding Beyer, Peacock responsible for the locomotive until it had been accepted.

With the locomotives, rolling stock and other items still to pay for and the remainder of the grant not due until after the final inspection, an £8,000 overdraft from Lloyds Bank was organised in September 1902, the directors indemnifying the bank against the company defaulting. In October the county council and Forden RDC asked for the first instalments of the repayments due to them; they were asked to wait until the railway had been opened.

Strachan appeared to be experiencing cash-flow difficulties at the same time; he was simultaneously building the Tanat Valley Light Railway. On 1 September 1902 he had asked the company for £1,000 to be paid on account of the retention money. The company could not oblige, he was told, as his contract was with the Cambrian.

With the exception of forming the slopes on three cuttings, the earthworks were completed, Collin informed the Cambrian directors on 29 September. The track had been laid to Llanfair and most of the sidings in the stations had been laid. Ballasting had been delayed because one of Strachan's locos had broken down and had been out of use for a month.

By 25 October, arrangements had been made to hire the first locomotive, named *The Earl* without any recorded discussion, to Strachan. Collin reported that the second locomotive had been received, that both were in good condition, and made according to the drawings and specifications. A trial with the required load was needed before they could be certified as satisfactory. A set of 95 cloth tracings of the drawings supplied by Beyer, Peacock were deposited with the Cambrian; they had cost £25. Pickering had delivered 11 goods wagons and Collin recommended hiring them and others due shortly, up to 20 in total, to Strachan 'to facilitate completion'. The wagons had been in transit on 1 October, when one of the carriages was awaiting despatch.

The GWR engine history cards record that *The Earl* had been delivered on 2 September and the second engine, named *The Countess*, had followed on 27 September. The names, of course, paid tribute to the Earl and Countess of Powis. Small oval ownership plates were affixed to their smokeboxes and they were numbered 1 and 2 in the railway's fleet.

The railway would be ready for inspection on 1 November, Collin had forecast at the meeting of the directors on 25 September. The company gave notice to the Board of Trade on 3 October. Sent separately from the engineer's data that accompanied the notice, were plans of the railway's structures and copies of the deposited plans. Sadly all that has survived of this bundle is a piece of the wrapping paper with an LNWR 'insured goods' label affixed.

On 3 October the directors, accompanied by Collin and Jones, enjoyed a trial trip over the railway, travelling on seats in an open wagon. The details were reported in the *Shrewsbury Chronicle* on 10 October. At first the new engine, *The Earl*, was used, then a second loco took over which broke down so a third was used. There was another, unspecified, mishap but the party reached Llanfair safely and were warmly greeted by Llanfair residents. They adjourned to the Wynnstay Hotel, where a toast was drunk in champagne, and returned to Welshpool without any mishap or delay. As the ballasting was incomplete, the description of changing locos indicates that *The Earl* was used until the ballast ran out, its place being taken by one of the three four-coupled locos Strachan used on the contract.

Collin had second thoughts about the line being ready for traffic and the notice was withdrawn on 14 November. As recently as 10 November he had reported good progress with ballasting, the track was being aligned, telephone wires and poles had been erected, point interlocking was in hand, and buildings and sheds were being erected.

On 1 November the *Montgomeryshire Echo* reported that Messrs J. Astley and Son had nearly completed the station buildings at Llanfair. Astley's relationship, if any,

with T.F. Evans, whose offer to construct the buildings had been accepted on 22 September, is not known.

During the same month the directors noted that check rails were to be added to the track over the Lledan brook and a hydraulic ram and tank were to be installed at Dolrhyd to supply locomotive water to Llanfair. A cheque for £40 5s was issued for payment to the ram's maker, W.H. Bailey & Company, in January 1903, but Collin asked for it not to be sent 'until it is found how the ram works'.

Apart from the outstanding works, another issue had become manifest. While Strachan had been using the new wagons there had been two cases of couplings breaking.

Jones had written to Denniss on 11 November and then to the company on 24 November; the points that he made have been merged in the following paragraphs. He denied that the couplings had broken and that they were unsuitable. Following investigation on the Festiniog Railway, Glyn Valley Tramway, Corris Railway, Abergynolwyn [Talyllyn] Railway, and the North Wales Narrow Gauge Railways, he determined that the coupling used by the last was the most satisfactory. He had originally specified an automatic, sprung, centre coupling for the passenger stock, intending to use a curved buffing plank with link and hook on the goods stock, an arrangement that would have caused 'very unpleasant shakings to the passengers' when the slack was taken up on mixed trains. The manufacturer was so convinced that using the same buffer on all the stock was the best thing to do that they installed it on the goods stock without charge.

The first case involved two wagons separating from the loco 20–30 yards after starting, and he had found no evidence that they had been coupled improperly. If the man who should have been riding on the last wagon had been in place, and not riding on the engine because it was raining, the damage would have been minimised.

In the second case, on 10 November, six wagons had run away from the loco. Jones was convinced that they had not been properly fastened and that the wagons were attached by a chain that was found broken afterwards, part on the loco and part on the first wagon. One of Strachan's men said that the chain had been used for lashing round the couplings as an added precaution and it had broken after the couplings broke apart, but Jones did not accept that.

On 19 November he had taken a train comprising an engine, four wagons and a brake van to Castle Caereinion and in the presence of representatives from the maker, the contractor and the engineer, had failed to 'break' a coupling on the sharpest curves or the steepest gradients. Propelling the train back to Welshpool at low speed, the wagon next to the loco derailed several times owing, he thought, to a combination of the track and the weight of the leading brake van. 'On no occasion did the derailments cause the couplings to become detached or loosened.' In many places it was not safe to go faster than 2mph.

A proper trial of the rolling stock could not be made due to the incomplete state of the track, he said. He was satisfied that the stock was superior regarding design, materials and workmanship than any to be found on other narrow gauge lines. He had contacted the Vale of Rheidol Railway, which used a similar coupling, and it was satisfactory, with no cases of 'break loose'. In view of the railway's gradients and curves however, he thought that the wagons should be fitted with side chains as an extra precaution. Pickering would supply them for 17s 6d per set.

Of the track, Jones said that several curves were sharper than the three chains specified, much of it was unballasted and the appropriate super-elevation had not been set. He could not tell if the maximum 1-in-30 gradient had been exceeded.

Denniss asked Collin for his observations on 14 and 24 November, but he did not visit Welshpool until the 28th, replying on 29 November 1902. He could not make an inspection because both of Strachan's engines had broken down, he said. After discussions with Strachan's son and Eric Byron, the resident engineer, he had

concluded that with satisfactory weather the line should be ready for opening by 1 January 1903. Two days had been lost to weather during the current week.

Regarding the track, he did not agree that it was in rough condition, except in two places where Strachan had temporary sidings connected. He admitted that the rails were not as true as on an established line, but there was nothing to cause derailments which had occurred on straight sections as well as on curves. Strachan had gangs straightening and adjusting the rails who would be adjusting the vertical alignments where the gradient changed as well. Since 'the new engine' had been running he had found it impossible to keep the track to gauge on curves up to 10 chains radius despite adding extra spikes on the outside rails. The company had therefore approved expenditure on his recommendation to fit tie bolts and bars on curves of up to six chains.

He was reassured, Denniss told Jones on 1 December, but required confirmation that the minimum curvature was not less than three chains and the gradient was not steeper than 1 in 30. He continued: 'Your remarks about the new engine and its effect upon the permanent way are ambiguous. Do you intend to infer that its wheelbase is too long? If this is your opinion will you please say so.'

Replying on 8 December, Jones was insistent that the locomotives could work on three-chain curves; they had a certain side play that would increase with use. They had been used on the partially completed railway without derailing despite some of the curves being sharper than three chains, one being as tight as two chains. If the curves were kept to three chains and the gradients did not exceed 1 in 30 he was confident that the locomotives would be satisfactory.

Writing on the same date, Collin said that he had had the curves and gradients checked 'in small lengths'. Some of the curves were slightly under three chains and there would be no difficulty correcting them when the final adjustments were made. Short lengths of gradients steeper than 1 in 30 were due to settlement; they would be adjusted in due course and would require more attention for some months after the railway was opened. The locomotives had a 10ft wheelbase and checking with other narrow gauge railways, the longest he had found was 6ft 1in on the North Wales Narrow Gauge Railways. Denniss had already, on 29 November, told the company that he thought the wagon chains should be adopted.

On 8 December 1902 Collin had informed the Cambrian directors that three miles of top ballast, metalling of station yards, point interlocking at two stations, and completing final track alignment were still required.

Returning to the rolling stock situation, on 12 November 1902 Jones had reported that thirty-six goods wagons and the brake vans had been delivered. The carriages and the rest of the stock were ready but he had deferred delivery because the carriage shed was not ready and it would get in the way.

When Collin told the directors on 22 December 1902 that the line would be ready for inspection in January they decided that a preliminary inspection should be conducted by the Cambrian's officers, accompanied by representatives of the locomotive and rolling stock builders, on 20/21 January 1903, followed by the Board of Trade inspection the next week. Collin, in the meantime, should explain why his final certificate of £25,350 varied from the estimate of £24,636 he had given in April. He did not respond to the request and it was to take some considerable effort to obtain clarification.

At the county council meeting on 19 December 1902 the company's request to defer repayment of principal and interest until the railway was completed was interrupted by a member expressing concern that he had been told that the railway would be unable to carry timber or cattle. Addie said that someone was

Payments to Strachan 1901-2		
1	29 June 1901	£663 19s 6d
2	29 August 1901	£1,502 9s 6d
3	26 September 1901	£1,161 4s 6d
4	31 October 1901	£1,050 1s 6d
5	28 November 1901	£1,858 7s
6	20 December 1901	£1,696 10s
7	23 January 1902	£1,469 6s 6d
8	20 February 1902	£661 1s
9	26 March 1902	£821 18s 6d
10	24 April 1902	£1,748 3s 6d
11	22 May 1902	£754 13s
12	11 July 1902	£1,281 3s
13	11 July 1902	£1,720 17s 6d
14	28 August 1902	£960 7s 6d
15	25 September 1902	£1,107 12s
16	23 October 1902	£877 10s
17	27 November 1902	£672 15s
18	17 December 1902	£697 2s 6d
		£20,705 1s 6d

pulling his leg but another member said the he had tried to send some timber and had been told by Denniss that it must be cut to shorter lengths. Denniss told the *Shrewsbury Chronicle* (26 December) that both cattle and timber could be carried. He had even gone so far as to quote through rates to inland towns for it. The request to defer payments was approved.

The preliminary inspection had been postponed until 13 January 1903, because Collin had decided that he was unable to certify the track as fit for use. Bad weather during December, including heavy rain, floods and frost, had stopped work for most of that month. He was to produce the certificate with the least possible delay, as the directors would view with displeasure any application for a further extension of time. Such a step would not only entail further expense but seriously prejudice the company's interests. On 23 January he replied that the line would be ready for the Board of Trade inspection from 31 January.

Druitt submitted his report on 6 February. The width at formation level was 10ft 6in on embankments and 9ft in cuttings. The deepest cutting was 15ft deep and the highest embankment was 29ft high. The sharpest curves were three chains radius and the steepest gradient 1 in 30, in one place continuously for one mile.

The flat-bottomed rails were in 30ft lengths, weighing 45lb per yd secured by dog spikes; soleplates were used at the joints where the rails were secured by three dog spikes. The rails were joined by fishplates with four bolts. The sleepers were of creosoted Baltic fir, 6ft x 9in x 4½in laid 3ft centre to centre. The ballast was broken stone and river gravel laid to a depth of 5in below the sleepers.

In Welshpool, along the Lledan brook some unclimbable iron fencing had been used. There were fifteen underbridges and one overbridge. Of the underbridges, that over the Banwy had three 40ft spans on the skew with masonry piers and abutments with steel girders under each rail. That over the Shropshire Canal had one span of 33ft 4in on the skew made of steel plate girders and iron rolled joists. Three underbridges were of brick arches with an 8ft span or less, and ten were formed by timber baulks under each rail with spans varying from 4ft to 10ft 6in. There were also wooden baulks carrying the rails across the gaps forming the cattle guards at either side of the roads where gates had not been provided at public level crossings.

There was one masonry viaduct with six 22ft 6in spans and three viaducts over the Lledan brook, the line being carried directly along the course of the brook for some little distance by means of longitudinal rail beams supported by cross girders (rolled joists) which in turn rested on the masonry sides of the stream. There were about forty-five of these joists of varying span, the longest being 17ft

3in. There were two culverts, of 3ft and 4ft diameter.

All the steel girders, baulks, joists etc had sufficient theoretical strength and proved fairly stiff under test load, but a few of the joists over the Lledan brook needed their bearings attending to.

There were eleven public road level crossings and the railway ran along the side of Smithfield Road for the first three chains of its length. Of the level crossings three were provided with gates shutting across the railway but not across the road and the remainder had cattle guards. The usual notices were positioned on the roads, but notice boards had still to be provided for Bebb's Passage, Bushalls Lane near Raven Square, and the road adjoining Cyfronydd station. With the exception of the roads in Welshpool across where the corporation of Welshpool had fixed the speed of 4mph under the powers conferred on them by Clause 52(3) of the order, the only important road crossed on the level was that adjoining Castle Caereinion station, where gates were provided so the train would stop on each side of it. Over the rest of the level crossings a speed of 10mph was to be allowed.

The gates across the railway at Castle Caereinion were hung to close inwards and not across the high road. It would have been an improvement if they were hung to open across the road which is on a fairly steep gradient as they would have then been visible to cyclists or people in charge of vehicles, and also the person opening the gates could attract the attention of such people.

There were stations at: Welshpool, commencement; Welshpool [Severn Stars], 0m 33ch; Raven Square, 1m 0ch; Golfa, 2m 66ch; Castle Caereinion, 4m 66ch; Cyfronydd, 6m 57ch; Heniarth Gate, 7m 54ch; Llanfair, termination. The first and the last had booking offices and waiting rooms, Castle Caereinion, Cyfronydd and Heniarth had shelters. All had gravel platforms at rail level.

Seven Stars was the railway's main passenger station in Welshpool. The former public house, demolished to make way for the railway, had been behind the photographer.

The crossing at Raven Square on 16 April 1938, Easter Saturday. The photographer must have been singularly unlucky to capture the scene without traffic or pedestrians.

Golfa station in 1956.

Castle Caereinion soon after the railway had opened.

Cyfronydd looking east.

Heniarth looking towards Llanfair.

Sidings and loops worked from two-lever ground frames controlled by the train staff were at: Welshpool, exchange siding points; the goods yard, double frame, four levers working the up facing points of the loop siding and the point leading to the goods yard; Standard quarry siding, not yet connected; Golfa loop; Sylfaen siding, points facing to up trains; Castle Caereinion, loop; Cyfronydd, loop; Heniarth, loop; Llanfair station, facing points at loop; the points at the end of the line for the engine run round were worked by hand.

The interlocking of the fifteen ground frames was correct. The quarry siding was not ready; the left-hand tongue of the facing points needed to be removed and the right-hand one clamped to the stock rail if passenger traffic was commenced before the siding was ready. There was also not quite sufficient clearance between the main line and the siding opposite the trap points at Sylfaen, Heniarth and Llanfair station. The sidings needed to be slewed further away from the line at these points. A buffer post was required at the termination of the line at Llanfair. At Cyfronydd the pit of the cattle guard at the road adjoining the station required draining.

Requirements were: check rails on all sharp curves situated on high banks; wheel guards on the bridges over the Banwy and the Lledan brook; the top ballast required breaking up; sleepers required additional packing in places; gauge widening was required on some curves to allow the engines with a fixed wheelbase of 10ft to get round without throwing considerable strain on the outer rail and grinding heavily against it; all sharp curves of three chains needed to be tied to their proper gauge by steel ties. Speed on the sharp reverse curves below Golfa station was not to exceed 5mph 'at present'.

The rolling stock was: two six-coupled engines, gross weight 19½ tons with a weight of between 6 and 7 tons on each axle; passenger carriages were on 4ft 6in wheelbase bogies, the total length over headstocks was 35ft. They had entrances at both ends with side steps and appeared suitable. They and the goods trucks were fitted with centre buffer couplings with Norwegian hooks, but no side play had been given to the couplings on the engines or on the trucks, although some had been given on the carriages.

Druitt had been unable to see the couplings in use so could not say if the hooks would make a satisfactory coupling, but thought that it would be dangerous to use the couplings as fitted owing to the want of side play, as they would be very liable to cause derailments when a train was on the sharp curves, which are very numerous on the line. Some modification by which the rigid outer buffer couplings would be quite free to move when the train was on a curve was considered absolutely necessary.

He concluded: 'Under these conditions I do not feel able to recommend the Board of Trade that the light railway has been completed to their satisfaction, although with the requirements completed the permanent way would be fit for traffic. But in any case, the conditions regarding the payment of the balance of the free grant would not be fulfilled until the line has been opened for public traffic. Until the couplings above mentioned have been modified I consider the opening of the railway would be attended with danger to the public using it.'

No explanation was provided for Druitt not having seen the couplings in use. He was satisfied with them when he returned to Welshpool at the company's request on 20 February. This time, a train was laid on for him. It comprised a locomotive, a carriage, two covered trucks, three open trucks and a brake van to represent what was expected to be a typical mixed train. Seeing that most of his requirements had been attended to, he conducted a formal inspection to save another visit.

The only outstanding issues were the check rails on the three-chain curves, the wheel guards on the Lledan and Banwy bridges, the gauge ties, gauge widening and the 'proper super-elevation' on the sharp curves; the last had not been mentioned previously. He recommended that as soon as Collin had certified that they had all been done the Board of Trade should sanction the line for passenger traffic subject to the following speed restrictions:

- A maximum speed of 15 miles an hour on any part of the line. This restriction could be revised at the discretion of the company's engineer when the formation had consolidated.
- The further restrictions of speed laid down in Clause 52 of the order.
- A speed of 5 miles an hour on the sharp reverse curves south of Golfa, and at Dolrhyd Mill.

Druitt pointed out that before opening for traffic it would be necessary to ensure that all the facing and trap points of the sidings were connected to the ground frames, as they had been disconnected for Strachan's convenience. The company should pay attention to Clause 28(4) regarding the gates at level crossings. He had asked the Cambrian to apply for the usual permission to run mixed trains.

Receiving Druitt's report, the directors met on 27 February and heard the resident engineer report his opinion that the requirements could be completed by 'next Tuesday night', 3 March. They hoped that Collin's certificate would be in the post the same day and started to make plans for an opening ceremony on 31 March.

During February the company had, incidentally, made it clear that it was not always going to be a pushover for every claim made against it. Denniss had asked it to provide wagon sheets, ropes, barrows and the other accoutrements required to run a railway. After a letter from the solicitor, he agreed that the Cambrian would supply them.

Collin had submitted a report on Druitt's visit dated 21 February to Denniss. Not mentioned by the inspector, the journey had not been without a little excitement. On straight line near Cyfronydd the brake

van had derailed. Collin had checked the gauge and found it correct but a joint near the point of derailment had been slack. This and the light weight of the van he thought was responsible for the derailment. The vehicle was quickly re-railed. Returning through the curves near Golfa, three wagons had derailed. After they had been re-railed and the train moved forward, Druitt had checked the gauge, ½in wide as required, and the curve, exactly three chains. Collin could offer no explanation for this derailment, telling Druitt that he would have all the three-chain curves checked for alignment.

On his previous visit Druitt had asked for the check rails to be laid with 3in clearance, which had been done. However, it was found that because the wagon wheels were narrower than those of the locos, the clearance was too great. Druitt's fresh recommendation of making the flangeway 2½in was put in hand.

Denniss submitted a special report containing copies of the correspondence with Collin and the Board of Trade to the Cambrian directors on 28 February. Collin had recommended opening the line for goods traffic on 9 March. Denniss had inspected the line himself and was satisfied with the couplings and saw that 'the engine went round the curves satisfactorily.' Taking into account the condition of the track and the possibility of subsidence [on the embankments], he thought that the goods service should be run 'for a short period' before passenger services were started, Denniss recommending the Cambrian directors sanction 31 March too. He added that Collin would have to pay close attention to the permanent way for a few months after opening.

A hidden drama accompanied the start of the goods train service on Monday, 9 March 1903, for it was the day after the extension of time expired. Was a further extension required? The solicitor telegrammed the Parliamentary agent asking the question on 7 March. Without further ado, explanation or questioning, an extension of two months was granted by the Board of Trade on 9 March.

The first train, reported the *Manchester Courier* on 10 March, left Welshpool 'in charge of the leading officials of the Cambrian Railways Company'; there was much enthusiasm. The formal opening, it added, had been fixed for 4 April, on the return of the Earl of Powis and his wife from India. Advertisements announcing the railway's availability for traffic were published from 10 March.

Strachan still had work to do, and on 17/18 March his men worked through the night. In the early hours of the second day a train hauled by one of his locos set off from Welshpool with two other men riding on the front of it. At Seven Stars one of them, John Williams, jumped off, falling under the loco as he did so and dying from his wounds. The inquest recorded a verdict of accidental death. Neither the Cambrian nor the directors made any recorded comment about the incident. Williams was 41 years old. Born in Kidderminster, in the 1901 census he had given his occupation as general labourer. He left a widow and two children.

The first three weeks' goods traffic, reported by Denniss to the Cambrian directors, is shown in the table. For the first week he calculated the average income per mile as £5 8s.

CAMBRIAN RAILWAYS.

PUBLIC NOTICE.

THE LINE between WELSHPOOL and LLANFAIR will be Opened for Goods, Mineral, and Live Stock Traffic on MONDAY, MARCH 9th.—Rates and other information may be obtained from the Company's Agents at Welshpool and Llanfair, or from Mr W. H. Gough, Traffic Superintendent, Oswestry..—C. S. DENNISS, Secretary and General Manager.

Two issues relating to the railway and water were dealt with by the town council on 19 March. In the town, a connection had been made to the town water supply for locomotive water without approval. It was agreed to ask the Cambrian to make a supplemental agreement to that prevailing for its existing water use; a charge of £5 annually was agreed in July. Outside the town, it appears that the construction works near Golfa Farm had damaged the underlying natural drainage and caused the farm's sewage to drain into the town's lower reservoir at Black Pools.

Other railway matters dealt with on the same date related to damage done by Strachan to the council's Smithfield (cattle market) siding, for which the council wanted £30 to repair, and the company's request to defer payments of principal and interest, which was agreed.

The Cambrian Railways' announcement of the railway's opening for goods traffic, actually published the day after the event. (*Montgomeryshire Express*)

Outwards	14 March 1903			21 March 1903			28 March 1903		
Description	Tons	cwt	£sd	Tons	cwt	£sd	Tons	cwt	£sd
Merchandise	28	18	£15 8s 3d	17	12	£9 8s 8d	18	3	£13 13s 1d
Grain etc.	40	11	£7 10s	28	11	£5 0s 8d	16	10	£4 7s 8d
Manure	17		£3 4s 4d	40	6	£7 1s 5d	87	8	£14 7s 8d
Slag	16	7	£3 14s 10d						
Coal and coke	109	18	£13 9s 6d	124	8	£15 5s 5d	83	10	£9 18s 3d
Other minerals	41	15	£5 7s 10d	35	17	£5 8s 1d	34	15	£4 10s 7d
Sawn timber							4	8	£1 2s
Total	254	9	£48 14s 9d	246	15	£42 4s 3d	254	15	£47 19s 3d
Inwards									
Merchandise				1		10s	5	8	£1 12s
Grain				7	10	£1 5s			
Total				8	10	£1 15s	5	8	£1 12s

Llanfair traders unhappy about the rates being charged also met on 19 March. Goods classified as 'sugars' cost 10s 6d per ton by rail and had to be collected from the station. By road they cost 10s per ton and the carrier delivered to the door. Some claimed that they had given instructions that goods arriving at Welshpool were not to be forwarded by train. They resolved to petition the Cambrian to seek reductions.

Denniss acknowledged the petition and his letter was read at a meeting on 27 March. He said that in fixing the rates he had to take into account the cost of working the line, but they should be regarded as tentative and some had already been reduced. 'In opening a new railway,' he wrote, 'it is difficult to accurately gauge the amount of revenue likely to be derived …' which was ridiculed. The reductions were considered inadequate. Surely, what he should have done was undercut the existing road rates by a small amount and assess the situation after the hauliers had gone out of business. Denniss had, apparently, given way on the question of carriage from the station and was now offering it free of charge.

The traders decided that until the rates were reduced to amounts they considered acceptable they would bypass the Cambrian where they could and have their goods conveyed to Llanfair by road, writing to Denniss, with a copy to the Cambrian's chairman, to tell him so. No more reports on this issue have been found so presumably some sort of rapport was established.

The *Montgomeryshire Express* had obtained a copy of the passenger timetable and published details on 24 March. Trains would leave Welshpool at 7.50am, 11.40am, and 4.55pm, and return at 9.40am, 2.20pm, and 6.30pm. On Welshpool fair days, the first and third Mondays in each month, additional trains would be run in both directions. There would be no trains on Sundays. Obviously, no one in Llanfair who wanted to do a day's work in Welshpool was expected to use the train.

On 4 April, the day of the 'grand opening', rain fell at first, but cleared later. In Welshpool the streets were decorated with streamers. On the Cambrian, a special train from Oswestry brought that company's directors and officers. The loco, *The Countess*, was decorated with red and green muslin, red rosettes with yellow centres and daffodils, the Prince of Wales' feathers mounted on each end of the loco were surmounted by leeks, and the slogan 'Success to the W&LLR' was displayed in white letters on the tank sides.

Shareholders with more than £15 invested had been invited to apply for free passes. Among the guests were representatives from the Shrewsbury & Welshpool joint line, the Shropshire Union Railways & Canal, and the Corris Railway, the last in the form of J.R. Dix, its manager.

Leaving at 11.15am, the inaugural train's passage through the town was a noisy affair. Fog detonators marked its departure and charges of dynamite were set off in the Standard quarry as it passed. More detonators marked its arrival at Llanfair, where three evergreen arches had been erected, one of them over the track. The landlord on the Wynnstay Arms had shown some initiative by obtaining a special license to sell intoxicating liquors at the station for two hours during the day.

Speaking at Llanfair, Lord Powis said that of the £50,000 spent on the railway so far little had been contributed from the Llanfair area, appealing for support in raising the £2,000 still required, explaining that shortage of funds prevented the installation of signalling and restricted the railway to 'one engine in steam' operation.

The only negative aspect surrounding the jubilation was the continuing threat by Llanfair traders to boycott the line over the rates. Denniss explained that the railway was being run as a commercial undertaking and dividends were anticipated. More facilities were still required, the accommodation at Llanfair was limited and the yard could be bigger. The rates set were authorised and would be reviewed in the light of experience.

Returning to Welshpool, the party gathered for lunch at the Royal Oak Hotel, joined by members of the public who had bought tickets for 3s 6d. More speeches followed and tribute was paid to the railway's predecessor, 'Johnny Jones and the Llanfair bus'.

He had often been seen perspiring while leading four horses hauling a heavy load and was not enjoying the best of health, having been hospitalised with a stroke the previous November. Denniss had said that the Cambrian would look after him now that his business had been removed, but as he died on 19 October he would not have required the company's charity for long. Buried in St Mary's churchyard in Llanfair, he was also better off than it appeared, for his effects were valued at £756 17s 2d.

During the speeches, Charles Thomas Pugh, the mayor, announced that a commemorative medal had been struck to mark the occasion. Cast in white metal, it had the town's arms on one side and Pugh's name and an inscription on the other. How widely the medals were distributed is not known but there are still families in the area who are proud to own one.

Forty years after the idea of a railway between Welshpool and Llanfair was first mooted the vision had been fulfilled thanks to the determination of the town to take advantage of the Light Railways Act in 1896. And unlike the promoters of the earlier schemes, it was prepared to put its own money in, and to persuade other authorities, including the Treasury, to contribute. The dream of making profits, repaying loans, paying interest and dividends was not fulfilled. But the promoters deserve great credit for bringing the railway into being.

Dignitaries, on the right, the Earl of Powis in the centre of the group next to the train, and interested members of the public await the departure of the inaugural train on 4 May 1903. Curiously, there are no women or girls to be seen.

CARRIAGES AND WAGONS 1960-2019

The railway obtained five carriages, seven wagons and two vans from the Admiralty's Lodge Hill & Upnor Railway in two batches in 1961. This is one of the four toastrack carriages in the red and cream livery adopted so that the train would contrast against the surrounding countryside. The vehicle on the right is the Lodge Hill breakdown van.

Two of the toastracks were enclosed to improve conditions for passengers when the weather was less than clement. In 1963 doors from the corridors of withdrawn GWR carriages were obtained from the dismantlers, North Wales Wagon Co, at Llanymynech, and fitted to No 204, seen here. These carriages were sold to the Sittingbourne & Kemsley Light Railway in 1978.

The 'combination car' was the fourth carriage obtained in 1961. It obtained its name because it comprised a brake compartment, and saloons for officers and other ranks. Until 1968 a 5p supplement was charged to travel in it. The body was sold to the South Tynedale Railway in 1989. Unused there, it was sold to the Welsh Highland Railway in 1997. Mounted on South African wagon bogies it found a new use as a mess car when the WHR was being rebuilt.

Llanfair looking eastwards in 1969, with all the railway's passenger stock in view. The four Austrian carriages had been donated by the Zillertalbahn and arrived at Welshpool by rail on 11/12 April 1968. The nearest brown carriage, B14, had been built for the opening of the Zillertalbahn in 1900; the other two were built in 1901. The green steel-bodied carriage, C572, had been built for the Salzkammergut Lokalbahn in 1925 and had made a brief appearance in a feature film made on that railway in 1956. On the right, construction of the workshop building, a volunteer project, has been started.

B20i is a replica of a Zillertalbahn vehicle obtained in 2007. It was built by S.C. Calea Ferata Ingusta S.R.L. in Criscior, Romania, for a customer who failed to complete the purchase, so the railway bought it to cover for its own vehicles being overhauled. Photographed alongside B27, the carriage donated by the Zillertalbahn in 1975, it had so recently arrived at Llanfair that its step boards, removed during transit, had not been re-attached.

Seen at Tanllan on 18 June 2000, B17, one of the carriages donated by the Zillertalbahn in 1968, had just returned from being rebuilt with an integral steel frame and modified to accommodate wheelchairs by a training centre in Appleby. B14 and B16 had been similarly rebuilt and modified by a training scheme based at the Cammel Laird shipyard, Birkenhead, in 1989-92.

Terry Turner donated a second Salzkammergut carriage to the railway in 2003. Like B25, donated to the railway by the Zillertalbahn in 1968, it was built in 1925. It had been stored outside, and out of use, at Austria's first heritage railway, the Gurktalbahn, for 24 years.

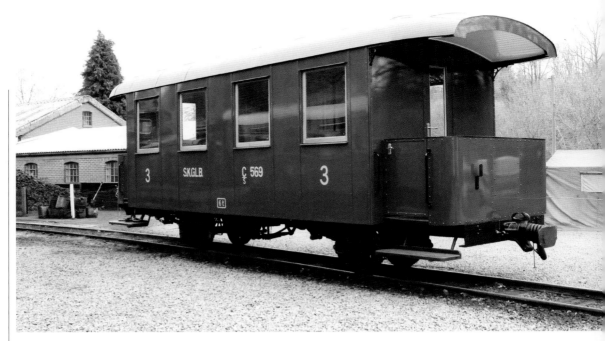

The railway's volunteers restored the carriage and it entered service in 2013.

The railway bought four bogie carriages, and Hunslet 2-6-2T No 85, from Sierra Leone in 1975. They were members of a fleet that had been built by the Gloucester Carriage & Wagon Company in 1961 but unfortunately the railway they had been built for was closed in 1974. Three of the carriages were 3rd class, the fourth was 1st class. Three were fitted with bus seats while the other was initially fitted out with an exhibition promoting the extension to Welshpool and never entered service. Nos 1048 and 1040, the exhibition carriage, were photographed at Llanfair in 1978.

Seen on 29 May 1999, No 1048 was the first of the Sierra Leone carriages to appear in this Pullman-esque livery. The application of women's names around the same time was a short-lived innovation.

One disadvantage of the Sierra Leone carriages was the small windows, suitable for the heat of Africa but not for admiring Montgomeryshire scenery, which led to a review of the railway's bogie carriage strategy. Nos 1207 and 1066 had insulation removed and their interiors restored to original condition in Romania, to be demonstrated as 'the African train'. No 1048 was sold to the South Tynedale Railway where it is used as a static buffet car at Slaggyford and No 1040 was scrapped. Now fitted with sumptuous leather armchairs, No 1207 was photographed at Llanfair on 15 July 2017.

Two carriages built for Hungarian State Railways in 1958 were purchased from the Ciernohronska forest railway in Slovakia in 1999, their large windows and suitability for modifying to have balcony ends making them particularly attractive. No 430 entered service in June 2003. Work on No 418, seen on 4 September 2005, was started at Llanfair and finished at the Ffestiniog Railway's Boston Lodge works.

The interior of No 418 when it was being fitted out at Boston Lodge, 21 May 2005.

No 418 at Llanfair on 4 September 2005.

The Earl hauls a train of two Hungarian and two Austrian carriages around the curve at Heniarth on 2 September 2017.

In 2018 both of the Hungarian carriages were modified at their western ends to improve accessibility for disabled passengers. The Department for Transport and the Rail Safety & Standards Board contributed to the cost with a £42,500 grant.

The body frame of the first Pickering carriage in the Ffestiniog Railway's Boston Lodge carriage works on 18 April 2003. The order included the manufacture of the steel underframe and bogies.

The first Pickering composite carriage shown to the author at Tanllan on 27 June 2004, before it had entered service.

A mixed train with the first Pickering carriage runs off the Banwy bridge on 25 March 2005.

The Earl with a mixed train that includes the three Pickering carriages at Heniarth on 6 September 2015. The first carriage has been repainted since the photograph was taken.

Castle Caereinion signal box open for business as a booking office. Two of the wagons obtained from the Admiralty are stabled on the left and there are two motor scooters parked on the platform.

The rear of a mixed train descending the Golfa bank in 1989. The goods stock comprises a Bowaters bogie wagon, a Lodge Hill bogie wagon and the Lodge Hill brake van.

Two modern ballast wagons were obtained from Romania in 2003. Made to the railway's requirements using parts from existing vehicles, the nearest one dispenses ballast between the rails while the other deposits it on the sleeper ends. (13 June 2004)

J. Lloyd Peate was a Llanfair merchant who sold coal from the railway's yard and whose family traded there until 1970. From 1903 until 1935 his coal was carried in the fleet of five Pickering wagons made to his specification, a move that meant he could use them for storage and not incur demurrage charges for using the railway's wagons. The wagons were scrapped when he started using road transport. In 2017 the railway's volunteers decided to make a replica of the wagons, obtaining sponsorship from his family, who still live in Llanfair, and from the railway's coal supplier. Peate's descendants pose for photographs when the wagon's completion was marked on 15 July 2017.

In 1895 Peate had been keen for a light railways Bill to be put into effect and he became an enthusiastic supporter of the Meifod route. He also owned standard gauge wagons. A plate from one of his wagons was found at Llanfair in 1966.

The volunteers who built the wagon also posed for photographs.

CHAPTER 4

THE INDEPENDENT YEARS

Thanks to the restrictions imposed by the shortage of funding the railway was minimally equipped. Two locomotives, three carriages, two goods brake vans, two goods vans, two cattle trucks and forty open wagons. With minimal additions to the wagon fleet and withdrawal of the carriages in 1931, this lasted until British Railways closed the line in 1956.

At stations, the termini were provided with an office, a goods shed and a tranship shed, all timber buildings. The locomotives had a 50ft-long shed and the carriages had one 80ft long. For passengers, protection from the weather was provided by verandahs attached to the office buildings and open-sided shelters at Golfa, Castle Caereinion, Cyfronydd and Heniarth. There was a urinal at Llanfair.

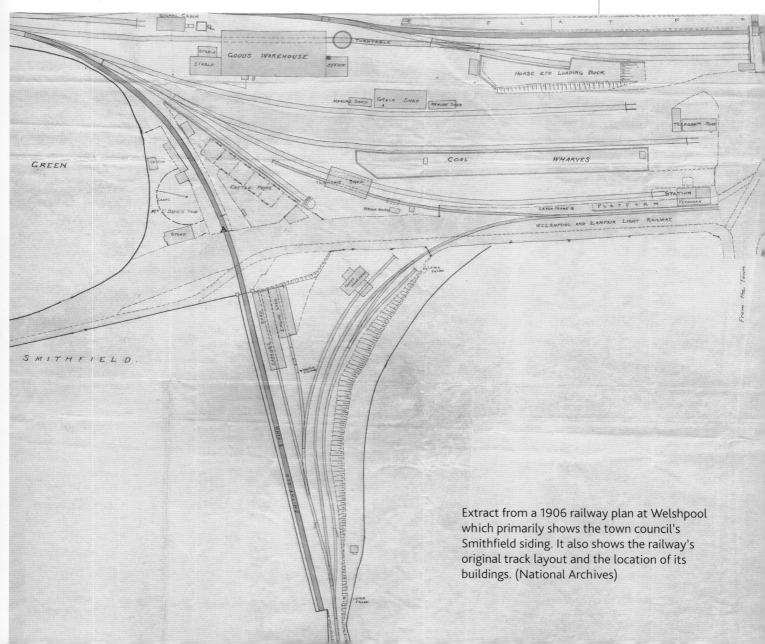

Extract from a 1906 railway plan at Welshpool which primarily shows the town council's Smithfield siding. It also shows the railway's original track layout and the location of its buildings. (National Archives)

A short mixed train at Llanfair soon after services commenced.

Ordinary passenger services started on 6 April 1903. The timetable indicates that despite the lack of accommodation passenger stock must have been left overnight at Llanfair. The Monday/Tuesday/Wednesday 5.5am goods to Llanfair returned mixed at 6.45am, for example, except on Llanfair fair days when the outward journey was mixed, and its return was goods only. The 7.5pm mixed from Welshpool returned as a passenger train leaving Llanfair at 8pm except on Saturdays when it ran mixed an hour later. Trains stopped at all stations and on Mondays they also stopped at Dolarddyn crossing, between Castle Caereinion and Cyfronydd, when passengers paid as if joining or leaving the train at Cyfronydd. Excursion tickets (1s 3rd class, return any train) were offered on the 11.40am from Welshpool on Thursdays and on the 2.20pm from Llanfair on Thursdays by the end of April. There were no trains on Sundays.

Finances were considered under several headings when the directors met on 7 April.

Two shareholders were to be asked to adhere to their conditional promises to subscribe to more shares; depending on the outcome, public support was to be canvassed. The final instalment of the Treasury grant was still awaited so the company was dependent on the goodwill of suppliers prepared to wait for payment. The overdraft stood at £6,260 12s 5d and about £2,000 was owed. Payments totalling £541 5s 5d to the investing authorities were approved. The opening ceremony had cost £38 19s 9d, an expense that could not be 'properly charged against the company', so donations were to be solicited from the directors.

On the railway, twenty minutes were lost by the morning train on 9 April when the loco 'slipped off the rails' at Heniarth. Unfortunately the one-line report in the *Montgomeryshire Express* (14 April) did not explain what had caused the derailment nor how the loco was re-railed so quickly.

The first two weeks' traffic was reported as shown in the table. It equated to £6 11s 3d per mile per week.

Goods	11 April 1903			18 April 1903		
Description	Tons	cwt	£ s d	Tons	cwt	£ s d
Merchandise	16	2	£8 19s 11d	29	10	10 11s 4d
Grain etc.	23	7	£3 16s 5d	12	12	£2 1s 4d
Manure	45	2	£7 15s 1d	37	16	£6 6d 10d
Coal and coke	51	19	£6 9s 2d	48	6	£5 16s 11d
Other minerals	19	15	£2 13s 4d	46	4	£6 7s 1d
Total	156	5	£29 13s 4d	174	8	£31 3s 6d
Passengers						
	1,274		£32 13s 10d	864		£31 3s 6d
Parcels			14s 8d			
Total			£63 1s 10d			£56 13s 4d

On 21 April, Denniss reported to his directors that if these figures were maintained then the railway would be a commercial success. He noticed that the traffic had dropped in the fourth week and attributed it to traffic being held for the railway's opening. The light railway order permitted the goods rates to be 25% higher than the equivalent Cambrian rates for five years, he reminded them. They had been set high because it was easier to reduce them to attract traffic if necessary. Following the traders' complaints, the class rates had been reduced and special rates quoted for heavy groceries, drapery, hardware, packed manure, grain and oil cake. There was scope for further adjustment if required.

The Treasury grant balance of £10,250 had been received by 5 May, when the company was £3,194 13s 4d in credit.

Half of Strachan's retention, £1,267, was approved for payment. Other payments authorised were £289 15s to Beyer, Peacock; £943 6s 4d to Pickering & Company; £685 8s 6d to the Cambrian, and the 21st payment due to Strachan. The solicitors were to sell the £1,000 India stock deposited in court as soon as it was released; it was sold for £1,016 3s 7d by 7 July. Additional shares to the value of £750 had been spoken for, although £500 was conditional on £1,357 being subscribed to trigger the authorised debenture issue.

Within a few weeks of the opening, problems had arisen at the interface between the locomotives' fixed wheelbase and the three-chain curves. Collin submitted a detailed report on 7 May, describing the problem locations and possible mitigation measures.

Location	Comment
Smithfield	Cannot be altered without taking a portion of the Smithfield.
Canal approach	Can be improved to 4½ chains without taking additional land.
Vicarage grounds	Route kept to Lledan brook due to cost of land. Curves can be eased to 4½ chains by building dwarf retaining walls to support embankments.
Llanfair side of Church Street	Three-chain curve necessary to follow Lledan brook; cannot be altered without purchasing property.
Hall Street	Severn Stars purchased to obtain three-chain curve; it might be improved to four chains by encroaching on the road.
Tannery	Curve might be improved to 4½ chains by widening the bank and building a short retaining wall.

Location	Comment
Allotments at rear of armoury	Curve cannot be improved without taking land.
Armoury – Standard quarry	Two curves which can be altered to 4½ chains by widening cuttings and banks and building a short retaining wall.
Golfa curves	Curves adopted to reduce the amount of [Reverend] Pughe's land required. Can be improved to four and five chains by widening cuttings, making slopes steeper, widening an embankment, and building a short retaining wall.
Dolrhyd	Curve cannot be altered without taking more land.

He estimated that the alterations described could be carried out for £1,000 without buying more land. There would still be five three-chain curves and twelve of 4 and 4½ chains. He recommended accepting Jones's suggestion of altering the locomotives to give extra side play on the leading and trailing axle-boxes. Ideally, he said, the minimum curve should be six chains, but that could cost up to £5,000 to achieve.

Jones's report had been submitted the day before. He had consulted with Beyer, Peacock and between them they had produced five options, as shown in the table.

Scheme	Proposed alteration	Time	Cost per engine	Where done	Comments
1	Convert to 4-4-0T	14 weeks	£195	Welshpool	Inside bearings on bogie, 1½in side play, rigid wheelbase reduced to 5ft 10in, bogie unsatisfactory due to position of frames and cylinders, steadiness of loco would be diminished, tractive effort reduced, weight increased, brake power reduced, capability reduced.
2	Convert to 2-4-0T	7 weeks	£80	Welshpool	Remove leading coupling rods, substitute sliding axle-boxes on leading axle to give 1in side play, rigid wheelbase reduced to 5ft 10in, leading wheels would have no radial action, engine would be more unstable, brake power and adhesion reduced.
3	Reduce wheelbase	16 weeks	£225	Manchester	Reduce wheelbase by 9in between leading and driving axles and by 1in between driving and trailing axles, cost out of proportion with possible merit.
4	Remove driving flanges	1 week	Nominal	Welshpool	Would be unsafe and make little difference on the track, increasing wear on leading and trailing tyres.
5	Additional play in axle-boxes	3 weeks	£10	Welshpool	Increase side play by ⅛in in the leading axle-boxes and by ¼in in the trailing axle-boxes, the equivalent of shortening the rigid wheelbase to about 8ft 6in, would increase wear and tear on the loco, no structural alterations required, haulage and brake power unaltered.

The final option was chosen and was completed on 15 May. By 10 June, Collin reported that the engines were running much better and not affecting the curves although 'there are two or three curves . . . when the engine . . . still moves the spikes a little.' He had arranged for soleplates to be used and for extra sleepers to be inserted to stiffen up the track.

Welshpool's May fair, on 4 May 1903, was the first big event since the railway opened and it attracted hundreds of visitors from the Llanfair area who thought to use the train. One train carried 230 passengers. The *County Times* (9 May) said that 180 were seated and the remainder travelled in the vans. For either group the overcrowding would have made for a most unpleasant experience. To take them home two extra trains ran during the evening, the last reaching Llanfair at midnight. According to the *Montgomeryshire Express* (12 May) many of the passengers had never seen a railway before, nor been to Welshpool.

Strachan's involvement with the railway moved closer to an end with an auction of surplus equipment at the Standard quarry on 15 May. Items listed included a locomotive, a stone breaker, 50 tons of rail, wagons, site buildings and eight draught horses.

On 19 May the train crew of the 11.40am from Welshpool was taken aback by the number of passengers leaving the train at Heniarth, especially when they were met there by the landlord of the Wynnstay Arms and his brake. They were bound for the laying of the Ann Griffiths' memorial chapel's foundation stone at Dolanog, about 4½ miles away. She had been the author and composer of popular Methodist hymns.

In June, Denniss produced details of the revenue for the first eight weeks. The average income of £7 1s 1d per mile per week was compared with £24 13s 6d earned by the Cambrian. He made no comment about the big dip after 9 May.

ANN GRIFFITHS' MEMORIAL CHAPEL DOLANOG.

THE MEMORIAL STONE

Of the above Building will be laid at 2 p.m.

On Tuesday, May 19th,

BY

MRS OWEN JONES, Llansantffraid,
MRS D. CHARLES EDWARDS, Llanbedr,
EDWARD JONES, Esq., J.P., Trewythen,
And the Rev. EDWARD GRIFFITHS, Meifod.

CONVEYANCES will run in connection with Trains arriving at Llanfyllin 11 50, and Heniarth Gate (Welshpool & Llanfair Light Railway) 12 40.

Tea will be provided at Dolanog.

Week ending	Passenger	Goods	Total
11 April	£33	£30	£63
18 April	£41	£34	£75
25 April	£25	£45	£70
2 May	£34	£36	£70
9 May	£44	£31	£78
16 May	£24	£28	£52
23 May	£28	£27	£55
30 May	£20	£35	£55
	£249	£266	£515

By the end of June, the gross receipts had reached £1,007 4s 5d, 40% (£402 17s 9d) of which was to be paid to the company. The cost of working had been £532, leaving £72 profit for the Cambrian, Denniss commenting: 'You will no doubt consider [it] is not unsatisfactory.'

July was a month of extreme contrasts so far as the company's finances were concerned. The overdraft was down to £46 11s 6d and unsecured borrowing of £1,000 had been arranged. The remaining share capital had been subscribed and steps were taken to issue the debentures. The sale of surplus land at Castle Caereinion and a house in Church Street, Welshpool, would help the financial position. Appendix 6 lists the capital expenditure incurred during the previous eighteen months.

An advertisement published in the *Montgomeryshire Express* by the sponsors of Ann Griffiths' memorial chapel at Dolanog, who provided road transport to the memorial stone ceremony from the nearest stations.

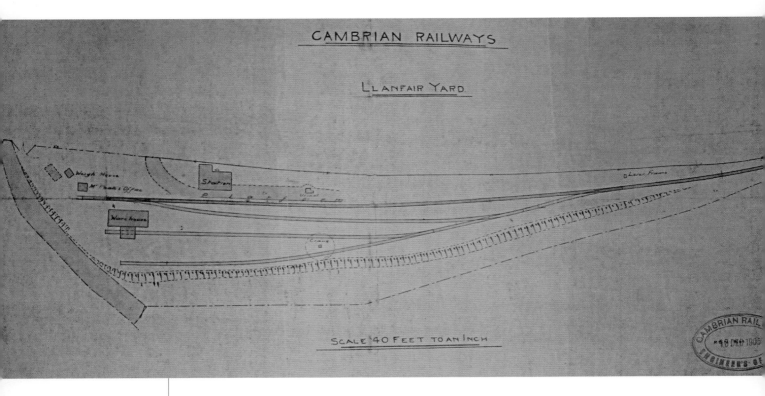

CAMBRIAN RAILWAYS

LLANFAIR YARD

SCALE 40 FEET TO AN INCH

A 1905 plan of the yard at Llanfair. (National Archives)

Just as the directors must have thought they were close to getting the company's finances into a state of equilibrium, on 7 July Collin submitted certificate No 23 for £2,850 18s, followed by a note on 16 July saying that £800 was due for extras. This was £3,560 3s 5d above the estimate he had given in January, which was itself higher than forecast. Collin was asked to explain the discrepancy. The 'missing' certificates, Nos 19-22, would have been for works undertaken outside the contract – buildings, for example.

The comment made on the opening day about inadequate facilities at Llanfair Caereinion was duly followed up, Collin estimating that it would cost £215 to enlarge the yard. On 11 August, Denniss informed the company that the Cambrian would do the work, including installing a siding, for 4½% interest, repayment being due when the debentures had been issued. He was informed that the debenture capital could not be used for this purpose and repayment would have to await the availability of funds from other sources. On 11 December, Denniss was informed that

until Collin produced his final certificate to justify Strachan's claim, no further expenditure would be incurred.

The terms for issuing the debentures had been agreed on 1 September at 20 years at 4½% although the directors reserved the right to redeem them at 103% after 10 years, giving six months' notice. A prospectus was issued on 28 November and applications for £1,550 had been received by 22 December.

A severe storm on 8 September 1903 that had washed out 200 yards of ballast near Dolrhyd mill was reported in the *Manchester Guardian* two days later. Until the damage was repaired trains terminated at Heniarth and passengers were transported to and from Llanfair by road. The same place was flooded on 6 October. The *Merioneth County Times* (8 October) advised the railway to raise the track or the location would be the source of endless trouble and expense during the winter months.

A few weeks later the 'greatest flood that has been known for over 20 years' (*Wellington Journal* 31 October 1903) occurred in Welshpool. The Lledan

On the Llanfair Railway, Welshpool

This coloured postcard of a train crossing Union Street in Welshpool was registered by the publisher in 1904. (J. Valentine)

brook burst its banks and the railway was flooded.

The appointment of John Pritchard as a passenger guard on the railway was noted by the *Merioneth County Times* on 10 September 1903. Born in Rhyl in 1864, he had been working as a signalman at Tywyn. The only appointment reported specifically for the railway, some posts would have been filled by existing Cambrian employees. One such was James Davies (1866-1939), transferred from Penmaenpool to be stationmaster at Llanfair in 1906 and staying there until passenger services were withdrawn in 1931.

On opening, Edmondson-style card tickets had been issued from booking offices at the termini. The *Montgomeryshire Express* (8 December) reported their closure from 1 January 1904, saying that in future tramway-style punch tickets would be issued on the train.

A card ticket issued to workmen to travel 3rd class from 'Saturday to Monday'.

A 3rd class tram-type ticket, valid as punched.

Addie's position as a director was terminated on 22 December 1903, when C.T. Pugh, his successor as mayor, replaced him. During the year, David Davies, the contractor's grandson, had been appointed to the board. Addie continued to act for the company as its valuer and on 20 April 1904 the directors paid tribute to his efforts on the company's behalf. He was reappointed to the board on 11 July 1905.

It was thanks to Addie that the directors eventually received information about Strachan's claim, several requests to Collin having been ignored. His 15-page typewritten report was dated 19 April 1904. Collin had written with explanations on 28 July 1903 and 26 March 1904. Some of the additional costs had arisen, he said, because the work carried out had been re-surveyed, establishing that more had been done than first calculated. Specific explanations from Collin's first report have been tabulated.

The Board of Trade requirements could not have been foreseen, Addie thought, but 'it is difficult to explain why [the other items] should not have been taken into consideration by the engineer in previous reports.' The works at Heniarth were unauthorised. The Dolrhyd water supply cost £398 14 10d, 'the importance of this work was not properly realised at the commencement.' Druitt's permanent way requirements, the gauge widening, the check rails, moving the check rails, the tie bars and adjusting the cants where a 5mph speed limit had been imposed, had cost £1,066.

In his second report Collin concluded that he considered the cost of the contract works to be £29,253 2s 11d plus £1,907 10s 10d for extras, nearly a 25% increase on the £25,350 he had given in January 1903. The extras included £238 for felling trees, which Addie thought was unreasonable. He said, however, that he had no reason to doubt the figures Collin had submitted, but thought that the engineers should have obtained approval for works not included in the contract and queried whether the charges for the slips were properly chargeable to the company.

With Strachan's claim for extras totalling £19,723 4s 6d the directors were happy that Collin could only justify £1,907 10s 10d, but were about to discover that Strachan was a very determined man who would not give up easily. No complete breakdown of Strachan's claim has been found; neither railway company thought

Item	Increase	Explanation
Earthworks	£700	£215 for widening and lowering road to Heniarth station; £300 to remove slips in cuttings following rain; balance for extra excavations in various cuttings.
Drains	£460	Following the landslips it was necessary to install drainage in the cuttings concerned.
Track	£870	Installing check rails on the three-chain curves, gauge-widening, fixing ties and extra soleplates; installing extra siding at Llanfair Caereinion requested by Denniss.
Metalling	£170	Surfacing the road at Heniarth after alterations.
	£135	Altering stiles at district council's request; fencing riverside to keep cattle from the track, the river having proved to be an inadequate barrier; fixing mile and quarter posts as required by the Board of Trade inspector.
	£90	Concrete footings to protect railway formation from scour at Dolrhyd.
	£40	Pulling down culvert over Lledan brook.
Stations	£635	Partly work carried out by Strachan previously estimated separately; increased works required installing water supply at Dolrhyd and extra gas supply at Welshpool.

it necessary to record details of it. Where details were mentioned, it is clear that in some instances he was trying his luck. He had been charged for the repair of some wagons that his men had damaged and tried to reclaim the expenditure, for example.

With £360 4s 5d in the bank, commitments totalling £672 17s 3d, the knowledge that there were still outstanding claims on the construction account to be met, and a full subscription list for the debentures exhausting the company's ability to borrow, the directors decided to return to the Treasury for further assistance.

Writing on 20 April 1904, Lord Powis asked the Treasury for a further free grant of £3,500 and a loan of £5,800 to clear existing liabilities and to effect certain improvements. Strachan's claim was judged to be exaggerated and was expected to be settled for the amount certified by Collin. The proposed improvements were as shown in the table.

Following an investigation into the company's situation, the Treasury replied on 4 August 1904, saying that an addition to the free grant was not justified but that a loan of up to £5,700 at 3¼% could be made if the remainder of the capital required could be found. The company was not informed that the reason the grant was refused was because it was making a profit and might pay dividends. Considering the matter on 13 September, the directors resolved to apply for an amendment to the light railway order to permit the loan to be taken and to increase the ordinary borrowing powers to £4,000.

Before the order application was submitted the company's Parliamentary agent informed the treasury that the loan would be sufficient to pay the cost of the works already carried out and put the company on a sound financial footing. The additional works would therefore be deferred until the money to pay for them could be raised. The application was advertised on 14 November 1904 and the Welshpool & Llanfair Light Railway (further borrowing powers) Order 1905 was made on 1 May 1905.

Despite the lack of funds for additional works a siding had been installed at Tanllan, near Llanfair, to handle timber traffic for E.O. Jones & Sons. It had been requested by Denniss on 18 April 1904. The merchant had purchased a large quantity of timber and was willing to load it if suitable facilities were provided. The work had been carried out by the Cambrian for £130, £70 of which would be repaid by the customer at a rate of 3d per ton loaded. The remaining £60 had been charged to the railway. The Board of Trade had been asked to inspect it on 30 June and Druitt submitted his report on 25 November. The siding, which faced trains from Welshpool, was controlled by a two-lever frame locked by the train staff. He recommended approval subject to the traffic being worked with the loco at the lower end of the train due to the gradient.

Improvement	Estimated cost
Additional sidings and enlargement of yard at Llanfair	£215
Altering signalling and provision of passing places so that more than one engine in steam can be run	£880
Platforms, goods sidings and metalling station yard at Castle Caereinion	£270
Timber wagons	£440
A third engine	£1,600
Additional passenger carriage	£235
	£3,640

The cover of the 1905 (further borrowing powers) light railway order.

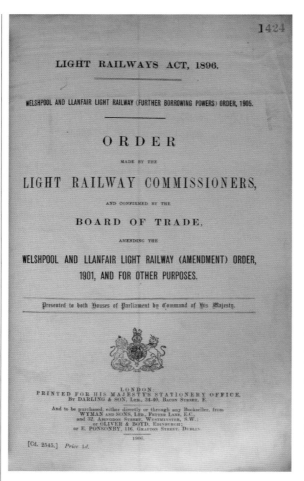

LIGHT RAILWAYS ACT, 1896.

WELSHPOOL AND LLANFAIR LIGHT RAILWAY (FURTHER BORROWING POWERS) ORDER, 1905.

ORDER

MADE BY THE

LIGHT RAILWAY COMMISSIONERS,

AND CONFIRMED BY THE

BOARD OF TRADE,

AMENDING THE

WELSHPOOL AND LLANFAIR LIGHT RAILWAY (AMENDMENT) ORDER,
1901, AND FOR OTHER PURPOSES.

Presented to both Houses of Parliament by Command of His Majesty.

LONDON
PRINTED FOR HIS MAJESTY'S STATIONERY OFFICE.
By DARLING & SON, LTD., 34-40, Bacon Street, E.
And to be purchased, either directly or through any Bookseller, from
WYMAN and SONS, LTD., Fetter Lane, E.C.
and 32, Abingdon Street, Westminster, S.W.;
or OLIVER & BOYD, Edinburgh;
or E. PONSONBY, 116, Grafton Street, Dublin.
1906.

[Cd. 2545.] Price 1d.

Provision of wagons for timber traffic had been a saga that had started in July 1903, when Denniss had said that the traffic would need 10 or 12 wagons. Jones had replied that he wanted paying to specify and procure them but the directors pointed out that they had been included in the list of stock required by the Cambrian to equip the railway and that although their purchase had been deferred, they were included in the fee already payable to him.

The directors gave up on dealing with Jones, though, and took over the order themselves, Addie visiting Pickering on 11 November 1903. He was told that wagons without springs or central couplers could be supplied for £25 each, but that they would be unsuitable. Wagons that complied with the Cambrian's requirements would be £44 each or £10 8s 10d per wagon per annum for five years. By 4 March 1904, six Cambrian-specification wagons had been ordered on a five-year lease contract, a nominal payment of 1s per wagon to be paid at the end of the term to complete the purchase. The wagons were delivered by 20 April but awaited acceptance by the Cambrian at that date. The lease with the

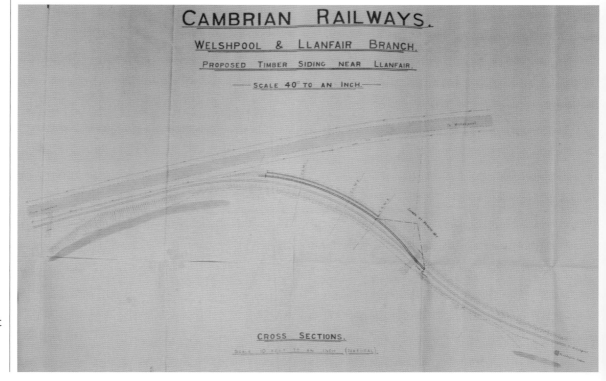

CAMBRIAN RAILWAYS.

WELSHPOOL & LLANFAIR BRANCH.

PROPOSED TIMBER SIDING NEAR LLANFAIR.

─ SCALE 40" TO AN INCH. ─

CROSS SECTIONS.

A drawing for the timber siding at Tanllan. Connected at the Llanfair end, the siding remained in place until 2014.

Scottish Waggon Company Limited was sealed on 13 September.

Strachan had given notice that his claim should be put to an arbitrator in April 1904. The contract had nominated Collin, or the Cambrian's engineer for the time being, to deal with any disputes. Collin had started to handle the case only to resign from the contract on 6 May and from the Cambrian for health reasons the next day.

He later explained to Denniss that as a receiver had been appointed to the Tanat Valley Railway, of which he was also the engineer, he stood to lose 'what is to me a very large sum of money', or would have to wait for many years before he was paid. The company had applied for further assistance from the Treasury and if it did not get all that it wanted there was also a possibility that a receiver would be appointed. As the railway had owed him money for about 12 months, he had a personal stake in the arbitration so he had to withdraw. £225 was paid on account of his claim for £324 11s on 12 April 1905.

Strachan's solicitors initially refused to accept Collin's successor as the Cambrian's engineer, G.C. McDonald, as arbitrator because Collin had resigned, but, after threatening to apply to a judge to make the appointment, they accepted him in July. Denniss and the Cambrian's solicitors decided that the remainder of Strachan's retention should be paid to prevent him from issuing a writ on that account; £1,355 5s 6d had been paid by 13 September 1904.

On 19 September 1904, Strachan wrote to the light railway directors objecting to repayments being made to the investing authorities 'considering the very large amount' due to the Cambrian. When the Cambrian directors met on 11 October, Denniss reported that not only had Strachan issued a writ for £1,509, he was also claiming damages for breach of contract, claiming that Collin had been dismissed to prevent him from issuing the final certificate. The solicitor expected the action to be dismissed with costs and recommended the light railway pay £975 18s 6d into court against the final

certificate. The light railway had recently paid £1,000 to the Cambrian and only had £200 to hand. If the Cambrian would pay the money into court, and the remaining £1,850 18s owed, it would be settled when the Treasury loan was received.

On 10 August 1904, Collin reported that one of the Banwy bridge piers had been 'dangerously undermined by the water'. He had put repairs in hand immediately at a cost of about £50. Sixty years later this pier nearly brought about the permanent closure of the railway.

A tragedy occurred on 8 September 1904 when John Powell, a carpenter from Castle Caereinion, was killed trying to board a moving train at Raven Square. With a friend, George Herbert Astley, he had been to the Welshpool show and at 8pm they had adjourned to the Raven Inn, intending to catch the return excursion train. Hearing it while they were still in the pub, they ran out to catch it as it was crossing Raven Square. Astley succeeded but Powell overbalanced and fell between the first and second carriages. Astley gave evidence that they did not know where the station was but thought the train was going to stop. The coroner thought that they must have had sufficient to drink to be muddled. The jury returned a verdict that death was caused accidentally while attempting to board a train in motion. The sense of tragedy must have been magnified because Powell's father, a rabbit catcher, had been on the train.

In the *Shrewsbury Chronicle*'s inquest report on 16 September, incidentally, the coroner was quoted as saying that the railway had carried 60-70,000 passengers since it had opened. Assuming the mid-point, 65,000, and three trains a day, that equates to an average of fifty passengers per train.

The train service was accelerated by ten minutes from 3 December 1904. Denniss had obtained the approval of both the locomotive and the civil engineers to this move, the journey time now taking 55 minutes. The Cambrian's working expenses for the half-year were £898 14s,

56.47% of the £1,592 7s 10d gross receipts. 'Considering the amount of ballasting and other attention which the permanent way has required I consider this by no means unsatisfactory,' Denniss reported in May 1905.

The Cambrian was reimbursed the £3,068 17s 5d by the company on 8 July 1905. As permitted by the working agreement, the company had been charged 5% compound interest (£264 10s 11d) on capital expenditure incurred on its behalf. In view of the difficulties caused by Collin, it asked the Cambrian to consider calculating interest on the simple basis. The difference was £11 8s 4d.

The deposit against the final certificate should not be paid into court, Strachan's solicitors had written on 29 October 1904, because they were intending to apply to have the matter referred to arbitration. If it was paid into court, it would be as if the action had been started and their claim for arbitration would not be heard.

Despite the earlier agreement over McDonald's appointment, the choice of arbitrator was prolonged. Eventually, Denniss recommended Charles Langbridge Morgan of the London, Brighton & South Coast Railway and Strachan put forward Walter Armstrong, new-works engineer of the Great Western Railway. In February 1905, Denniss agreed to the final selection being 'by means of drawing a piece of paper from a hat' and Armstrong was chosen. Addie had told Denniss that he had tried to negotiate a settlement with Strachan but had found him impossible to deal with. He had, however, established that Strachan was prepared to accept £6,000 in settlement of his claim.

Armstrong accepted the appointment and a preliminary hearing was held on 18 April. Strachan attempted to launch his case only for an objection to be upheld that he had not submitted his statement of claim. His original claim of £19, 636 13s 9d had been reduced to £9,876 14s 5d. He was also claiming £17,893 17s 3d from the Tanat Valley Railway. Engineers for each side were to discuss the claim and produce lists of agreed and disputed items by 18 May. The Cambrian's counterclaim would be presented on the same date.

Agreement was reached on items valued at £1,574 6s 11d, but the statement of differences was not produced 'owing to Strachan's obstinacy in regards to proposed meetings'. The value of the counterclaim was £1,685 15s 11d, mostly represented by £50 per week for the thirty weeks the railway was incomplete after the date specified, 1 September 1902; the remainder represented locomotive hire, repair of wagons and other items.

Collin probably saw the arbitration as an opportunity to recoup some of the money that he was fearful of losing. He had refused to return or give access to the contract documents that he had taken when he left the Cambrian's employment, and now he made what were perceived as extravagant demands to act as a witness against Strachan; 25 guineas retainer, 4 guineas a day for office work and 20 guineas a day to appear. Denniss approved of the retainer and offered 5 guineas a day to attend, including office work and producing any plans. In his accounts of the arbitration, Denniss did not refer to any contribution being made by Collin so possibly no agreement was reached.

The hearing was continued on 4 August, when Strachan 'resumed his case in a very excited manner'. He had subpoenaed Denniss and questioned him about a letter he [Denniss] was supposed to have written on 17 December 1902, refusing to take delivery of rolling stock. When Denniss denied having written such a letter Strachan 'completely lost control of himself', claimed that the letter had been supressed and demanded an adjournment for it to be produced. When he refused to behave, the Cambrian's counsel walked out. Investigation established that the letter related to the wagons being fitted with chains that had been dealt with by the light railway directors on 17 December.

Concerning Strachan's behaviour, the Cambrian wrote to Armstrong, copied to Strachan via his solicitors, on

10 August 1905. 'Reckless expenditure', 'waste of time', 'considerable inconvenience', 'quite unprecedented' and 'emphatic protest' were amongst the phrases used, calling upon Armstrong to use his influence 'to ensure the reasonable expeditious conduct of the proceedings with due regard to the expenditure and to avoiding the waste of time, both of which hitherto have been so recklessly incurred by Mr Strachan's action.' Armstrong replied: 'I quite concur with your expressions, and hope Mr Strachan will try to conduct his case in a more reasonable manner. His conduct at the last sitting was very objectionable.'

When the hearing was continued on 23 November, Strachan's counsel took two days to read letters that both sides agreed had no bearing on the case, but which revealed an 'unfortunate interference' by Byron, the resident engineer, in matters being dealt with by Strachan and the railway. 'It is unfortunate that so many letters on this subject were written,' Denniss informed the Cambrian directors, adding that the exercise had cost about £300 in fees.

Resuming the arbitration on 15 December, Strachan's solicitors made an informal offer to settle for £5,000, each side paying its own costs, which was refused. Strachan put up Arthur Cameron Hurtzig (1854-1915), a London-based engineer, as his expert witness but it soon became apparent that his knowledge of the railway was limited to what he had been told by Strachan, which resulted in Strachan withdrawing £1,200 of his claim because Hurtzig could not support it. Denniss was cross-examined on 16 December, a Saturday, for 2½ hours about allegations that the Cambrian had not treated Strachan properly, none of which were relevant to his claim.

On 18 December evidence for the railway was given by Morgan. Proceedings were not resumed on 19 December as expected, because Armstrong was ill. Two more days were taken for closing speeches on 5/6 February 1906. Awaiting the decision, Denniss reported that he thought that Strachan's claim was based on feeble evidence. His claim had been reduced to £6,600 and 'would probably be substantially reduced by the award.'

Indeed, Armstrong awarded Strachan £4,251 10s 4d, and allowed the counterclaim, on 14 June. The railway, with only £1,200 available and unable to borrow from its bank without directors' guarantees, asked the Cambrian to advance the remainder which it did grudgingly to stave off more threats of action from Strachan. The Cambrian also paid the arbitrator's charges of £321 17s 6d, to avoid them being included in Strachan's expenses claim and thereby saving £8 in taxation fees.

One item that Strachan did succeed with related to spoil removal, his contractual responsibility. However, he had made a verbal agreement with Collin to load it into Cambrian wagons so that it could be used to widen the embankment near Forden in preparation for doubling the track there. He had used his loco to transport the spoil to site and had unloaded it, charging £348 11s 5d for doing so. The directors thought that they should not be responsible for the entire charge as the spoil benefited the Cambrian, suggesting that they be credited with £300. The Cambrian offered £200. It appears that neither the Cambrian nor the company thought to claim against Strachan in respect of his unfulfilled obligation to maintain the railway for twelve months after its completion.

It is not unknown for contractors to boost their profits by claiming for extras, claiming to have undertaken extra work not specified by the contract. As a strategy, that might work if a client is well-funded. When the client has limited funds then there is more likely to be resistance. The outcome, with an award close to the railway's original calculation of the amount due, suggests that Strachan's claim was more than a little enhanced.

Overall, a better result for the railway would have been obtained by accepting the settlement offer, as the costs incurred, including Strachan's expenses,

One of the bolster wagons at Pickering's works. There were six of them made.

amounted to £2,847 12s 9d. As precedents established during the hearings simplified the handling of Strachan's complaint against the Tanat Valley Light Railway, the Llanfair railway directors thought that company should stand some of the expenses. The sum of £134 11s 1d was agreed upon.

In 1906, Pickering, the rolling stock manufacturer, enquired about the outstanding order for four timber wagons. When Denniss said that the Cambrian could work the traffic without them, a request was made for the order to be cancelled. On 24 September 1906, Pickering wrote that the order could only be cancelled if it were replaced by orders for other rolling stock. A decision was deferred and nothing more was said about it.

Another derailment occurred on 22 September 1906, during shunting operations reported the *Montgomeryshire Echo* (29 September). Most likely at Welshpool, although the paper did not say, it was obviously more severe than the incident at Heniarth in 1903 as it required the Cambrian's Oswestry breakdown gang

to sort it out. The passengers made their journey by road.

The question of capacity at Llanfair arose again at the end of 1906. W.H. Thomas, an Oswestry timber merchant, had bought timber in the area which was being transported to Welshpool by road. Enlarging the yard at a cost of about £170 would attract this traffic, some of which would be bound for destinations beyond Welshpool, and provide coal storage space, avoiding keeping wagons under load.

Concerned about the lane to Heniarth station at the end of 1906, Llangyniew parish council asked Llanfyllin Rural District Council to attend to it. On 29 November the latter authority established that the road had been made by the owner of Heniarth mill and had been used when the railway was being built, the railway putting it into repair and widening it for half its length, about 100 yards, but having no liability for its ongoing maintenance. It had fallen into disrepair and was now impassable. Denniss had refused to do anything about it as it was not railway property. Establishing that it was

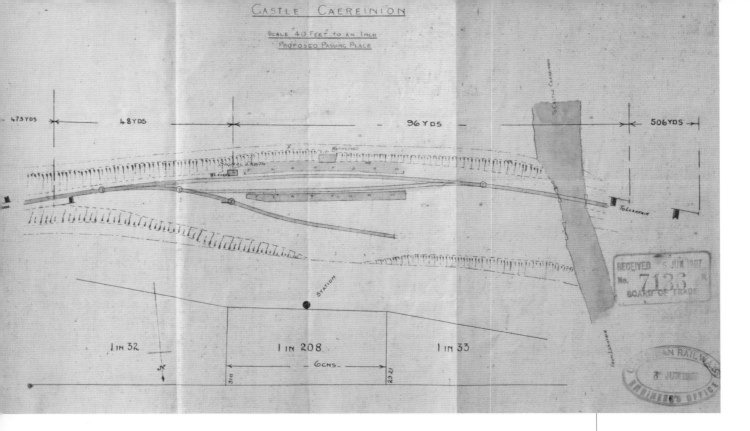

The 1907 plan of Castle Caereinion produced when the Cambrian Railways wished to cross timber trains there. (National Archives)

still a private road, notwithstanding its use by the public to access Heniarth station, the district council resolved to take no action.

More timber traffic was responsible for an examination of the facilities at Castle Caereinion, reported on 2 January 1907. Jabez Barker, a Shrewsbury timber merchant, had bought an estimated 1,400 tons of timber in the locality which could be hauled by road to Llanfair and then by rail to Welshpool. At 5s per ton, gross revenue would be £350, 40% of which would be £140. On a Sunday, when the railway was closed, a successful trial had been undertaken with some 60ft timbers and trucks connected with chains acting as bolsters; the timber's length prevented it from being carried in the ordinary (mixed) trains. Therefore two-train running, requiring the installation of signalling and a siding for the local traffic, was required to handle the traffic. The cost of the alterations and installing signalling was estimated at £160.

The directors agreed to the work being carried out on 23 March 1907 and on 4 June Samuel Williamson, Denniss's successor as secretary from 1906, gave notice to the Board of Trade that the station was ready for inspection. Submitting his report on 15 June, Druitt said that a small signalbox

had been equipped with a 10-lever frame, one lever spare. He explained that one-engine-in-steam working was to be replaced by train-staff-and-ticket combined with absolute block telegraph except that the telephone would be used instead of block instruments. He saw no objection to this, requiring only to see a copy of the working instructions and a fresh undertaking as to the method of working, signed by both companies, to approve its use.

The regulations were dated 23 September 1907. Of note was the requirement that when any train was assisted by a second engine it was to be attached to the rear of the train, no double-heading. Sending Druitt the regulations on 18 September, McDonald explained that it was only intended to use the crossing for a month or two at a time, 'chiefly for ballasting or maintenance purposes', and that at other times the points would be disconnected from the signalbox and reconnected to the ground frame. Druitt required that the staffs for the system not in use be locked up.

The company's liabilities had been the subject of a report that Addie submitted on 18 March 1907. Including £100 as working capital, the total was £4,145 5s 2d.

A quiet day at Raven Square.

He suggested issuing the remaining £200 debenture stock and borrowing by mortgage or a fresh debenture issue a further £3,850. The Treasury was to be asked to remit the interest due to it for five years and on 7 August 1908 the local authorities were asked to forego redemption payments due to them for seven years.

Concerned about the rail deck on part of the Lledan brook, on 17 May 1907 the town council suggested that the section near the tannery be covered in concrete. A contribution of £5 towards the estimated £10 cost was approved. On 19 July the council asked for help in carrying out a 'further small portion to make the improvement complete'. Referring to the 'present dangerous open space', the request was passed to the Cambrian.

Llanfair District Education Committee included the railway in its invitation for tenders to supply coal to the elementary schools under its control in September 1907. Would-be suppliers were asked to quote for delivery to Llanfair station and for delivery to the schools.

Explaining the company's financial position to shareholders at the annual meeting on 11 October 1907, Lord Powis said that it was unfortunate that the company was obliged to redeem its loans, as the payments, taken out of net receipts, would otherwise be available for dividends. He pointed out that if the large railway companies had to redeem their borrowings, they would be unable to pay dividends. On the other hand, he concluded, in time the mortgages would be wiped out and the revenue available for shareholders. The railway would be in a very different situation in fifty years, when the redemption was due to be completed.

In an attempt to reduce the debt, originally nearly £3,000, incurred in contesting Strachan's excessive claims at arbitration, Addie led deputations to the investing authorities in August and September 1908, appealing for the suspension of the loan repayments, not the interest, for seven years in order that it might be reduced. There was no difficulty in securing the councils' approval as the concession incurred no immediate expense for them. The annual amount concerned ranged from £42, Welshpool, to £7, Forden.

The debt made the Cambrian the company's largest creditor. Reviewing the situation in March 1909, Williamson, the Cambrian's secretary, calculated that unless the railway's finances improved considerably, the £3,174 13s owed would only be reduced to £2,569 17s 10d in seven years' time.

John Strachan, the argumentative contractor, died in Kent on 2 April 1909 and was buried in Newmonthill cemetery, Forfar, Angus, the location of his grave known but unmarked. As his effects were valued at £29,660, shortage of funds is unlikely to explain the lack of a memorial.

On 30 July 1909 the light railway directors asked the Cambrian to relieve the company of the interest charged on the £190 expenditure incurred on adapting Castle Caereinion to pass trains. Two years after the work had been done, they had discovered that the facility was not being used. Denniss told John Conacher, the Cambrian's manager, that it had not been used because the railway could keep up with the pace of timber delivery without it, carrying timber either before or after the ordinary service, the longest lengths being about 73ft. 2,113 tons had been carried, earning £587 16s 11d, £235 2s 9d of which accrued to the railway. In addition, the Cambrian had earned £412 3s 8d from timber despatched to destinations beyond Welshpool. Druitt's requirement for a repeater of the distant signals to be located in the signalbox, not mentioned in his report, accounted for the £30 increase in the cost over the estimate.

Barker's timber had been loaded at Tanllan but in May 1909 he had been given notice to quit by E.O. Jones & Sons, owners of the loading dock, so alternative arrangements were required. With minimal alterations the timber could be loaded at Heniarth or it would be lost to the railway; about 300 tons was still expected. The Cambrian offered to reduce the interest charged to 2½% until the crossing was brought into use, or to cancel the interest when the company cleared its debt. If the railway had been unable to accommodate this traffic it would have been hauled to Dinas Mawddwy for conveyance via the Mawddwy Railway.

A 10-year-old boy no doubt rued the day that he decided to use the railway as a playground in May 1909, placing a length of timber across the line 'for sport'. Fortunately the driver of the next train was able to stop and remove the obstruction without any damage being caused. The Cambrian's solicitor prosecuted the child at Llanfair magistrates' court where he was ordered to be given six strokes of the birch.

Raven Square crossing was the location of another incident, a collision between a train and a horse and trap on 7 September 1909. The 9.00pm from Llanfair was crossing at 4mph, reported the *Montgomeryshire Express* (14 September), when a farmer heading briskly out of Welshpool collided with the train, which stopped immediately. The loco's paintwork was damaged, and the horse and trap were turned over, the shaft broken. The farmer was knocked unconscious and hospitalised for two days. No injuries to the horse were reported.

A charge of animal cruelty brought against a farmer by the RSPCA and which involved the railway was heard at Welshpool magistrates' court on 19 October 1909. It was the practice to transport calves in sacks because they were carried as dead weight, attracting a cheaper rate. John Thomas, Dolarddyn, had despatched a calf from Castle Caereinion in this manner on 12 August. On arrival at Welshpool it was seen by a passenger who thought that it was in poor condition. He noticed that its eyes were 'gelatised' and decided that it had white scour, a fatal disease, and should not have been transported thus. He reported it to the RSPCA. The Welshpool station master saw the animal and refused to tranship it, sending for the farmer to take it back. Evidence was given that it had been born partially blind, which accounted for the condition of its eyes, and had not been injured during its train journey. As its health did not improve after several days the farmer put it down. The case was dismissed without hearing the defence, each side paying its own costs.

It appears that the Castle Caereinion crossing might have seen more use than the directors, and possibly some Cambrian management, knew about. On 2 May 1910, McDonald reported that the Standard quarry had in stock a large quantity of chippings that he wished to use as ballast on the light railway. He had used this material before, but the quarry did not have enough stone in stock for the work to be finished. He raised the matter with the directors because to work the ballast trains at the same time as the 'ordinary' trains the Castle Caereinion signal box and loop would have to be brought into use. 'This was done on the previous occasion, but I understand that there may be some question of policy involved in re-opening the crossing place for this purpose,' he wrote.

Only four ordinary shareholders attended their meeting on 26 September 1910, noted the *Montgomeryshire Express* (27 September), and the three directors nominated by the town council to represent the town's interests did not attend either. Except for passengers, which was within a few shillings of the 1908 amount, revenue had increased under all headings. One of the shareholders suggested that the rates on cattle should be reduced but could not say if doing do would increase the amount of traffic, which was only worth £35 a year anyway.

Dealing with the re-election of directors, R.C. Anwyl, a director, pointed out that not only did they receive no fees but no expenses either. Perhaps they should be considered the railway's first volunteer directors?

The transport of livestock was the subject of correspondence between the light railway and the Cambrian in 1911. Charles Leonard Conacher, the Cambrian's traffic manager, one of John Conacher's sons, wanted to modify six wagons for the purpose. After obtaining more information,

£18 10s 10d expenditure was approved on 20 February 1911.

Increasing timber traffic at Heniarth in 1911 prompted Conacher to ask for the siding to be lengthened at a cost of £27. The company offered £20 on the basis that part of the work was maintenance. In October 1912, Barker's timber traffic warranted the entrance at Cyfronydd being widened. The railway companies were to share the £2–3 cost of a crane.

At Seven Stars a waiting room was provided in a cottage that had been bought and adapted to accommodate the line during construction. It was let to the Cambrian, which sub-let it to a guard.

In 1903 Collin had certified that repairs valued at £106 7s 4d had been carried but by 1912 the building was in a very poor state, the front and rear first floor walls were leaning, the floorboards were rotten, the entire first floor wanted taking down and rebuilding at a cost of up to £40. The light railway directors thought that the work could not have been done properly in the first place and wanted a contribution from the Cambrian. On 24 June it gave notice to quit but wanted to keep a section of land attached to the property as a site for a waiting room. By 14 October 1912, the building had been sold to a builder for £70 and a tender for £24 17s accepted for the construction of a waiting shelter.

A protracted correspondence about the right to stop trains at Dolrhyd, between Heniarth and Llanfair, during 1912, had its origins in the railway's construction, when the conveyance gave the former owners the right to erect 'a shelter as a waiting place for passengers by the railway', but no right to stop, join or leave trains. In 1903, permission had been given to stop trains at both Dolrhyd and Eithnog boathouse, 120 yards closer to Llanfair, and in 1908 the directors had approved the erection of a platform at Dolrhyd by the occupants. When the locomotive water stop was moved from Dolrhyd to a point closer to Llanfair Caereinion in 1911/2, trains were

**LOCAL EXPRESS—
WELSHPOOL to LLANFAIR
back the same day. Perhaps!**

sometimes delayed by having to stop three times within a short distance. Neither the shelter referred to in the conveyance nor the platform approved in 1908 appear to have been built.

A 1912 request for a platform and shelter at the boathouse prompted the Cambrian to review the number of stopping places in the locality with the intention of reducing them, but the proposal was dropped by August 1913.

A strike by miners seeking a minimum wage in March and April 1912 affected all railways and led to reduced services, the Cambrian using the *Cambrian News* (8 March) to advertise the withdrawal of certain trains to reduce consumption. The 'Welshpool and Llanfair branch' was affected only by the cancellation of the Thursdays only 7.5pm from Welshpool and return, which would not have had much effect on the amount of coal being used. It was restored on 22 April.

Considerable damage in the county was done by 'a terrific gale' (*Hartlepool Northern Daily Mail* 10 February 1913) on 31 January. The 8.30pm train from Llanfair ran into a tree that had fallen across the line near Golfa. Fortunately the train did not derail and there were no injuries.

The Cambrian Railways obtained powers to make a minor diversion of the railway at Welshpool in its 1913 Act, which, among other things, sanctioned its amalgamation with the Vale of Rheidol Railway. At the instigation of the council, authority was given to 'reconstruct' 136 yards of the railway to remove the terminal track from the road. The standard gauge tranship siding and the narrow-gauge station building were shortened to make room for it. Cartwright (see Bibliography) records that the town council had been seeking the change for seven years; it had certainly resolved to approach the Cambrian about it in August 1908, claiming that it was a danger to the public and the traffic using the road.

Agreeing to the diversion, which was within the original limits of deviation so it could have been made by agreement and without fresh powers, must have been the price paid to gain the council's agreement for an easement permitting a third rail that had been laid over its Smithfield siding giving narrow gauge access to a cattle dock, which was retrospectively approved by the Act. The light railway directors had given their approval to it on 2 May, providing the Cambrian was responsible for its cost.

For ten years from 1902 the artist Martin Anderson published postcards using the pseudonym 'Cynicus'. One of his designs was adapted to illustrate his view of bucolic country railways, rarely in a manner that would be recognised by a railway's users.

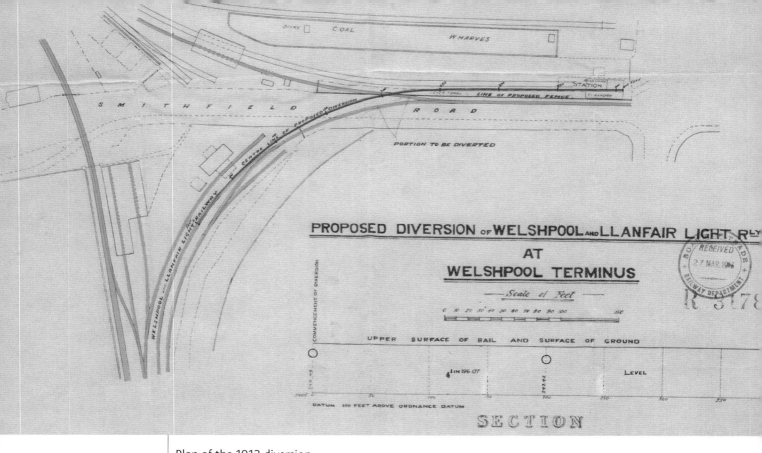

Plan of the 1913 diversion.

This photograph shows the narrow gauge siding diverging from the standard gauge line and looking as though it also might be heading for Oswestry or Shrewsbury instead of the sawmill.

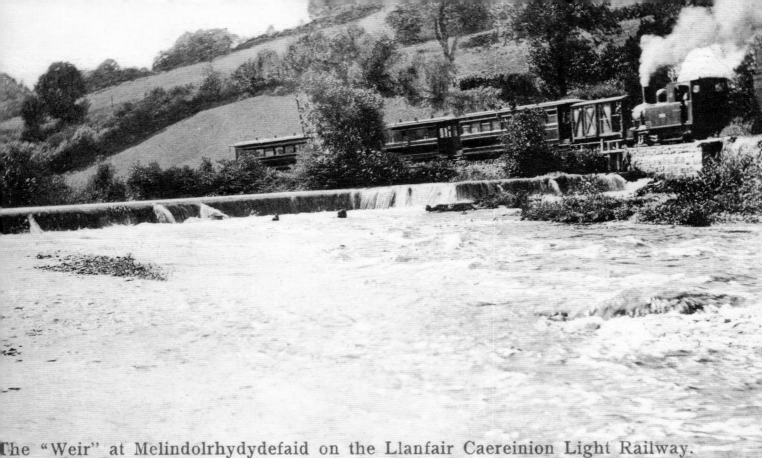

The "Weir" at Melindolrhydydefaid on the Llanfair Caereinion Light Railway.

A market day train of three carriages passing the weir at Dolrhyd. The sluice for the race for the nearby mill is just below the brake van. (L.K. Jones, Llanfair)

Reviewing this aspect of the Bill, an officer at the Board of Trade wrote, 'It does not appear that through running over the systems of the two railways is intended as the gauges are apparently different.' The royal assent was given on 4 July.

W.A. Jehu, a shareholder, had complained to the Cambrian about the inadequacy of the carriages in February 1913. On Welshpool fair days, the first and third Mondays of each month and every Monday from June until September, there was considerable overcrowding. The three carriages in use had a nominal capacity of 100 although in practice they were overcrowded with 90 passengers. The directors had rejected the Cambrian's proposal to obtain another carriage on 2 May. When Williamson pursued the idea, 'an estimate of the additional income that might reasonably be expected' was requested on 12 September but no more carriages were obtained.

Complaints about the carriage oil lighting were eventually considered by the Cambrian on 13 February 1914, when it was reported that acetylene lighting equipment could be purchased for £25 14s and installation costing about £5. This minute is rather strange, because the railway had already rejected a proposal to adopt acetylene lighting on 2 May 1913.

The 1899 order had exempted the railway from being assessed for rates beyond the land's original value for ten years from its opening, with allowance made for an extension. Forden RDC must have had a good filing system, for on 3 April 1913 its clerk wrote to ask if the railway intended to apply for an extension. Receiving the Cambrian's request for a ten-year extension, the Board of Trade sought opinions from the funding authorities. Both Forden and Llanfyllin said they would accept five years, which was communicated to the Cambrian in December, when the extension was backdated to 4 April 1913, applicable to all the authorities. On 2 May 1913, the light railway directors had resolved to apply for a further extension of the time allowed for the repayment of the loans.

The Cambrian's negotiations for a motor service between Llanfair Caereinion and outlying districts were referred to

The Sylfaen shelter seen in 1931. When it was subject to vandalism in 1960 the preservation company had it removed to Castle Caereinion. (R.K. Cope)

Williamson for a further report on 8 May 1914. Without the forthcoming war's intervention preventing the implementation of this development the end of the passenger service might have been hastened.

Approval was given to extending Llanfair goods shed by 50ft, at a cost of £120, and to spend £15 improving the siding space there on the same occasion. The Cambrian directors were feeling quite generous, for they agreed to fund the work, have the repayments spread over five years, and not charge interest. Meeting on 15 April 1914, the directors agreed to pay £50 from balances and asked for ten years to repay the remainder. The work was reported as completed on 21 June 1915.

Work at other stations saw a shelter erected at Sylfaen, which had been deferred

in 1905 because the £12 estimate was deemed unaffordable when the Strachan arbitration costs had priority, and in 1916 facilities for handling milk traffic at Heniarth were improved at a cost of £1 10s.

A crisis occurred in May 1914, when axles on both locomotives broke within three weeks of each other. Williamson informed the directors 'by special letter' and Jones was asked to explain. The trailing axle of *The Earl* had broken on 4 May and the loco was still at Oswestry being repaired, when the driving axle of *The Countess* broke on 25 May. One of *The Earl*'s wheelsets was sent to Welshpool and, by dint of working overnight, *The Countess* was ready for service at 6am on 26 May. The locos had a history of broken axles as shown in the table.

Loco	Date	Axle mileage	Comment
The Earl	June 1908	73,161	Original axles, steel cast by Beyer, Peacock, replaced with carriage axles from stock, made by Patent Shaft & Axletree Company and machined to Beyer, Peacock dimensions.
	April 1911	39,488	Driving and leading axles broke, replaced with new Patent Shaft & Axletree Company axles with diameter at wheel seat increased by $\frac{1}{8}$in.
	4 May 1914	77,429	Trailing axle broke. Nickel chrome steel replacement obtained from Thomas Firth & Sons, Sheffield. Wheel bosses bored out to accommodate wheel seats increased by $\frac{1}{4}$in. Replacements for the other axles ordered for fitting when received.
The Countess	July 1908	73,862	Original axles, steel cast by Beyer, Peacock, replaced with carriage axles from stock, made by Patent Shaft & Axletree Company and machined to Beyer, Peacock dimensions.
	January 1911	32,109	Driving axle broke, replaced with new Patent Shaft & Axletree Company axle with diameter at wheel seat increased by $\frac{1}{8}$in.
	July 1911	38,202	Trailing axle broke, replaced with new Patent Shaft & Axletree Company axle with diameter at wheel seat increased by $\frac{1}{8}$in.
	25 May 1914	40,825	Driving axle broke. Nickel chrome steel replacement obtained from Thomas Firth & Sons, Sheffield.

All the breaks had occurred in the same place, about ¼in inside the wheel boss, where they could not be seen. Jones commented that the original axles had been the best but did not explain why they had been replaced. He thought that the railway's sharp curves with excessive super-elevation and steep gradients 'set up severe and unusual strains on the axles.' The failures occurring at similar mileages, with one exception, suggested that the steel quality was consistent. With the exception of the axles, he said, the engines had given very little trouble and had been quite satisfactory. The fireboxes were getting worn but did not need replacing for the present, he added.

When the cost of coal used by the railway was increased in 1915, Williamson asked for an explanation and was told that it was due to price increases. Further investigation revealed that actually consumption had increased, to 455 tons from 393 tons. Jones was unable to offer an explanation and further investigations were put in hand without a recorded output.

The local authorities agreed to defer the repayment of loan principal for a further seven years in 1915. The Treasury had also agreed, providing that when payments to the local authorities was resumed it was treated the same.

A timber merchant, Boys & Boden, started trading in Welshpool in 1915. On 6 April, Williamson informed the light railway directors of proposals to realign a siding to accommodate a standard gauge siding being laid to serve the woodyard. He emphasised that the Cambrian would receive little benefit from the arrangement because most of the traffic was expected to be routed over the joint line to Shrewsbury. The directors gave their approval to the work, but nothing more was said or done about it. A standard gauge siding was put in and the firm continues to trade.

Alfred Jones Collin, the engineer who had overseen the railway's construction but who had failed to manage Strachan effectively and to assist the company to resist his claim for further payments, died in East Sheen, Surrey, on 5 February 1916, aged 54.

Another death in 1916 was that of Viscount Clive, who had cut the first sod in 1901, on 13 October. A captain in the Welsh Guards, he died of wounds received in the battle of the Somme.

This memorial in the churchyard of Welshpool's Christ Church records the death of William Herbert Waring VC, MM, in action in Ronssoy, France, on 8 October 1918. A lance-sergeant in the 25th Battalion, Royal Welch Fusiliers, leading an attack on a machine gun post, he killed four men and captured twenty. Regrouping, he led another advance for 400 yards before he was mortally wounded. From August 1904 until July the following year he had been a goods porter at Welshpool, appointed to work on the light railway. (Appendix 11)

Lord Clive, who had dug the first sod in 1901 aged 9, was returned home before succumbing to wounds sustained during fighting in the Somme in 1916. He is buried in the Christ Church churchyard, not far from Waring's memorial.

In 1916, the Cambrian incurred its biggest loss in running the railway to date. Williamson explained that the increased costs were due to the payment of war bonus and the higher cost of coal and materials, rates and taxes and wages. Coal consumed was 467 tons. Costs continued to rise during the war and the Cambrian's losses increased.

In 1919 the government called on local authorities to propose reconstruction schemes to aid recovery after the war. In Montgomeryshire, Meifod parish council thought that there would be benefit in constructing the previously proposed Meifod route to Llanfair, while in Welshpool the town council was interested in having the railway extended from Llanfair to Llanerfyl, five miles. Neither proposal came to anything.

An alternative proposal arose out of the county council's complaint to the Ministry of Transport about damage being done to roads by the haulage of timber in 1920, the railways still being under government control. At issue was 5,000 tons of timber still to be carried. On this occasion, the response involved extending a narrow gauge siding into the merchant's yard at Welshpool, the provision of further wagons and minor alterations at 'one or two' stations.

The ministry did not think the matter was of sufficient importance to justify it covering the £140 expenditure required, although it would pay 5% interest if the expenditure was incurred on the capital account. The merchant was prepared to pay half of the cost, but as the railway had no funds, the Cambrian was asked to advance the £70. The Cambrian did not want to advance any more money to the railway, proposing instead that it paid for the work and was reimbursed 7d per ton from the extra traffic until it was recouped. As the extra wagons would have cost an estimated £400 the whole idea was not as worthwhile as it was represented. It must have been cheaper to have repaired the roads.

The return made to the Light Railways (Investigation) Committee in 1920 provides an insight into the railway's operation.

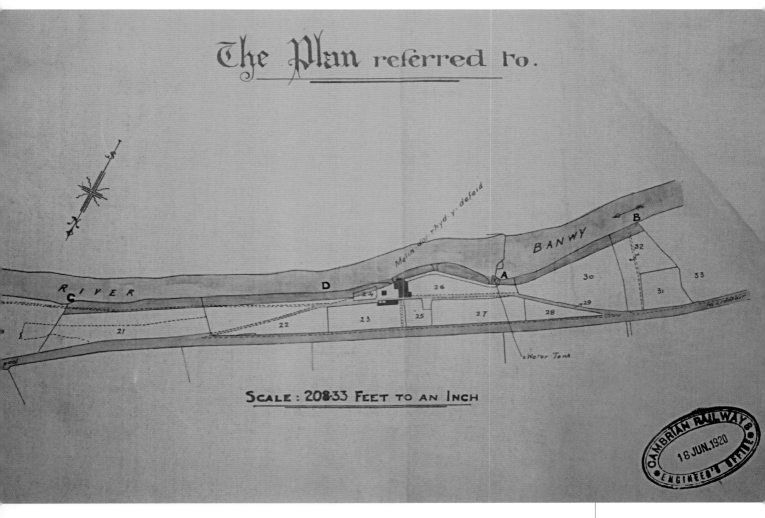

The Plan referred to.

SCALE : 208·33 FEET TO AN INCH

There were two drivers, two firemen, one cleaner, one passenger guard, one porter guard, one stationmaster, one clerk, one porter and two goods porters. Standard conditions of service, rates of pay and hours of duty applied. The track was maintained by two gangs of four platelayers working under the supervision of a Cambrian inspector.

There were no through rates for passengers, 53,449 of whom had been carried in 1913 and 55,227 in 1919. Goods rates were 25% higher than the equivalent Cambrian rate. Wagon capacity at stations was: Welshpool, 45; Sylfaen, 4; Castle Caereinion, 10; Cyfronydd, 8; Heniarth, 20 and Llanfair Caereinion, 45. Only the first and the last could handle cattle and sheep.

The issue of trains stopping near Dolrhyd was raised again in June 1920,

because the owner, R.C. Anwyl, the director, wanted to sell Eithnog with the right to stop trains. Now called Eithinog Hall, the house was being offered with three reception rooms, eleven bedrooms, one bathroom, stabling, garage and an adjoining cottage. Williamson pointed out that although the conveyance gave the right to erect the shelter it left out the obligation to stop trains: 'It is easy to be wise after the event.' Making much of the point that the land occupied by the railway at Dolrhyd had been given to it by his wife without charge, Anwyl received the assurance he required on 22 October. The previous day instructions had been given that trains should only stop at the boathouse and not at Dolrhyd.

The unexpected consequence of his efforts of 1920 had Anwyl writing to

A 1920 plan showing land taken by the railway at Dolrhyd. The location of the water tank is indicated. (National Archives)

the Cambrian again on 23 December 1921, because he had sold Dolrhyd to its occupant who was no longer allowed to stop the train. He now went to Welshpool by road. 'Would it not be a gain to the company to get the fares, as the train goes so slowly?' The Cambrian offered to allow the Dolrhyd owner and his family to stop trains at the boathouse, 120 yards away. Being told of this, the owner, D.O. Jones, coal and corn merchant, wrote that he did not see why the trains should stop at the boathouse and not at Dolrhyd. He used to look out for passengers stopping the train there to avoid it having to stop twice, someone from Dolrhyd used the train every week but the boathouse stop had only been used three or four times since Eithnog had changed hands, 'but I don't regret your offer.' That was the end of it.

A complaint made at the annual meeting on 7 November 1921 attracted the attention of the *Hull Daily Mail* (15 November). One of the councillors complained that two stations in Welshpool were named after public houses, Seven Stars and Raven Square. 'The public house is an important institution,' he added, 'but should we name our stations after them?' Lord Powis said that the directors would consider changing the names, but they obviously had no need to.

Suspension of the loan repayments had allowed some respite on the outstanding capital commitments. Liabilities had been reduced by £2,777 2s 2d since 1904 but the Cambrian was still owed £2,437 15s 1d. Resumption of the repayments was due in 1922 and Llanfyllin Rural District Council had written on 12 November calling for payment to be resumed with immediate effect. The directors resolved to meet the authorities to plead their case for a further extension, and on 27 January 1922 Lord Powis attended the town council on the railway's behalf.

Without debate, the council accepted the request providing the other authorities and the Treasury did likewise. By 31 March the county council and the Treasury had agreed to the extension and responses from Llanfyllin and Forden were awaited. It was, in any event, an academic exercise as the consequences of the Railways Act, enacted on 19 August 1921, meant that the company's future was very limited.

The Act provided for the grouping of railway companies and the distribution of £60 million compensation for the losses incurred by the railways while they were under government control from 1914 until 1921. On 22 March 1922, the directors resolved that the company should be represented by the Association of Smaller Railway Companies and claimed a total of £2,296 9s 10d under three headings, 'arrested growth of traffic', loss of income because of traffic being diverted to road transport, and loss of income because of the increased cost of administration and taxes. After a modified claim of £3,636 9s 10d had been submitted the company was awarded £2,667 7s.

Concerning the Grouping, both the railway and the Cambrian had been included in the 'western group', for absorption into or amalgamation with the GWR. The Cambrian had been amalgamated with effect from 1 January 1922 but it was still necessary for the railway and the GWR to reach an agreed valuation.

A meeting with the GWR on 21 June resulted in a cash offer of £19,345 being made, based on the net revenue for 1913 of £1,915, less rent charges and interest payable on the Cambrian's advances (£131), being capitalised to produce 5½%. Writing on 27 June, the GWR explained that it recognised that the sum offered did not represent the nominal value of the debenture stock or the loans, implying that they were worth less and that if they were scaled down for less than their face value the company would be able to make a distribution to its shareholders. The GWR pointed out that the Lampeter, Aberayron & New Quay Light Railway's investing authorities and the Treasury had accepted a third of their advances in 2½% GWR debenture stock; a cash offer should improve the scope for negotiation.

The directors, however, thought that the offer was too low and asked for more, appointing David Davies's agent, W. Burdon Evans at Llandinam, to act for it, which might explain why, considering the poor state of the company and small size of the undertaking, the appeal was successful. The cash offer was increased to £20,000 and the GWR took over responsibility for the £2,387 15s 1d owed to the Cambrian and the rent charges payable. The company would retain all the compensation and the balance of the net revenue account on 31 December 1922, producing £23,236 7s for distribution.

Payments of 80% to the investing authorities and 90% to the debenture holders would permit 5s per share for shareholders. The Treasury, however, wanted 90% as none of its loan had been repaid while the local authorities had been repaid 5% of theirs. It settled for 81%. This change, and a deduction for income tax due on the traffic receipts that had been overlooked, cost the ordinary shareholders 1d per share. The money was handed over to the GWR to make the distribution on the railway's behalf.

The directors met for the last time on 14 December 1922. Three of them, J.C. Hilton, A.R. Pryce and Lord Powis, had served throughout the company's existence. W.F. Addie, who had worked tirelessly on the railway's behalf, had retired on health grounds at the general meeting on 6 August 1920 and died on 16 April 1921, aged 70. R.C. Anwyl had died on 21 February 1921, aged 82. Hilton died on 21 November 1925, aged 83, Pryce on 3 June 1926, aged 76, and Lord Powis, the 4th earl, on 9 November 1952, aged 90.

David Davies, who had been appointed a director in 1903, although the only indication of his position was the inclusion of his name in the list of directors in the shareholders' reports, had been very much a figurehead, attending neither board nor shareholders' meetings. He died on 16 June 1944, aged 64.

William Forrester Addie, who as mayor persuaded Welshpool's residents to back the railway, was buried in the Croft cemetery in Welshpool.

This ornate memorial marks the resting place of Athelstane Robert Pryce, Cyfronydd, in St Garmon's churchyard, Castle Caereinion. The angel's missing arm lies on the ledge at the right of the memorial.

Company secretary John Evans was buried with his wife in the Croft cemetery, only a short distance from the spot where W.F. Addie was buried.

John Evans, the company's secretary since its inception, had died on 9 March 1922, aged 76, the directors minuting a tribute to him on 31 March. His successor, Isaac Watkin of Oswestry, one of the company's auditors, had been appointed on 22 March.

The shareholders also met for the last time on 14 December, twelve in person and thirty by proxy. They approved the resolution required for the company to participate in the absorption scheme and gave thanks to the Davies's agent for negotiating their compensation and to the solicitor for negotiating the settlement with the investing authorities. They also resolved that 'in view of the great loss of traffic owing to the delay, inconvenience and expense attending the transhipment of goods, the Great Western Railway Company be urged to consider the desirability of converting the line from narrow gauge to standard gauge', before thanking the directors for the care and attention they had given to the company during its existence. Few companies could have had such a send-off.

From 1 January 1923 their enterprise was a part of the GWR. Having taken control of the Cambrian from 25 March 1922, the GWR was already responsible for the railway's operation.

As an independent concern the railway had been hampered on several fronts. The grant qualification, that the railway be built and operated by an existing company, was intended to save money, the cost of administration being absorbed by the existing company, but it probably increased costs too, for the employees were paid the same as their main line counterparts. There was no local manager to canvass for business and to ensure that operating patterns reflected changing demands. It is notable that the railway did not cater for tourists – there must have been a market for the residents of Welshpool, Oswestry and Shrewsbury to visit Llanfair Caereinion at the weekend or on holidays, if only someone had thought to develop it.

The lack of capital and Strachan's claim for extras prevented the railway from being fully equipped, but the provision of the enhancements sought in 1904, and the fourth carriage later, is unlikely to have had much influence on the outcome. Judged by the almost straight line of annual income, traffic levels varied little and there is no evidence that it was unable to meet the demands placed upon it, except that passengers on market days would have appreciated more space.

As an investment, the railway was marginally successful. Loan interest was always paid and most of the loans were repaid, but that was more by luck than judgment. The ordinary shareholders did less well but that is always the case. Without the free grant, though, the situation would have been very different, for the railway could not have been built. With the continued existence of the railway it could be argued that the Treasury is still seeing the benefit of the grant.

The railway was a marginal enterprise for the Cambrian too. Over the years until 1914, the accumulated loss was a mere £36. During the following five years the losses amounted to another £5,343, no doubt largely due to the government's policy of not allowing the railways to increase rates in line with increasing costs.

There was a measure of tidying up required before the company's affairs were disposed of. In January, Lloyds Bank in Welshpool was instructed to change the

GREAT WESTERN RAILWAY COMPANY. No. *1.*

LONDON, *1st February* 1923.

Warrant for Payment in respect of *Mortgages* of the *Welshpool &* *Llanfair Light* Railway Company.

Messrs. GLYN, MILLS, CURRIE & Co., 67, Lombard Street, LONDON.

Pay *The Corporation of Welshpool* _____ or Order,

Three thousand eight hundred & twenty six pounds 3/5 _____

For the Great Western Railway Company.

£*3826 : 3 : 5.*

Signature of the person or persons to whom the warrant is made payable. } *Corporation of Welshpool*

Ex⁴. *WW*

NOTE.—This Warrant must be presented to the Bankers upon whom it is drawn with'r six months from date.

The warrant issued by the Great Western Railway in respect of the town council's loans in 1923. This payment, and similar made to the other investing authorities and the shareholders, marked the formal end of the light railway company's independent existence.

name on the railway's account to that of the GWR. Watkin, the secretary for only a few months, was awarded a cash payment of £60 for his loss of office by the GWR in March 1923.

A final word, for this chapter, about the locomotives, from the *Western Mail*

(28 December 1922). *The Earl* was out of action for repairs and on 26 December *The Countess* failed climbing the Golfa and became immovable. The passengers completed their journey by road and the paper anticipated that services would be resumed on the day it was published.

FEATURES ALONG THE LINE

Welshpool from the air circa 1950, with the terminus, loco and carriage shed and the town council's Smithfield siding visible.

The entrance to the tranship yard, 12 October 1951. (F.W. Shuttleworth)

Coaling up alongside the Smithfield siding. (Brian Morrison)

Climbing past the end of the Smithfield siding towards the bridge over the canal. The board on the right instructs drivers not to exceed 5mph between it and mile post one.

The canal bridge following its restoration funded by the supermarket development scheme. It was removed from site to be repaired. (14 May 2011)

The Earl crossing Church Street in 1956.

In 2013 murals were commissioned to remind residents and visitors of the railway's route through Welshpool. In this view the railway crossed from a point in front of the first bollard on the left. (31 August 2013)

A train passing through Bron y Buckley, a post-war development, in August 1954. (F.R.M. Fysh)

Countess at Raven Square, circa 1950. This is one of the earliest colour photographs of the railway. (David Elliott)

Looking towards Llanfair from Raven Square. Just beyond the permanent way hut is the sign instructing drivers that they can proceed at 'normal speed'.

Descending the Golfa on 24 April 1951.

Seen after the railway was closed, the sign near Golfa summit instructed drivers
not to exceed 5mph between it and Welshpool station.

The 'black pools', right centre of this 1904 postcard view, are no longer visible from the train. When the photograph was taken they served as Welshpool's water supply. (J. Valentine)

Countess crosses Cwm Lane to reach Golfa station on 5 April 2015.

The low sun catches track renewal work at Sylfaen on 11 February 2010. The stock stabled beyond the works includes the Baguley-Drewry railcar and the permanent way mess carriage made up in 1998/9 using the underframe of an ex-Upnor flat wagon and parts from Zillertalbahn carriage B17 made surplus by its refurbishment.

When Sylfaen was a terminus in 1964 this Pickering brake van was used as a booking office. The photograph shows that it was left in place and the line returned to nature after the service was withdrawn to Castle Caereinion.

The Earl whistles for Coppice Lane level crossing, near Castle Caereinion, on 2 September 2017.

On the Llanfair side of Castle Caereinion, the railway crosses Dolarddyn Lane, where *The Earl* was seen on 2 May 2016.

To replace the original shelter that had gone missing during the closure period, Cyfronydd gained a shelter in the form of an LNWR brake van body that had been on the Shropshire & Montgomeryshire Light Railway. When trains cross here the stationmaster uses it as a control office.

A works train hauled by *The Earl* crosses the Brynelin viaduct with a works train. Fifty years of tree growth now conceals this view. Cyfronydd, the home of R.D. Pryce and A.R. Pryce, is visible in the distance.

An excursion crosses the Banwy bridge on 9 June 1956.

Joan passes out of service stock stored at Heniarth in 21 June 1978.

The Earl arrives at Llanfair with a passenger train comprising a Pickering van and four Lodge Hill carriages in 1963. The area to the right was later developed as an industrial estate.

Llanfair circa 1950. The shed on the left was the weighbridge office. The black building is the original station building, which contained booking office and waiting room; its canopy had been removed in 1938. The building with the double doors was erected by the GWR in 1937 and the carriage was a brake composite installed circa 1947. It concealed a former Cambrian Railways carriage installed in 1940. The back of the weighbridge office is in the distance.

CHAPTER 5

CHANGE OF MANAGEMENT, AND CLOSURE

Under Great Western Railway control, the railway carried on much as before. As a part of a much larger organisation less information about its operation remains in the public record.

Repainted in GWR livery, the locos were renumbered 822 and 823, standard GWR-style cast numberplates being mounted on the tank sides, their nameplates being relocated to the cabsides, *The Countess* shortened to *Countess* to make the plates fit. In 1929/30 *The Earl* was out of service for 125 days while it received a heavy intermediate repair, which included fitting a new boiler with standard GWR fittings at Oswestry shed. Later in 1930 *Countess* also received a heavy intermediate repair, some work being carried out at Welshpool before the loco was moved to Oswestry works; it was out of service for 181 days. The carriages and wagons were also painted in GWR livery and renumbered.

A typical mixed train at Welshpool in the 1920s. The stock is in GWR livery, but the loco retains its original boiler. Locating the number plate on the tankside has forced the nameplate to be moved to the cabside, and in this case *The Countess* has become *Countess*. By this time, two carriages was probably sufficient for market day traffic. The little shed on the left seems to have served as the tiniest of waiting rooms.

The Earl ready to leave Llanfair. The steam heating equipment was fitted in November 1923. The loco's chimney has been replaced at some point.

Seen when shunting at Llanfair, *The Earl* was fitted with a Swindon-built boiler, including smokebox and chimney, at Oswestry in 1930.

A branch line review carried out in 1926 recommended the line be closed. The report included figures for 1924/5, as shown in the table, although a complete comparison was not compiled.

During 1925 the railway had handled 5,639 tons of minerals, 2,579 tons of merchandise, 1,368 cans of milk, and 344 trucks of livestock. Reducing the train service to single-shift, eight hours, and abolishing the post of stationmaster at Llanfair Caereinion were proposed as economy measures, but complete closure would save £6,502 annually. This figure was actually the annual expenditure and took no account of any residual expenses or consequential losses arising from closure. The recommendation was not acted upon.

An unusual incident must have occurred with *Countess* in August 1928, for it was stopped for five days for light repairs carried out at Heniarth. The location suggests that it must have failed in traffic and had been in such a condition that it could not be moved.

The locomotive committee approved the expenditure of £147 to replace the wooden water tank near Llanfair Caereinion by one of iron on 25 April 1929. Still in situ although disused, this tank gives the appearance of having been manufactured from an old tender.

On 12 February 1931, the traffic committee accepted the general manager's report recommending the withdrawal of passenger services 'as from 9th instant', a decision taken after the event. Passenger receipts had fallen by 37% in 1930 (*Llanfair Railway Journal* No 79). The town council complained to the Ministry of Agriculture, on the basis that it had certified that the railway was essential for agricultural purposes to qualify it for the Treasury grant, and to the local MP. Llanfair parish council petitioned in support of the eighty regulars who used the train on market days and the Welshpool Municipal Association tried to get the GWR to agree to run passenger trains on market days. The public appeared to be unconcerned and few turned out to ride on the last train on a wet 7 February. The loco was *Countess*, which had hauled the first train in 1903.

A party returning from a funeral was nearly responsible for another, or more, when the car in which they were travelling was in a collision with a train at Castle Caereinion on 17 June 1932 (*Manchester Guardian* 18 June). One of the four occupants was detained in Welshpool hospital with unspecified injuries, the other three had cuts and bruises. The car was destroyed, 'practically' cut in two, the paper explained.

| Traffic department staff | 1924 | 1925 | 1924 | Expenditure | | | |
| | | | | 1925 | | | |
				Passengers	Parcels	Goods	Total
Welshpool	£435	£435	£1,129	£750	£298		£1,048
Llanfair	£356	£382	£3,537	£501	£417	£2,544	£3,462
	£791	£817	£4,666	£1,251	£715	£2,544	£4,510

Loco department, engine and train running expenses	£3,557
Engineering department, maintenance and renewal	£1,930
Signal department	£138
Clothing	£10
Fuel, lighting, water and general stores	£5
Rates	£45

Taking water from the riverside water tank authorised by the GWR in 1929. The original water tank had been on the other side of the line, closer to Dolarddyn.

LLANFAIR RAILWAY CROSSING, CHURCH STREET, WELSHPOOL

Although *The Earl* is moving too quickly for the photographer's camera and film to freeze its motion, the image is of interest for showing a train with passenger stock crossing Church Street in 1928. Only the building nearest the church remains, the others being demolished to make way for the extension of Brook Street after the railway was closed. Notice also the kerbside petrol pump.

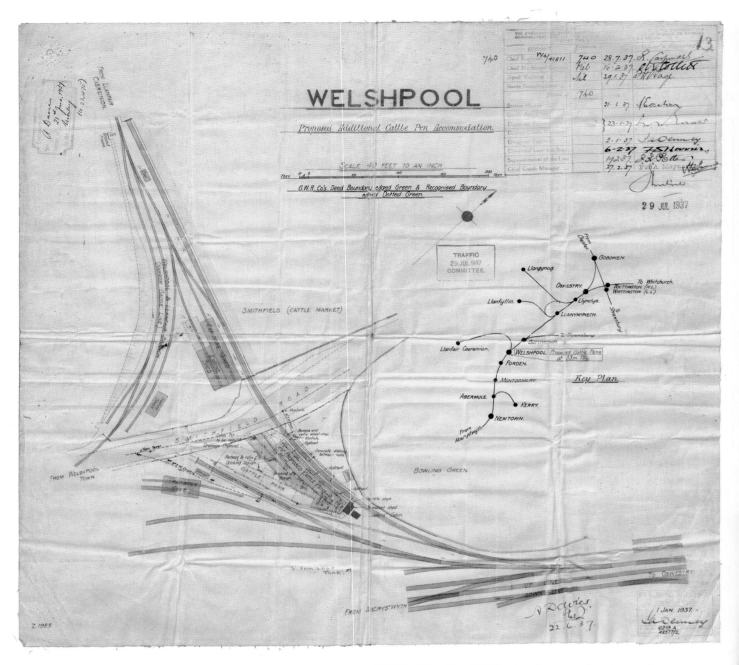

The GWR's plan for extending the cattle pens at Welshpool in 1937. (National Archives)

Standard gauge cattle vans stabled on the mixed gauge siding alongside the 1937 cattle pen extension. With the restored canal bridge, the mixed gauge track is all that survives of the narrow gauge railway in Welshpool. The cattle pens were restored in 2019.

The locomotive history sheets show that both locos required heavy maintenance during the war and afterwards. The details are given in the table.

Loco	Date stopped	Date set to work	No of days stopped	Location	Notes
822	23 October 1941	14 March 1942	142	Welshpool	Intermediate, Swindon 16-18 December
822	30 April 1942	19 May 1942	19	Oswestry shed	Repair
823	12 November 1946	13 February 1948	458	Oswestry shed	General, Swindon 28 November – 3 December 1947
822	30 November 1947	11 December 1947	11	Welshpool	Light
822	1 March 1948	24 June 1948	115	Swindon	General
823	27 May 1953	3 July 1953	37	Oswestry shed	Unclassified
822	20 July 1953	15 March 1956	977	Oswestry shed	Heavy intermediate, awaiting decision
823	29 August 1953	31 August 1953	2	Oswestry shed	
823	1 February 1956			Oswestry	
823	15 March 1956			Oswestry	In store
822	24 November 1956			Oswestry	In store

The train service was cancelled when both locos were out of service in December 1947.

One of the locomotives dismantled for overhaul at Oswestry in the 1950s.

On 28 March 1946 the traffic committee had approved the expenditure of £90 for the conversion of ten narrow gauge timber trucks into open-side wagons.

Nationalisation on 1 January 1948 had no immediate effect on the railway beyond repainting the locos and fixing LMS-style Oswestry shed plates to them. The only records to survive from this era relate to closure proposals.

The British Transport Commission sanctioned closure twice. The Railway

A street-side view of the Welshpool terminus in the 1950s.

Castle Caereinion's little-used signal box in 1951. The loco retains its steam heating connectors.

Executive's first proposal to close the line to save £2,729 annually was approved on 25 November 1950, although no explanation was recorded for not putting the policy into effect. Cartwright (see Bibliography) states that the corporation submitted a motion asking for the policy to be reconsidered but that in itself was unlikely to have caused a reversal. The 1955 'case for closure' stated that none of the local authorities had objected to the 1950 proposal. The report recommending closure included details of the traffic carried during the year ended 31 August 1949.

The Road Haulage Executive would arrange an alternative road service at an annual cost of £2,900. To facilitate the transfer of traffic from rail to road vehicles the standard gauge transfer siding at Welshpool would be extended by 80 yards at a cost of £270. Recovering the assets, mainly the track, would cost £768 more than they were worth. The land and redundant buildings were valued at £357. Re-sleepering in 1950/1 was expected to cost £5,000, which tends to suggest that track maintenance had not been a priority during the last GWR years or the first of the nationalised railway.

		Through			Through	
	Local to branch	Outwards	Inwards	Local to branch	Outwards	Inwards
Parcels		257	3,405		£27	£582
Freight	Tons	Tons	Tons			
Merchandise	5	62	812	£6	£109	£1,607
Coal			3,155			£1,659
Other minerals			2,647			£2,283
Total	5	62	6,614			
	Wagons	Wagons	Wagons			
Livestock	109	148	18	£92	£837	£30
Tenancies and transhipping charges at Welshpool				£572		
Total				£670	£973	£6,161
						£7,804
Increases from May 1950						£1,278
						£9,082

The coal yard at Llanfair Caereinion, photographed on 15 March 1951. (R.E. Tustin)

Loading the Birmingham Locomotive Club's excursion on 9 July 1949, with benches and chairs from the mainline station used to accommodate passengers travelling in open wagons.

During the early 1950s the railway became a magnet for enthusiasts attracted by a goods-only narrow gauge steam railway being run by the state. Indeed, on 2 July 1949, the Birmingham Locomotive Club had been the first of several organisations to arrange for the operation of special trains where the passengers travelled in open wagons. On ordinary operating days enthusiasts received a warm welcome with many riding in the brake van, either officially, having signed an indemnity, or unofficially.

The second and final closure proposal was approved on 20 July 1955 although the railway was to continue operating until 5 November 1956. Traffic carried in the year to 30 June 1954 formed a part of the case for closure.

Revenue likely to be lost to rail was calculated at £1,400, but if 1,000 tons of slag and fertilizer and 2,000 tons of coal destined for Llanfair Caereinion were diverted to road haulage throughout then a further £3,110 would be lost. Savings would be £3,764 employment, £3,095 maintenance and £2,489 interest. The railway employed two goods porters at Welshpool, one goods checker at Llanfair Caereinion, one ganger, two lengthsmen, one driver, one fireman, and a guard. As a sign of inflation, extending the standard gauge siding at Welshpool would now cost £550.

Permanent way renewals, including 3¼ miles of re-sleepering, over the next three years were expected to cost £7,100. Locomotive repairs estimated at £1,600 had been deferred pending a decision on the line's future. *The Earl* had been at Oswestry receiving a heavy intermediate repair since 20 July 1953, returning to Welshpool on 15 March 1956, just in time for the line's closure. Out of service since 1 February, *Countess* was taken to Oswestry for storage on the same date. Their nameplates had been removed to protect them from 'souvenir hunters' in 1951.

	Forwarded	Received	Revenue
Parcels	106	2,280	£712
Merchandise	27 tons	2,612 tons	£4,875
Coal		3,263 tons	£3,535
Livestock	45 wagons		£95
Total			£9,217

A typical 1950s scene at Castle Caereinion. (C. Gregory/Michael Bishop collection)

The Earl leaves Welshpool with a good load on 21 June 1956. For its last months in service the loco has been fitted with a baffle plate to divert steam from the safety valves. (F.M. Gates)

A meeting objecting to the closure, held in Llanfair, was reported in the *Liverpool Echo* on 19 January 1956. One speaker said that with the railway closed, road haulage costs would be higher than for the existing through rate and the price of coal and fertilisers was likely to be increased, a reversal of the situation in 1903. The protest was to no avail, especially as Welshpool town council, which had fought so hard to get the railway in the first place, now wanted to see the back of it. The last commercial narrow-gauge steam-hauled goods train run by British Railways was run on 2 November.

An uncommon view of an empty train descending the Golfa bank in the 1950s. (C. Gregory/Michael Bishop collection)

The photographer captioned this photograph as illustrating the last freight train, on 2 November 1956. Ownership of a car would have allowed him to reach this spot close to Llanfair. (J. Ransom)

Several special trains had run during the last few months, the Stephenson Locomotive Society running the last one on 3 November 1956. With 120 passengers on board, the train left Welshpool at 2.30pm and returned from Llanfair at 4.15pm, accompanied by the Newtown Silver Band at several locations. Returning to Welshpool at dusk, the train exploded detonators, fireworks were let off, car drivers sounded their hooters and flashed their lights. *Railway Magazine* (January 1957) reported that on arrival the sound of *The Earl*'s whistle was answered by those of locomotives on the main line, a 22xx 0-6-0 and a 'Manor' 4-6-0. Then there was silence as the band played Handel's funeral march from *Saul*. It must have

been quite emotional. Some of those present had seen the first train in 1903, and very likely the first sod being cut too.

After clearing wagons and equipment back to Welshpool, *The Earl* was stored in the loco shed until 7 May 1958, when it was sent to Oswestry to be stored with *Countess*. Applications to purchase nameplates and a chimney were recorded on the loco history sheets.

SPECIAL TRAIN COMMEMORATING CLOSURE OF WELSHPOOL LLANFAIR LIGHT RAILWAY
The last 2' 6" gauge public railway in the British Isles
NOVEMBER 3 1956
Stephenson Locomotive Society Midland Area
Welshpool to
LLANFAIR CAEREINION
and back
via Golfa, Sylfaen Halt, Castle Caereinion, Dolarddyn Crossing, Cyfronydd and Heniarth
(W) (1266)   For conditions see over

142   142

A ticket for the train commemorating the railway's closure.

The Newtown Silver Band entertains the crowd before the special train left Welshpool.

Photographers push to find positions to photograph *The Earl* climb the Golfa bank with fare-paying passengers for the last time until 1975.

Two schoolboys and a couple of photographers watch the train arrive at Llanfair. The 'last train' board was attached to the smokebox during a stop at Castle Caereinion.

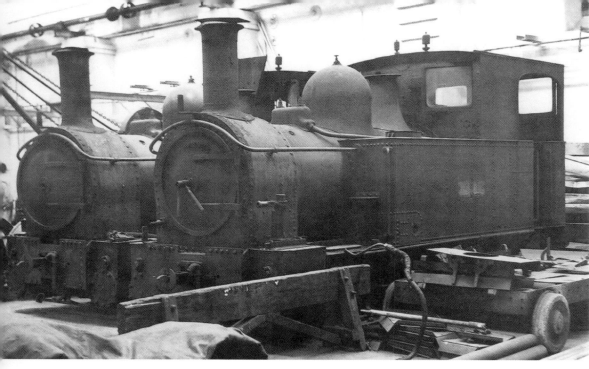

The locos seen in store at Oswestry on 16 September 1958.

Rolling stock at Welshpool after the line had closed.

Castle Caereinion abandoned to nature after the line had closed. The shelter had already gone.

Soon after services had ended BR extended the standard gauge transfer siding over the site of the narrow gauge terminus and closed the gap in the railings. The road crossing was left in place for the town council to remove.

VISITORS

In 1991 the railway played host to its first visiting loco, Manning, Wardle 0-6-2T *Chevallier* from Whipsnade Zoo, as a gala attraction. It was captured crossing Brynelin viaduct with the zoo's railway manager's Land Rover in the wagon behind.

The zoo's Kerr, Stuart 0-6-2T *Superior* visited in 1992. This end of Llanfair station has changed considerably since.

The Bredgar &
Wormshill Light
Railway, Kent,
supplied this La
Meuse 0-4-0T in
1993. The loco is
now on display at the
Statfold Barn Railway.

In 1994 and 1995
Henschel 0-6-0T
Siam also visited
from the Bredgar &
Wormshill Light
Railway.

Also on display in 1994 were two Parry People Movers, demonstrating the concept of flywheel-powered transport.

A short length of temporary track was laid at Raven Square on which No 7 gave rides.

This people mover did not participate in a gala but undertook trials on the railway for a brief period in 1995.

Pakis Baru No 5 has been the most unusual visitor, being a Mallet articulated locomotive built by Orenstein & Koppel in Germany for export to Indonesia in 1905. Visiting in 2015 and restricted to running between Llanfair and Cyfronydd, it is a member of the Statfold Barn Railway collection.

Under new ownership, the Manning, Wardle 0-6-2T *Chevallier* made two more appearances, in 2010 and 2015. On the second of these occasions it was photographed with the goods train at Heniarth.

The Sittingbourne & Kemsley Light Railway's Bagnall 0-6-2T *Superb* also made two appearances, in 2017 and 2018. On the second occasion it was photographed at Heniarth.

Hired for two years, the Zillertalbahn's 0-6-2T *Zillertal* made its first public appearance during the 2019 gala. It was photographed at New Drive as it climbed the Golfa bank out of Welshpool.

CHAPTER 6

A NEW LIFE

Preservation of the railway had first been suggested in 1952 and a society was formed shortly after the line was closed. Agreement was reached with BR for volunteers to work on the line, and the first working party, which appears to have been a half-day affair, took place on 13 July 1959. The track was badly overgrown in parts, some of it was waterlogged and some of the fencing was in poor condition.

The Welshpool & Llanfair Light Railway Preservation Company was registered as a company limited by guarantee on 4 January 1960, taking over the society's objectives and assets. The town and county councils were invited to maintain, and continue to maintain, their links with the railway by appointing directors. By 1961, 350 members had been recruited; in July an appeal was made for each of them to contribute £15 to purchase stock and provide working capital.

At the time of the closure, there were only the Talyllyn and the Festiniog Railways operating as what are now called heritage railways, with the participation and support of volunteers. No-one had taken over a branch line from British Railways and officialdom was not quite certain how seriously it should treat such proposals.

In the face of increasing traffic, the town council made it quite clear that it was no longer prepared to tolerate the Church Street crossing. Considering that latterly the crossing had only been used twice a day and that any traffic problem was more likely caused by the traffic than the crossing, the council's stance was probably generated by a desire to be seen to be 'modern', and supporting steam railways was not, in the 1950s, considered to be the right thing to do. At the same time,

the Ministry of Transport was equally determined that it would no longer tolerate trains crossing the trunk road at Raven Square.

An editorial in the *County Times* of 21 June 1958 supported the council, saying that 'with the great increase in road traffic the time has gone past for permitting the Llanfair narrow gauge trains to go trundling through the town and across Church Street, one of the busiest thoroughfares in Mid Wales . . . there is also the conclusive fact that the area near the main line station is required for municipal development and there is no space there for a Llanfair train terminus.' The paper also objected to the railway's supporters being from London, Birmingham and elsewhere, and objected to them thinking 'it possible to make a nuisance . . . by bringing the Llanfair trains through the town,' adding that the council should not talk to them about their proposals.

Bearing in mind that the only facilities for storing or maintaining rolling stock were in Welshpool and the main source of traffic was expected to be from the town, the preservation company wanted to retain as much of the route as possible.

It seems to have abandoned the Church Street crossing quite early on but fought to retain the Raven Square crossing so that a terminus could be established in the Standard quarry. Both the county council and the Ministry of Transport raised objections to this, the former saying, in July 1960, that it would 'render impossible the completion of the Back Road [Brook Street] scheme as designed'. It also said that the 'retention of the crossing of the trunk road at the island is most undesirable in view of the visibility conditions for trains emerging from the Llanfair direction, the general interruption of traffic flow …'

First considered in 1946, the Back Road/Brook Street scheme included making alterations to the roundabout, which was considered to be sub-standard for reasons that were not explained in the surviving documentation. It appears to have been planned as if the railway had already been removed. Despite there being no known incidents involving trains and traffic at Raven Square, and the number of trains using the crossing having very little impact on traffic flows, the authorities were determined that its continued use should not be permitted.

Primarily interested in acquiring the narrow gauge yard in order to increase car parking space near the cattle market, the town council's £2,350 offer to buy the trackbed from the terminus up to Raven Square, and to recover the redundant assets, saving BR £380, was accepted by BR Western Region on 17 February 1961 although the sale was not completed until 1963.

The notice of the company's intention to apply for a Light Railway (Leasing and Transfer) Order published on 17 November 1961 maintained its position regarding Raven Square, describing the railway as 'situate between a point on the north west side of Brook Street near the Standard quarry Welshpool where the railway … diverges from Brook Street aforesaid and Llanfair Caereinion ...'

On 21 November 1961, the company's managing director, F.S. Mayman, met members of the divisional road engineer's staff in Welshpool. He told them that 'their' preferred station site at Raven Square barely had space for a loop and platform. Passengers' cars parked on the trunk road would also be more dangerous than using the crossing. As the company had no funds to acquire additional land to change the alignment or to provide its own car park he asked if consideration could be given to allowing the crossing to be used for a limited period, up to five years, while it accumulated funds to develop a terminus short of the roundabout.

One of the engineers promised to consider this, while emphasising that his department would never agree to the crossing being accepted in perpetuity, but Mayman seemed to think that he had got what he wanted.

In an internal minute dated 4 January 1962, the railway inspectorate's Colonel John Richard Hugh Robertson said that he could not see the crossing being acceptable to the local and road authorities and he did not think that the company would be willing to incur the cost of a public inquiry to force the issue. If the company was to succeed at a public inquiry then the inspectorate would insist on 'at least full flashing red light control' of all the roads approaching the crossing, 'the cost of which . . . would be considerable'. It could be, he speculated, that the road use was so heavy that 'something more elaborate (and costly) would be necessary'.

Objections to the proposal to reopen the line across Raven Square were made by the county council, Welshpool Engineering Company and Mid-Wales Motorways Limited, the company was informed on 14 February 1962. The nature of the objections and the company's response to them were summarised in a letter from the company's solicitor a month later.

In other correspondence the county council had made much of the speed of the traffic on the trunk road while also pointing out that Raven Square was a junction of four roads and a private drive. The company pointed out that therefore the traffic was already slowed, and the passage of a few trains would not constitute a hindrance or a serious hazard. The same applied to the proposed new roundabout, where plans showed the railway in situ. There would be no difficulty in adjusting the level of the railway to match that of the new road.

With regards to Brook Street, the county council appeared to be wanting to appropriate the railway formation to widen the road; the authority's needs, the company contended, could be met without taking any railway property.

Mid Wales Motorways parked its buses in the quarry on market days. It had not been inconvenienced when BR ran the train service and it should not be inconvenienced, as it averred, when the preservation company ran the trains.

Welshpool Engineering was seeking to develop its property in the quarry as a petrol filling station and car showroom without first establishing that the railway that ran along its boundary had been formally abandoned. Not having done so, they could hardly complain if they were inconvenienced by the resumption of train services.

All three objectors asserted that terminating the train service on the south-west of Raven Square would be less dangerous than crossing the roundabout and terminating in Brook Street. On the contrary, the company declared, it would be more dangerous. Passengers would emerge onto the trunk road and there were no footpaths. There would also be a tendency for vehicles to stop to pick up or set down passengers there. In Brook Street passengers and their transport would be out of the way of the traffic.

The company had already made the point about vehicles stopping in the vicinity of a station in Raven Square, which led the road engineer to consider imposing a 'no waiting order' on both sides of the trunk road and possibly on other roads in the locality.

Faced with the loss of the buildings and sidings in Welshpool and accepting that it did not have the resources to reopen or operate the complete line at once, the company had already said that reopening would occur in stages, starting from Llanfair, so it was clear that it would be several years before narrow gauge trains returned to Welshpool.

On 14 February 1962 a highways official noted that the application placed the minister in an awkward position. On the one hand he was expected to deal with it impartially, on the other he would want to object to it on highways grounds. The existence of the other objections could save him the embarrassment of making a formal objection though.

A high-level meeting was held with both railway and highways divisions represented on 27 March 1962. Its purpose was to coordinate views and to decide on a common course of action. The 'west of Raven Square' terminus was reasonable; the future possibility of widening the adjacent trunk road should not be used as a bar to it. The meeting's chairman felt that the company was not aware of the 'very strong objections' the ministry had and Robertson confirmed that, having met company officers, he thought that they expected the order to be made as it stood.

Before consulting the Treasury solicitor on the propriety of the minister holding an inquiry where he would be making an objection, it was agreed to make another approach to the company. By 4 April 1962 however, the highways branch had decided 'to take a rather more positive line than hitherto'. It would point out that there were strong trunk road objections to the idea of a level crossing, any level crossing was a serious impediment to the free flow of traffic, and new impediments could not be permitted. The previous existence of a level crossing, its low usage and 'that the trunk road is relatively lightly trafficked' were not material. The company would be told that it would be responsible for the cost of signalling the four roads that met at the roundabout and that consideration was being given to imposing a parking ban on the trunk road alongside the department's preferred station site!

Officials took the view that their objection to the crossing would prevail at a public inquiry, but felt that it would be wrong to put the company to the trouble and expense of an inquiry if the result was a foregone conclusion. The Treasury solicitor gave his opinion on 9 April 1962. The minister could refuse the application or amend its provisions to ensure public safety. He was not bound to hold an inquiry if he was in possession of such information as was material or useful to determine the application. If an inquiry were held the agent authority, Montgomeryshire County Council, could present the minister's objection as its own.

Meeting in Welshpool on 10 May 1962, Mayman restated the case for limited use of the Raven Square crossing, to enable a station and car park to be established in the quarry, the situation being reviewed after five years. They were told that the ministry was bound to support the county council's objection to the crossing, even on a temporary basis.

On 6 June 1962, the ministry informed the company's solicitor that the minister would be recommended to modify the order, eliminating the crossing, that there should be no difficulty in terminating the railway to the west of Raven Square, and that the ministry and the local authorities would cooperate as much as possible. The company was invited to submit any further information or arguments that the minister should consider before making up his mind. If it required a public inquiry to be held it would be responsible for the costs.

The company had made its first formal contact with the railway inspectorate on 28 June 1961, explaining its ambition to run passenger services over part of the line from April 1962, and requesting a site meeting so the company could be informed of likely requirements. On 26 July the railway's civil engineering director met Robertson in Welshpool. They agreed to the following:

- Install stop block on the Llanfair side of Raven Square immediately and a trap point as soon as possible.
- Determine status of New Drive crossing; install cattle grids on both sides of the road.
- Install handrails on underbridges on Welshpool side of milepost 2 and on Llanfair side of Castle Caereinion level crossing.
- Investigate condition of abutments of temporary bridge installed by BR following culvert blockage on Llanfair side of milepost 2 and replace temporary structure as soon as possible.
- Install a line of pegs on site of apparent landslip between milepost 2 and 3 and monitor for movement during the winter.
- Investigate cause of morass on the Llanfair side of Golfa level crossing.

- Fit gauge ties to track over skew underbridge on Welshpool side of milepost 4 and examine waybeams.
- Provide new cattle grids at Cyfronydd level crossing and on the Welshpool side of Heniarth crossing.
- Repair embankment above Banwy near milepost 7 [Pontsycoed] and erect handrails to direct footpath users to the foot crossing.
- Fit gauge ties to track on underbridge on Welshpool side of milepost 7½ [Banwy bridge], examine bridge, replace in due course, speed limit to be 5mph.
- Examine two timber span bridges between Heniarth and Llanfair.

Robertson emphasised that the railway's gradients and level crossings made good couplings and braking arrangements essential, insisting that each passenger train be marshalled with a manned brake van equipped with a ratchet handbrake. Safety chains should be used in addition to strong couplings. If continuous brakes could not be fitted before the start of passenger operations, then 'some kind of automatically applied and effective run-back brake should be fitted … to each passenger carriage.'

Regarding operations, 'one engine in steam' would be used initially. At level crossings, trains should whistle on approach, stop and be flagged across by a crew member. At Castle Caereinion the gates should be worked by a crew member or a member of station staff, and flagged across. Robertson undertook to obtain the approval of the divisional road engineer to this method of working. The question of speed limits was left until more was known about the condition of sleepers where the line was badly overgrown and until after brake tests had been made. In his report he noted that the use of the Raven Square crossing was not discussed, adding that he had expressed the personal view that the company would be 'well advised' not to press the issue.

In his 30 August 1961 letter to the divisional road engineer in Cardiff,

The Countess returns to Welshpool on 6 October 1962.

Robertson said that the proposed method of working the level crossings was 'somewhat more restrictive than the method followed by British Railways'.

He had second thoughts about whistling on the approach to level crossings though, and on 7 November 1961 informed the road engineer that 'in deference to the noise abatement committee, a train need not whistle while approaching the crossing but need only do so when starting from rest, to cross the road,' which would be covered by rules that require a driver to whistle before moving his engine.

During the course of the afternoon – he did not arrive at Welshpool until after 2pm – he produced a straight-line diagram of the railway, with all crossings, underbridges and other features noted. He also saw the two toastrack carriages and five bogie wagons the company had acquired from the Admiralty's Lodge Hill & Upnor Railway in Kent.

This line had been unusual amongst 2ft 6in gauge military lines in having run a passenger service and its closure on 29 May 1961 made its stock available just at the right time for the railway. Delivered to Welshpool by rail on 28 July, *The Earl*

had been steamed to remove the vehicles for storage in Golfa loop; BR had provided the driver and a company member fired for him, the first steam movement since the last train in 1956. The purchase of the toastrack carriages had been announced the year before (*Coventry Evening Telegraph* 29 August 1960). Three more carriages, two more wagons and two four-wheel vans were obtained from the same source and delivered on 24 November 1961.

The original locomotives had been offered to the company for £654 each in 1960. Despite not being formally withdrawn from stock until 17 August 1961, *The Earl* had been returned to Welshpool and transferred to company ownership on 28 July. At Oswestry it had been stripped down and given a light overhaul by apprentices. Its purchase price was covered by a matching donation from John Wilkins, a Midlands industrialist and owner of the Fairbourne Railway; he became company chairman for two years from 1967. *Countess* was 'condemned' on 27 July 1962, sold on 28 September and delivered to Welshpool on 6 October. Some repairs, including retubing, were carried out at Oswestry.

The new company used the occasion of the return of *The Countess* to run a members' special train to Llanfair. With a flag draped over *The Earl*'s smokebox, and a train comprising a brake van, three ex-Admiralty toastrack carriages, the combination car and the diesel locomotive *Upnor Castle*, the ensemble was captured at Raven Square. The photograph illustrates how it was possible to improve the road and provide a footpath without taking any railway land. The Admiralty stock is in its original livery.

In addition to the locomotives, the company bought the two brake vans, two covered vans, a cattle van and five wagons from BR. Track materials from Welshpool yard were purchased and stored at Castle Caereinion.

Delivery of the new stock and materials to Welshpool provided the company with several opportunities to run trains through the town before the tracks were lifted. The first transfer had actually taken place in 1959, when a member hired a pair of horses to pull stock purchased from BR to Raven Square. The arrival of *Countess*, painted in Cambrian Railways livery, provided an opportunity to transfer the stock to Llanfair, both locos being steamed and members invited to travel.

If the transfer order was made in time, reopening between Llanfair Caereinion and Castle Caereinion was to be on 19 May 1962, Mayman told Robertson on 31 January. The latter conducted two more inspections, that on 20 March being described as unofficial and that on 1 May described as official, but the order was not made in time for the line to be reopened.

Robertson was in hospital when he sent Mayman two pages of handwritten observations on the company's proposed rules in May; Mayman sent them back to Robertson's office saying that he could not read them, 'no doubt he was writing under great difficulty', and asking for a typewritten version to be produced, 'you are probably used to his style.'

Although the company had given in to the ministry's pressure to abandon the Raven Square crossing, Mayman was clearly unhappy about the situation when he wrote to Robertson on 25 July asking for help in getting the county council to provide signs for the level crossings without charge. After telling the company that it [the company] would have to pay for the signs the council had ignored all letters. A colleague of Robertson's persuaded the council to cooperate.

The British Transport Commission (Welshpool and Llanfair) Light Railway (Leasing and Transfer) Order 1962 was made on 3 October 1962, effective from 10 October. A single double-sided sheet, the order provided for the lease or transfer of the railway from the south-west of Raven Square to Llanfair Caereinion on such terms and conditions as could be agreed, and required the approval of the minister in writing before any part of the railway was used for the carriage of passengers.

Subject to certain conditions, provisional written permission to carry passengers between Llanfair Caereinion and Castle Caereinion was given on 5 October 1962. The first fare-paying passenger trains ran on 1 December, three trains from Castle Caereinion being advertised in connection with a fair at Llanfair.

A 25-year lease was agreed, effective from 25 December 1962, with an annual charge of £100 for the first five years, increasing in stages thereafter. There was no renewal option. It was expected that before the term expired the company would be in a position to purchase or would negotiate an extension. In agreeing to lease the line, BR and the British Transport Commission had dealt with the company in a sympathetic manner, for they could have insisted on outright purchase on terms that were extremely difficult if not unsurmountable, which could have delayed the railway's revival or prevented it altogether. It was fortunate that, outside Welshpool, no landowners were clamouring to acquire railway land for non-railway purposes.

Heavy snow and below-zero temperatures in January 1963 prompted a decision to steam *The Earl* to clear the line and carry feedstuffs from Welshpool to snowbound farms. Unfortunately, ice in the flangeway of the Cyfronydd level crossing caused the loco to derail, the driver being quoted (*Birmingham Daily Post* 7 January 1963) as saying, 'We skidded so smoothly that I didn't realise we were derailed until we hit the fence.' The road was closed for several hours until a diesel locomotive effected a rescue.

A resident of Leighton, near Welshpool, was anxious to have the rails removed from the Raven Square crossing 'before Easter, as they are a great danger to motorists', he told

The 1962 light railway order.

the ministry of transport on 4 March 1963. He had apparently had a near miss with a train on the crossing 'some time back' and was pleased to notice that the railway had been 'abolished'. There is no record of what he thought of being told that the railway had not been abolished and that the rails concerned were still vested in BR.

With the opening date set for 6 April 1963, an invitation was sent to Robertson. He returned it on 11 March, pointing out that the intended operation of trains between Welshpool and Castle Caereinion would be illegal and he could have no part of it. As the guests were not fare-paying passengers and the company leased most of the line and had BR's approval to use the remainder, his claim that the opening day operation would be illegal must be questionable.

His final inspection took place on 26 March and he submitted his report on 2 April. Subject to attention being given to some points before the opening and to others as soon as possible thereafter,

The opening train passing along the Lledan brook on 6 April 1963.

he recommended that the provisional approval given for the carriage of passengers between Llanfair Caereinion and Castle Caereinion be confirmed.

Notwithstanding Robertson's concerns about its legality, the reopening train did run from Welshpool on 6 April, sixty years since the railway was opened. Once again, the Earl of Powis, the 5th, was the principal guest. At Llanfair he drove *The Countess* through a ribbon before the train returned to Welshpool where the guests took lunch at the Royal Oak Hotel, another link with the past.

Completing the purchase of the route through the town on 4 April, the council told the new railway operators that it could not be used after August. On 17 August the final last train was run, and track lifting was started two days later. The Church Street crossing was removed on 24 August.

Unlike the Talyllyn and Festiniog Railways, the railway had no facilities for storing or maintaining its rolling stock.

With passenger services having finished in 1931 there was no background of tourism to draw on. Finding out if a business could be made was going to be a long and difficult process, especially as there were years of arrears of track maintenance to be overcome.

The first year's operations earned £675 from 9,000 passengers, sufficient to cover costs but leaving little spare for overheads and maintenance. A £300 loss on the year contributed to a £353 deficit at the year-end. In response the £1 1s membership subscription was doubled.

Progress was made with Robertson's requirements when a detachment of the 60th Railway Regiment, Royal Engineers, Army Emergency Reserve, seventy-seven men, spent eight days on the railway in April/May 1964. Tasks included fettling the track between Castle Caereinion and Sylfaen and laying a run-round loop at Raven Square. A member of the divisional road engineer's

staff passed on 6 May and submitted a note for file to say that a stop block had been built at Raven Square 'and the concrete was still wet'. Noting that 27ft of boundary wall or hedge had been removed and replaced with a post-and-wire fence, he thought that there was insufficient space for passengers to wait to board the train. He had nothing to fear though, for the loop was never brought into regular use.

Services were extended to Sylfaen on 6 June1964, the longer journey expected to

On 16 July 1963 the opportunity was taken to pose *The Earl* with a newly overhauled 0-4-2T on a test run from Oswestry. (B. Roberts)

The lack of weeds suggests that this photograph of the first Raven Square loop was taken not long after the Royal Engineers had built it in 1964. It is probably not well, even at this distance, to draw attention to the serious spelling error made by the creator of the sign on the right. The site of the stop block was lost to the railway when the roundabout was rebuilt in the 1970s.

Upnor Castle shunts the train at Sylfaen on 22 August 1964, a few days before the company decided that the extended service could no longer be sustained. (R.E. Tustin)

increase fare revenue, but in August the difficult decision was taken to cut back services to Castle Caereinion because, despite the army's efforts, the track beyond was inadequate. Despite that setback, 12,935 passengers were carried.

The hardest blow came in the winter, with the discovery that heavy rain on 12/13 December 1964 had increased river levels so much that one of the piers on the Banwy bridge was undermined. Evidence of scouring had been found in 1963 when a repair using bagged concrete had been implemented. It was just over sixty years since A.J. Collin had first dealt with a problem there. With support from members and the public contributing to the £2,750 bill, and the practical support of the Royal Engineers, the bridge was repaired in three phases in April, June and July 1965. It was to be 1997 before the underlying problem was identified, and 1999 before an effective repair was completed.

While the bridge works were in progress trains ran between Llanfair and Heniarth. In the absence of a loop, the loco was detached on arrival and ran into the siding. The train crew then pushed the carriages past it by hand, enabling the loco to be re-attached to return to Llanfair. Passengers were encouraged to inspect the bridge repairs.

Services to Castle Caereinion were resumed on 14 August 1965 and after the track had been relaid and two culverts rebuilt, services were extended to Sylfaen again on 15 July 1972. A series of members' specials to Welshpool to mark the 10th anniversary of reopening run on 12/13 May 1973 coincided with BR's offer to sell the line, a price of £8,000 being agreed. The Wales Tourist Board made a 15-year loan of £3,500 and Welshpool Borough Council contributed £1,000 to the appeal fund. The sale was completed on 12 March 1974.

The Banwy bridge as it was found after the left-hand pier had been undermined in December 1964.

Seen in April 1965, the bridge beams have been jacked up to enable the engineers to build a new pier. (Cutting Edge Images)

The temporary terminus at Heniarth enabled a short journey to be offered, and some revenue earned, while the Banwy bridge was repaired. *The Earl* is seen running forward to rejoin its train after the train crew had pushed the carriages into the siding by hand. In the background passengers can be seen walking up to view the bridge. April 1965. (Cutting Edge Images)

These badges of the Royal Engineers and the Royal Corps of Transport were mounted on the bridge to commemorate its repair. Unfortunately, they were subsequently stolen.

The replacement pier is visible in this view of the railway's Sierra Leone train crossing the bridge. The Hunslet 2-6-2T and four carriages were obtained from the West African state in 1975. The locomotive was built in 1954 and the carriages in 1961, so very modern compared with the remainder of the railway's stock.

A train terminating at Castle Caereinion. As most of the men in sight are wearing jackets and ties the undated photograph might have been taken on the occasion of a company event.

This photograph was taken soon after services to Sylfaen were resumed on 15 July 1972. The hedge was lost to roadworks in 1973. Following the purchase of additional land, a loop was constructed in 1976, removing the need for a second locomotive to shunt the train past its engine before the train could return to Llanfair.

After a five-year rehabilitation project, which included the use of government-sponsored labour from the Manpower Services Commission's Community Enterprise Programme and a £20,000 grant from the Development Board for Rural Wales, the first public trains ran to Welshpool on 18 July 1981 and the 6th Earl of Powis performed the official opening on 16 May 1982.

Ten years later, the station was completed by the addition of an 1863-built timber building relocated from Eardisley station on the Hereford, Hay and Brecon Railway in Herefordshire. A modern toilet block constructed to a sympathetic design and incorporating the roof and doors from the North Staffordshire Railway station at Horninglow was erected alongside it. The building was opened to the public on 17 April 1992 and the Earl of Powis performed the official opening on 25 July. During the speeches the local MP called for the town section to be reinstated, anticipating that with construction of a bypass imminent

the town would need something distinctive to attract visitors. To date his call has fallen on deaf ears but the proposal has been raised, unofficially, on several occasions since.

The development was rewarded twice: a first-class award in the Ian Allan Railway Heritage Awards, and the Montgomeryshire Design Award for 1992. The latter, awarded by the district council, acknowledged its positive contribution to the local environment and the attention to detail.

Soon after it started running trains, and while trying to stabilise its operations, the company had realised that its two original locomotives needed support, and that additional motive power should be obtained. In 1966 a member funded the purchase of *Monarch*, an articulated Bagnall built in 1953, from Bowaters paper mill, Kent, in 1966 but it did not enter service until 1973. Two bogie wagons obtained from the same source in 1975 were adapted to carry ballast.

For its next steam acquisition, the railway looked overseas, to Austria,

Additional land was leased from the Powis estate to enable the railway's ambitions for a terminus at Raven Square to be fulfilled. After the stream was diverted to the edge of the enlarged site a contractor provided the fill to create the level ground needed for the new station, seen here in August 1980.

Raven Square station on 21 September 1981. Although the station infrastructure was incomplete, services had started here on 18 July. The van visible beyond the unfinished signal box acted as a temporary booking office and the locos took water from a tank mounted on a wagon. The signal box, which incorporated a booking office window, was complete when the Earl of Powis performed the official opening ceremony on 16 May 1982.

It was ten years before a scheme to provide permanent passenger facilities at Raven Square was put into effect. Seen on 1 November 1991, the former Midland Railway station building from Eardisley, Herefordshire, is being re-erected while a toilet block is erected behind.

The Countess arrives to disgorge passengers at the completed station on 28 July 1992. The new buildings had been in use from 17 July.

Running in matt black and unnamed, the Franco-Belge 0-8-0T stops at the riverside water tower in September 1970. The tank has been replaced by another at Llanfair. (Cutting Edge Images)

for a locomotive capable of entering service straight away. In 1969 members raised £1,200 to buy an 0-8-0T from Stiermärkische Landesbahnen (Styrian Provincial Railways). Built as a tender loco by Franco Belge for the German military railways in 1944, No 699.01 had been rebuilt as a tank engine in 1957 and was found to be ideally suited to the railway when it entered service in 1970. Its origins, however, did prompt the *Birmingham Daily Post* (6 November 1969) to run the headline 'Rail company buys engine built by Nazis.'

Named *Sir Drefaldwyn* (Montgomeryshire) in 1971, it was not the first rolling stock obtained from overseas, for in April 1968 the Zillertalbahn, also in Austria, had donated four four-wheeled carriages. Six carriages were offered but only four were obtained. In recognition of the links between the two railways, the Austrian line named one of its locos *Castle Caereinion*.

Subsequently, more locomotives were obtained from Antigua, Sierra Leone, Finland, Romania and Taiwan, and carriages from Austria, Sierra Leone and Hungary, the trains gaining a very cosmopolitan appearance as a result. Between 2003 and 2010 a rake of new-build Pickering carriages was added to the fleet, recreating the train that was lost when the GWR withdrew the passenger service in 1931.

One of the highlights of the railway's achievements since 1963 must be the recreation of a Pickering passenger train, replacing that scrapped by the GWR after passenger services had been withdrawn in 1931. The brake composites, the first and last in order of construction, were funded from the railway's own resources. The 3rd class carriage, built second, was funded by a donation from a member, the late John Andrews. Including the underframes and bogies, they were built at the Ffestiniog Railway's Boston Lodge works between 2004 and 2010. Operating during galas, vintage weekends and photo charters, the train is very popular.

A Sierra Leone train arrives at Castle Caereinion on a fine September afternoon in 1999.

The return of *The Countess* to service after sixteen years out of use was marked by a ceremony at Raven Square on 16 August 1986, the dowager Countess of Powis, widow of the 5th Earl, performing the honours in a spritely manner. She was photographed with Ken Fenton, the railway's chairman.

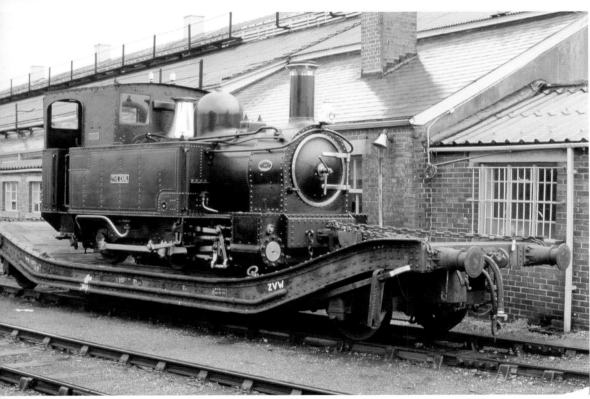

The Earl at the Great Western Society's Didcot depot.

After eight years in service, *The Countess* was withdrawn in need of an overhaul in 1971. Work started in 1978 and was completed in 1986. The dowager Countess of Powis, the widow of the 5th earl, launched it back into service in a ceremony at Raven Square on 16 August 1986. The other original loco, *The Earl*, which remained in service until 1978, had to wait longer to return to service, but in the meantime, from 1979 until 1991 it was displayed at the National Railway Museum, York, the Birmingham Railway Museum, Tyseley, and the Great Western Museum, Didcot, also making an appearance at the Rocket 150 celebrations at Rainhill in May 1980.

Construction and restoration work in progress at Llanfair on 25 September 1993. The western end of the building became the railway's tearoom.

As the company's position stabilised, a programme of building work was carried out to provide facilities and accommodation for all parts of the business, including a workshop, a machine shop and a carriage shed. In 1993 the European Regional Development Fund awarded £139,000 to the £250,000 project to develop Llanfair station. The 1903 goods shed was extended and transformed into a booking office, shop and tearoom, the original station building was renovated, and the temporary buildings dotted around the site removed. The project was completed in 1994.

The tearoom had its origins in a refreshment service that had been started on 27 August 1966, when a mobile tea van equipped with three gas burners had been put into use on the platform at Llanfair. Obtained from British Railways at Shrewsbury, it had been a wartime gift from railwaymen of the Buenos Ayres Great Southern & Midland Railways to their GWR colleagues. Income from catering, and souvenir sales, has made an essential contribution to the railway's vitality over the years.

Another project, carried out in 1994/5, was the construction of a two-storey 32-bed hostel for use by the railway's volunteers. Known as Keyse Cottage, it was named after Stanley Keyse, a volunteer and director, a solicitor by profession, who was a great help to the railway in its early revival days and left it a substantial bequest that was used to fund the building's construction. It replaced a railway sleeping car that had been obtained in 1984.

Good fortune and good neighbours shone on the railway when an electrical fault in a refrigerator started a fire in a van stabled next to the shop at Llanfair on 27 April 1998. Although the fire alarm did not operate the occupants of the house opposite heard the noise and called the fire brigade, which extinguished the fire within thirty minutes. The shop and booking office were gutted and the tearoom sustained smoke damage. The company's insurance covered the damage to the building and its contents, including the establishment of temporary facilities while the repairs were carried out, but not to the van. The premises were reopened in August.

Keyse Cottage, the railway's volunteer hostel, was still being fitted out when photographed on 15 July 1994. The quality of the accommodation plays a big part in encouraging volunteers to engage with the railway and in maintaining their interest.

Seen on 1 May, the aftermath of the fire at Llanfair on 27 April 1998. The interior was gutted.

The Banwy bridge on 5 September 2004 after the underlying problems affecting the troublesome pier had finally been resolved and a replacement constructed and clad. The locomotive is the smallest on the railway, a Barclay 0-4-0T built for Glasgow Corporation's Provan gas works. Acquired by two members in 1969, it was subsequently donated to the railway. Naturally, its small size precludes it seeing much use, but it can still play a useful role. In 2018 it promoted the railway when it visited Taiwan as the guest of the Taiwan Sugar Corporation.

Some members complained when they learned that the summit of the railway's notorious 1 in 29 Golfa bank had been lowered by 30 inches during track works in October 1997, saying that the change had damaged one of the railway's historic original features. The author is unaware of any comments being made when the alignment at the foot of the gradient was altered in 2004, both changes being made to improve conditions for locomotive crews.

After nearly 100 years of use, some of the original rail was in need of replacement. In 1998, 75 tons of nearly new 60lb railway was obtained from South Africa. Later renewals used new rail rolled in the UK, Poland and China. To assist in renewals and maintenance a tamper designed for use in gold mines was obtained from South Africa in 1999 and two bogie ballast wagons were obtained from Romania in 2004. By 2019 72% of the railway's rail has been replaced with heavier material. Some of the original rail has been retained for use in sidings and some was sold to a Romanian railway equipment supplier.

The first new passenger rolling stock since 1973 was obtained in 1999. Two 40ft-long steel-bodied bogie carriages built for the Hungarian State Railways were obtained from the Ciernohronska Forest Railway in Slovakia. Requiring extensive overhauls before they could be put into traffic, the first (No 430) was dealt with in-house, while the second (No 418) was contracted to the Ffestiniog Railway's Boston Lodge works. Both were modified to have open balconies, a popular feature of the Austrian stock, and entered service on 5 June 2003 and 25 August 2005 respectively.

No 418, one of the railway's Hungarian carriages at Llanfair shortly after it had been modified to improve its access for disabled passengers. Both carriages have been adapted in the same manner.

A bequest enabled the issues with the Banwy bridge pier that had caused problems in 1904 and threatened the railway's survival when it was undercut by the river in 1964 to be resolved. Although a repair had been made in 1995 it showed signs of failing. The new work, carried out early in 1999, included removing the base and the army-built pier and building a new base properly anchored to the riverbed, a new concrete pier and cladding with stone. The contract also included shotblasting and painting the bridge's beams and renewal of the walkways.

Charitable status obtained in 1990 opened the way to a £785,000 five-year programme supported by a £495,000 award from the Heritage Lottery Fund that started in 1997. The quality of the application was such that the railway also benefitted for several years from its bid team acting as consultants to other grant applicants.

The biggest investment in the railway since it had been built, these works,

which included overhauling the original locomotives and equipping them with new boilers, tanks and cylinders, and providing a loco shed at Llanfair, were completed in time for the railway's centenary on 5 April 2003, when *Countess* hauled the commemorative train, just as it had done in 1903 and 1963. The 8th Earl of Powis participated in the celebrations, planting a tree at Raven Square station.

Built in 2000/1, the 90ft loco shed accommodates three locomotives. Previously they had been stored outside. With its corrugated cladding, the building is like the original Welshpool shed. It is equipped with a smoke-extraction unit for use when locos are being lit up. With the locos stabled under cover, the railway was able to insulate its locomotive boilers for the first time since 1963.

More storage was added to the railway's estate in 2006 when a single-road carriage shed was erected at Welshpool in 2006.

During centenary celebrations at Raven Square on 4 May 2002, the Earl of Powis poses with the spade and wheelbarrow used in the first sod ceremony in 1901. He was accompanied by company chairman Ken Fenton. In the background is the ex-Pwllheli water tank that had been erected in 2001.

Subsequently enlarged to create a mirror image of the original loco and carriage sheds in Welshpool and then extended westwards in 2019, the building was adapted to provide a space that could be used for rolling stock storage and events.

E.R. Calthrop's intention that the railway should be equipped with 'transportation' wagons was fulfilled in 2009. Not to facilitate transhipment though, but to carry a tractor equipped to trim the railway's lineside hedges, the vehicle's low centre of gravity made it ideally suited for this purpose. The vehicle concerned is 'rollwagen' No W303, which carried standard gauge wagons on the 750mm gauge Zillertalbahn in Austria. It found on a scrap heap in Romania and was overhauled before being delivered to Llanfair.

A serious incident occurred on 3 March 2010 when the railway's Baguley-Drewry personnel carrier ran away for 2.1 miles on the Golfa bank during track works and collided with wagons stabled at Raven Square. Two of the three people on board sustained minor injuries. Built as a standard gauge vehicle, the railcar had been converted to 2ft 6in gauge shortly before the railway acquired it in 2008.

The incident occurred when the driver was in the process of changing ends. An investigation by the Rail Accident Investigation Board established that the interlock designed to prevent movement in this situation could be easily overridden, preventing the brake from being applied when the vehicle started to move. The bulletin issued by RAIB was critical of the railway's processes for assessing the risks of putting the vehicle into service but it did not mention that the railway had consulted with one of the rail industry supervisory bodies before it did so.

Afterwards, the railway's manager was invited to address several industry groups on safety and managing risk. Acting for the railway, he also undertook several consultancy commissions on the same subject. The railcar was repaired and remains in use.

In Welshpool, development of the former Smithfield, cattle market, site by a supermarket funded the restoration of two features of the former railway route through the town. The canal bridge, which the railway had stopped British Railways from demolishing it in June 1963, claiming that an imminent coal delivery would need to be delivered to Llanfair, was restored in 2011 and restoration of the surviving mixed-gauge siding and associated cattle dock was completed in 2019.

Two regular events in the railway's calendar are the annual gala and the operation of Santa specials. The gala is held over the weekend following the August bank holiday and features extra trains, unusual workings, the occasional visiting loco, attractions and stalls. Run during December, the Santa trains are targeted at families and include a journey from Llanfair to Cyfronydd. Both make a worthwhile contribution to the railway's finances.

The 50th anniversary of the railway's revival was commemorated by events held during the annual gala weekend in 2013. A highlight was bringing the original locomotives into Llanfair station, *Countess* pulling the Pickering carriages and *The Earl* decorated as it had been for the last train in 1956.

During a gala it has become customary to arrange the locomotives for a floodlit photography session. On 31 August 2019 visitors were treated to Beyer, Peacock 0-6-0T *Countess*, Franco, Belge 0-6-2T *Zillertal* and Kerr, Stuart 0-6-2T *Joan*.

Santa train operation has been a regular feature of the timetable since 1967. On 19 December 1999 the author was favoured with appropriate conditions for photography. When cold, passengers benefit from the operation of steam heating, one of only two narrow gauge railways in the UK known to provide this type of comfort.

The level crossing at Castle Caereinion was automated in 2015. Following a collision with a car at New Drive crossing on 16 September 2010 the railway reviewed the risks associated with its crossings and this one had been assessed as requiring attention as soon as possible. The road is straight and the traffic fast, and for vehicles leaving the village the crossing is out of sight until the last minute. The lifting barrier installation cost £120,000. The rail at this crossing, and at Coppice Lane and Cyfronydd, had been renewed and laid on concrete foundations in 2011.

In 2016 the railway took the opportunity to buy a factory unit next to its land at Llanfair, paying £280,000 for it, using funds from reserves. Announcing the purchase, the railway said that it intended to develop the site to improve its workshop facilities, including a machine shop, lifting gantry, a woodwork shop and paint shop. Although a plan was produced to show how this could be achieved the railway subsequently scaled back its ambitions and decided to use the building for other purposes.

External funding was obtained for developments in 2018/9. Modifications to the railway's Hungarian carriages to accommodate wheelchair users and the purchase of wheelchair lifts located at Llanfair and Welshpool to use with them was funded by a £42,500 grant awarded by the Rail Safety & Standards Board and brought into use in 2018. The installation of two electric car charging points at Llanfair in 2019 was funded by the tourist amenity investment scheme, a development programme sponsored by the Welsh Government and European agricultural fund for rural development. The £89,000 award included elements for the reinstatement of Cyfronydd's siding and cattle dock and the restoration of a grounded LNWR van body located there,

On 26 March 2016 *The Earl* passes the reinstated waiting shelter at Castle Caereinion. The Heniarth shelter was reinstated at the same time.

The level crossing automation at Castle Caereinion was commissioned in 2015. *Joan* was photographed on 5 April.

HRH Prince Charles, the Prince of Wales, visited the railway on 19 July 2002, meeting staff and volunteers, unveiling a plaque and travelling on the train to Welshpool. He was photographed with chairman Ken Fenton before being presented with the book about the railway.

reinstatement of the loop at Cyfronydd and enhancements to the display/storage sheds at Welshpool.

Innovative and imaginative solutions were found to the prospect of a locomotive shortage in 2020/1. The situation had arisen because both of the railway's original locomotives, which had been reboilered in 2001/2, and the Kerr, Stuart 0-6-2T *Joan*, which had been re-boilered in 2011, required overhauls in quick succession and beyond the capacity of the railway's own resources to deal with in a timely manner. The overhaul of the Franco, Belge 0-8-0T No 699.01 also took longer than expected when faults dating back to its manufacture in 1944 were discovered and addressed.

Two ways through the likely difficulty were found. Firstly, the Vale of Rheidol Railway was contracted to overhaul *The Earl* at its Aberystwyth workshop; with a target completion date of summer 2020, the loco was despatched in June 2019. Then, arrangements were made with the Austrian Zillertalbahn to hire its 1900-built Krauss 'U' 0-6-2T No 2 *Zillertal* for two years.

The arrangement revitalised the railway's relationship with the Austrian line, which had donated four carriages in 1968 and a fifth in 1975. The loco, which had just emerged from an overhaul after a period of use as a hire loco, and one of the carriages had been built for the Zillertalbahn's opening. After four members had been to Austria to be trained

in its operation *Zillertal* arrived in Wales on 13 August 2019. In the next fourteen days it was dismantled to enable its boiler to undergo an out-of-frames examination to ensure compliance with UK requirements and reassembled in time to operate during the annual gala on 30 August-1 September, a remarkable achievement much appreciated by the visitors who saw it and rode behind it over the weekend.

Appendix 12 shows how the railway has been rewarded by the effort in restoring services to Welshpool and in improving facilities at Llanfair, where the tea room attracts passing motorists on non-operating days. It has also benefited from improvements to the road network, prospective passengers in the West Midlands and the North West finding the journey to Montgomeryshire a more pleasant experience than in times gone by.

Over the years the railway's achievements have not gone unnoticed. In December 2002 HRH the Princess Royal presented its representatives with the 'independent railway of the year' award, the judges saying that the railway had 'made great strides and has after many years become a complete railway . . .

with good facilities at each end and plenty of interest in between.' Another royal accolade was bestowed on 19 July 2003 when HRH the Prince of Wales visited the line, travelling from Llanfair to Welshpool.

As noted on page 6, one more accolade was announced in the *London Gazette* on 2 June 2019, the grant of the Queen's Award for Voluntary Service for 'operating an eight-mile steam railway to demonstrate how it served its rural Mid-Wales community from Edwardian times.' Described as 'the MBE for volunteer groups', the award not only provided another link with Buckingham Palace but confirmed the railway's connection with Welshpool, the town that was determined to have a railway to Llanfair, for the nomination had been made by the mayor, Stephen Kaye.

With the benefit of some generous bequests, the railway has reached maturity in a manner unimaginable either to its original promoters or to those who fought so hard for its preservation. Apart from the early years, when finance was a struggle, it has never been through a financial crisis and has money in the bank, a claim that cannot be made by many heritage railways.

The Queen's Award for Voluntary Service was presented at Llanfair on 14 September 2019. On the left, Lord Lieutenant of Powys, Tia Catherine Jones, and railway company chairman Steve Clews hold the certificate. To their left are Deputy Lieutenants Trevor Trevor and David Trant, the award assessors, the latter holding the crystal presented to the railway with the award. (Kevin Heywood)

LOCOMOTIVES

Purchased from British Railways

No 1 0-6-0T *The Earl* Beyer, Peacock 3496/1903, No 822 from 1922; mileage when sold – 213,887

No 2 0-6-0T *The Countess* Beyer, Peacock 3497/1903, No 823 *Countess* from 1922; mileage when sold – 223,162

These locos were not numbered in Cambrian Railways' stock.

PWM1906 Wickham 2904/1940

Acquired by Preservation Company

Number	Name	Wheel arrangement	Builder	Works number	Date	Acquired	Notes
3	*Raven*	4wDM	Ruston	170374	1934	1961	Sold 1974
4	*Upnor Castle*	4wDM	Hibberd	3687	1954	1962	Sold to Festiniog Railway 1968
5	*Nutty*	4wVBT	Sentinel	7701	1929	1964	Owned by Narrow Gauge Museum Trust. Returned in 1971.
6	*Monarch*	0-4-4-0T	Bagnall	3024	1953	1966	Sold 1992, repurchased 2003.
		4wDM	Ruston	191680	1938	1967	Obtained as spares for *Raven*
7	*Chattenden*	0-6-0DM	Baguley	2263	1949	1968	
8	*Dougal*	0-4-0T	Barclay	2207	1946	1969	Visited Taiwan 2018/9
9	*Wynnstay*	0-6-0DM	Fowler	4160005	1951	1969	Sold 1969
10	*Sir Drefaldwyn*	0-8-0T	Franco Belge	2855	1944	1969	Imported from Austria
11	*Ferret*	0-4-0DM	Hunslet	2251	1940	1971	
12	*Joan*	0-6-2T	Kerr, Stuart	4404	1927	1971	Imported from Antigua
14	No 85	2-6-2T	Hunslet	3815	1954	1975	Imported from Sierra Leone
		0-4-0DM	Hunslet	2245	1941	1981	Scrapped 1999
15	*Orion*	2-6-2T	Tubize	2369	1948	1983	Sold to Jokioisten Railway, Finland, 2006
16	*Scooby/Scwbi*	0-4-0DM	Hunslet	2400	1941	1992	Rebuilt 1992, new cab
17	No 764.423	0-8-0T	Resita		1955	2004	Exported to Romania in 2016
		4wDM	Hunslet	6651	1965	2004	Hired April-September
18		6wDM	Diema	4270	1979		Imported from Taiwan
19	No 764.425	0-8-T	Resita		1954	2007	Imported from Romania, exported there in 2016

WELSHPOOL & LLANFAIR RAILWAY ESTIMATE 1887

	Cu yd	Price/yd	£ s d	£ s d
Length of line				10m 2f 8ch
Construction of line	Cu yd	Price/yd	£ s d	£ s d
Earthworks				
Cuttings - rock	13,950	1s 9d	1,220 12 6	
Cuttings - soft soil	158,800	10d	6,616 13 4	
Total	174,050		7,902 5 10	7,902 5 10
Embankments, including roads – 151,800 Cu yd				
Accommodation bridges and works (9)				2,750 0 0
Culverts and drains				900 0 0
Metalling of roads and level crossings				300 0 0
Gatekeepers houses at level crossings				90 0 0
Permanent way, including fencing: cost per mile: 10m 2fg 8ch @ £1,083 0 0				11,210 0 0
Permanent way for sidings and cost of junctions				800 0 0
Stations				2,000 0 0
				27,152 5 10
Contingencies at 5%				1,357 14 2
Total for construction				28,510 0 0
Land and buildings – 45 acres				2,700 0 0
Total cost of construction and of acquisition of land and buildings				31,210 0 0

23 December 1886
Simpson, Davies & Hurst
Engineers

LLANFAIR & MEIFOD VALLEY LIGHT RAILWAY ESTIMATE

Railway No 1				13m 7f 7.5ch
Gauge				4ft 8½in
Construction of line	Cu yd	Price/yd	£ s d	£ s d
Earthworks				
Cuttings - rock	19,870	3s	2,980 10 0	
Cuttings - soft soil	74,915	1s 3d	4,682 3 9	
Roads	750	1s 3d	46 17 6	
Total			7,709 11 3	7,709 11 3
Embankments, including roads – Cu yd	69,738			
Bridges – Public Roads – Number 2				700 0 0
Accommodation bridges and works				1,614 0 0
Viaducts (Bridge over Shropshire Union Canal)				457 0 0
Culverts and drains				750 0 0
Metalling of roads and level crossings				100 0 0
Gatekeepers houses at level crossings, including gates and signals				1,684 0 0
Permanent way, including fencing cost per mile: 13m 7fg 7.50ch @ £1,400/mile				19,556 5 0
Permanent way for sidings and cost of junctions				2,026 0 0
Stations				1,680 0 0
Contingencies at 7½%				2,720 0 0
Land and buildings: 78a 1r 24p				2,346 10 0
Total cost of construction and of acquisition of land and buildings				£41,343 6 0

John E. Thomas
Engineer

ESTIMATE OF PROPOSED LIGHT RAILWAY 1897

Railway No 1				9m 1f 1½ch
Gauge				2ft 6in
Construction of line	Cu yd	Price/yd	£ s d	£ s d
Earthworks				
Cuttings - rock	3,880	3s	582 0 0	
Cuttings - soft soil	37,551	1s 4d	2,503 8 0	
Roads	160	2s 6d	20 0 0	
Total			3,105 8 0	3,105 8 0
Embankments, including roads – Cu yd	33,720			
Accommodation bridges and works				275 0 0
Viaducts				800 0 0
Culverts and drains				614 0 0
Metalling of roads and level crossings				567 0 0
Gatekeepers houses at level crossings				
Permanent way, including fencing and heavy permanent way through streets: cost per mile: 9m 1fg 1.5ch @ £950/mile				8,682 0 0
Permanent way for sidings and cost of junctions				1,275 0 0
Stations				1,390 0 0
				16,690 8 0
Contingencies at 10%				1,669 0 0
Land and buildings				2,950 0 0
Total cost of construction and of acquisition of land and buildings				21,309 8 0

Calthrop & Ward
Engineers

AMENDED ESTIMATE 1901

Railway No 1				9m 1f 1 1/2ch
Gauge				2ft 6in
Construction of line	Cu yd	Price/yd	£ s d	£ s d
Earthworks				
Cuttings - rock	3,000	3s 6d	525 0 0	
Cuttings - soft soil	61,000	1s 4d	4,066 13 0	
Total			4,591 13 0	4,591 13 0
Embankments, including roads – Cu yd				
Accommodation bridges and works				3,973 11 0
Viaducts				1,899 12 6
Culverts and drains				1,350 0 0
Metalling of roads and level crossings				600 0 0
Gatekeepers houses at level crossings				
Permanent way, including fencing and heavy permanent way through streets: cost per mile: 9m 1fg 1.5ch @ £950/mile				10,926 10 0
Permanent way for sidings and cost of junctions				1,500 0 0
Stations				2,000 0 0
				26,841 6 6
Contingencies at 10%				2,688 13 6
Total for construction				29,530 0 0
Land and buildings				2,950 0 0
Total cost of construction and of acquisition of land and buildings				32,480 0 0

This Cambrian Railways point lever is still in regular use at Llanfair.

WELSHPOOL & LLANFAIR LIGHT RAILWAY STATEMENT AS TO TOTAL COST SHOWING INCREASES ON STATEMENT FURNISHED TO HM TREASURY IN MAY 1902

Railway No 1	9m 1f 1½ch	
Gauge	2ft 6in	
	Estimate 1902	Actual cost
Construction of line	£ s d	£ s d
Earthworks	7,240 0 0	8,990 0 0
Accommodation bridges and works	3,854 0 0	2,224 0 0
Viaducts and bridges	2,683 0 0	5,100 0 0
Culverts and drains	1,070 0 0	1,650 0 0
Metalling of roads and level crossings	785 0 0	730 0 0
Permanent way, including fencing, interlockings and telegraphs Permanent way for sidings and cost of junctions	15,554 0 0	17,212 0 0
Stations	1,575 0 0	2,664 0 0
Land and buildings	6,300 0 0	6,753 0 0
Sum expended on house retained		105 0 0
Rolling stock	5,500 0 0	5,500 0 0
Expenses, engineers fees, legal and other expenses	3,400 0 0	3,630 0 0
Miscellaneous, including interest on loans during construction and costs of local authorities in connection therewith and other incidental expenses	1,900 0 0	1,386 0 0
	50,271 0 0	59,345 0 0
Value of land given by landowners	2,400 0 0	2,400 0 0
	52,671 0 0	59,345 0 0
Additional works required not yet executed		3,540 0 0
Total cost of railway and equipment		62,985 0 0

CAPITAL ACCOUNT 1902/3

Income

	To 31 December 1902 £ s d	To 26 June 1903 £ s d	Total £ s d
Share capital – cash received	13,546 10 0	232 5 0	13,778 15 0
Bank interest allowed	111 8 11		111 8 11
Sundry receipts for registration fees etc.	15 0	7 6	1 2 6
Rents received	17 17 6	5	22 17 6
Sale of timber, hay etc.	38 0 6		38 0 6
Loans (less instalments of principal repaid)	15,350 0 0	101 1 6 cr	15,248 18 6
Law costs recovered	4 16 0	1 0	4 17 0
Treasury free grant	7,250 0 0	10,250 0 0	17,500 0 0
	36,319 7 11	10,386 12 0	46,705 19 11
Lloyds Bank Limited (General a/c) amount at debit			4,715 3 1

Outgoings

Legal and preliminary expenses – payments made	1,002 4 5		1,002 4 5
General and office expenses	110 9 3		110 9 3
Engineer – payments on account	1,350 0 0		1,350 0 0
Board of Trade – fee on applying for amendment order	50 0 0		50 0 0
Bank charges	119 19 9		119 19 9
Deposit with Board of Trade	1,000 0 0		1,000 0 0
Salaries – secretary and auditors	77 2 4	6 5 0	83 7 4
Land claims and compensation	5,295 3 2	443 17 2	5,739 0 4
Expenses cutting first sod	22 10 9		22 10 9
Construction – payments made per Cambrian Company - £23,837 5 6			
Construction – other payments - £36 18 6	20,705 2 0	3,169 2	23,874 4 0
Permanent way materials	5,202 8 7	34 9 1	5,236 17 8
Locomotives and rolling stock	3,669 10 9	2,236 15 4	5,906 6 1
Shropshire Union Railway & Canal Company – for stoppage of navigation	10 0 0		10 0 0
Costs re loans	269 11 0		269 11 0
Rates and taxes	6 5	2 17 8	3 4 1
Signalling and telegraphs	200 0 0	150 0 0	350 0 0
Engine and carriage shed	280 0 0		280 0 0
Stations and buildings	350 0 0	50 0 0	400 0 0
Weighbridge	60 0 0		60 0 0

Seven Stars cottage		106 7 4	106 7 4
Interest on loans		455 5 2	455 5 2
Income tax on interest	15 15 5	15 15 3 cr	2
	39,875 5 6	6,689 18 6	46,565 4 0
Lloyds Bank Limited (Construction a/c) amount at credit – £4,775 6 10			
North & South Wales Bank Limited amount at credit – £67 9 9			
Secretary – cash in hand – £13 2 5			4,855 19 0
			£51,421 3 0

Countess at the end of the line in the 1920s.

LOANS

From whom received	Amount £	Rate of Interest	Terms
Montgomery County Council	1,000	3⅛%	50 years from 2 December 1901
Montgomery County Council	6,000	3½%	50 years from 23 December 1901
Welshpool Town Council	5,000	3⅛%	50 years from 16 July 1902
Llanfyllin Rural District Council	2,600	3¾%	50 years from 27 December 1901
Forden Rural District Council	750	3¾%	50 years from 21 February 1902
Treasury	5,700	3¼%	Ten years from 5 July 1905
	£21,050		

The Birmingham Locomotive Club's 1949 excursion stops for water, an unusual view that shows the top of the water tank. (Cutting Edge Images)

REVENUE 1903-22

	1903	1904	1905	1906	1907	1908	1909	1910	1911	1912	1913
Passenger traffic	£1,167	£1,352	£1,365	£1,406	£1,323	£1,84	£1,265	£1,239	£1,226	£1,213	£1,318
Mail, parcels &c	£108	£219	£177	£180	£176	£170	£184	£189	£182	£184	£178
Merchandise	£852	£1,057	£735	£723	£824	£871	£936	£922	£1,016	£883	£782
Minerals	£521	£566	£631	£640	£669	£548	£557	£551	£520	£714	£674
Livestock	£9s	£12	£10	£15	£19	£30	£35	£54	£94	£88	£90
Rent and miscellaneous		£1	£1	£1	£2	£2	£3	£3	£4	£5	£7
	£2,659	£3,209	£2,920	£2,967	£2,913	£2,907	£2,981	£2,960	£3,046	£3,088	£3,049
Working expenses	£1,595	£1,925	£1,752	£1,780	£1,748	£1, 744	£1,788	£1,776	£1,828	£1,853	£1,829

	1914	1915	1916	1917	1918	1919	1920	1921	1922
Rent and miscellaneous	£1	£1	£1	£1	£2	£36	£17	£10	£46
Share of operating revenue	£1,188	£1,232	£1,234	£1,235	£1,234	£1,240	£1,239	£1,235	£1,236
Received by company	£1,189	£1,233	£1,235	£1,236	£1,236	£1,276	£1,255	£1,245	£1,282

The Earl at Golfa with a good load of coal in 1956.

CAMBRIAN RAILWAYS PERSONNEL EMPLOYED ON NARROW GAUGE RAILWAYS

Locomotive department (RAIL92/142)

Welshpool

	Date of birth	Joined		Wages/day	
George Owen	2 October 1882	18 August 1902	Cleaner Fireman Passed fireman	2s 4d 3s – 12s 17 December 1919 – 12s	Joined at Oswestry, fireman at Welshpool from 1910. Did not strike in August 1911. On strike 26 September – 6 October 1919
Frederick William Evans	6 January 1885	22 March 1904	Cleaner Passed cleaner Fireman (9 April 1910)	2s 4d 2s 4d – 2s 8d 2s 8d – 12s	Most of service at Welshpool with spells at Oswestry and Kerry. Transferred to Kerry as passed fireman on 12 January 1922. Did not strike in August 1911. On strike 26 September – 6 October 1919
Parey Ernest Evans	9 July 1890	18 May 1908	Cleaner Passed cleaner Fireman	2s 2s 4d – 2s 8d 3s 4d 12s	Most of service at Welshpool, three years at Oswestry. Did not strike in August 1911. On strike 26 September – 6 October 1919
David Harold Humphrey	23 September 1890	16 July 1908	Cleaner Passed cleaner Fireman	2s 2s 4d 3s 4d – 11s	Most of service at Welshpool, two years at Oswestry. Did not strike in August 1911. On strike 26 September – 6 October 1919
William Henry Humphreys	24 July 1893	21 June 1910	Cleaner Passed cleaner Fireman	2s – 2s 4d 2s 4d – 2s 8d 3s 2d – 11s	All service at Welshpool. Did not strike in August 1911. On strike 26 September – 6 October 1919

These were the only loco crew based at Welshpool so might be assumed to have worked on the light railway. Drivers were presumably rostered from Oswestry. Before 1910 George Owen's service as cleaner and passed cleaner alternated between Oswestry and Welshpool. While he was a passed cleaner at Welshpool in May 1904 he was suspended for two days 'for neglect of duty by failing to test gauge taps on their [sic] engine, thus causing boiler to be short of water and lead plugs to drop', an incident which might, therefore, have occurred on the light railway.

OUTDOOR STAFF – GOODS DEPARTMENT

Welshpool station – new appointment in connection with transhipment of Llanfair traffic (RAIL92/145)

	Date of birth	Joined		Wages/week	
R.H. Parry	18 May 1873	10 March 1903	Goods porter	16s	Resigned 5 January 1904
David E. Davies	24 October 1884	20 May 1902	Goods porter	15s	Dismissed for pilfering 29 August 1904
William [Herbert] Waring	13 October 1885	23 August 1904	Goods porter	16s	Resigned 7 July 1905
John Evans	1 February 1875	14 April 1919	Temporary goods porter	£2 17s - £3 3s	Resigned 9 May 1921. Maximum pay £3 7s on 1 January 1921.
Donald McTavish	21 October 1888	11 July 1921	Temporary goods porter	£2 18s	Services dispensed with on 18 November 1921
John Eveson	18 May 1890	3 December 1919	Goods porter	£2 14s - £2 8s	Ellesmere 26 February 1923

Llanfair Railway – Welshpool station

	Date of birth	Joined		Wages/week	
George Griffiths	12 March 1875	19 January 1903	Transhipping goods porter	17s - 18s	Resigned 1 August 1904
Thomas Walker Jones	8 July 1883	9 November 1903	Transhipping goods porter	17s	Resigned 26 July 1905
Henry Edwards	28 September 1883	19 September 1904	Transhipping goods porter	17s	Resigned 12 May 1908
Albert R. Watkins	30 May 1884	16 July 1908	Transhipping goods porter	16s - 17s	Resigned 19 October 1909
George Griffiths	12 March 1875	19 October 1909	Transhipping goods porter	17s - 18s	Called up 9 November 1914
Walter A. Beedles	25 September 1892	9 November 1914	Goods porter	17s - £2 10s	Pay increased to £3 6s by 1 October 1920 then reduced
George A. Lloyd	12 November 1893	30 April 1919	Goods porter	£2 10s	Pay reduced to £2 8s on 1 July 1922

Llanfair Caereinion

	Date of birth	Joined		Wages/week	
H. Tudor	10 June 1879	5 November 1919	Temporary goods porter	£2 17s - £2 18s	Pay increased to £3 6s by 1 October 1920 then reduced. Services dispensed with on 3 December 1921.

Station staff uniform men (RAIL92/146)

Welshpool station, Llanfair staff

	Date of birth	Joined		Wages/week	
Charles Done	4 June 1882	7 May 1898	Train porter	18s	Services dispensed with 9 June 1905
Clement Lewis	9 June 1882	5 July 1899	Train porter	18s	Talgarth 1 February 1906
David G. Blockley	4 October 1883	April 1900	Train porter	18s - £1	Shunter 2 February 1912
W.F.G. Lloyd	3 May 1876	12 December 1904	Train porter	18s	Pool Quay 16 May 1912
Charles E. Preece	6 September 1890	2 April 1907	Porter guard	17s - 18s	Porter 8 July 1918, foreman 19 August 1919.
Fred E. Thomas	9 August 1894	14 June 1910	Porter	15s	Platform porter 13 February 1919
Edward Foulkes	22 November 1895	7 October 1914		16s - £2 9s	Pay peaked at £3 9s 6d on 1 January 1921
George J. Phely	28 July 1871	11 February 1886	Relief man	£1 - £1 1s	Porter, Pool Quay 7 November 1900
John George	8 September 1875	4 November 1890	Relief man	£1 3s	Machynlleth 14 March 1901
D. Gilbert Blockley	4 October 1883	April 1900	Booking porter	13s 5d - 16s	Train porter 1 February 1906
John Smith	18 July 1884	21 January 1901	Booking porter	16s	Incapacitated owing to ill health 5 February 1906
Richard Jones	19 November 1884	6 October 1902	Booking porter	16s	Resigned 1 November 1906
Richard J. Leighton	26 April 1887	2 April 1902	Booking porter	15s	Resigned 28 March 1908
William H. Roberts	27 November 1888	29 December 1905	Booking porter	14s	Incapacitated owing to ill health 20 August 1908

Llanfair Railway – Welshpool station

	Date of birth	Joined		Wages/week	
Evan H. Humphreys	11 June 1872	16 November 1892	Guard	£1 4s	Checker Oswestry 13 July 1903
John Pritchard	17 January 1863	1 July 1890	Guard	£1 4s	Talsarnau 3 December 1913
Henry Lewis	29 November 1872	1 October 1895	Guard	£1 8s - £3 5s	Pay peaked at £4 3s 6d on 1 January 1921

Llanfair Caereinion station

	Date of birth	Joined		Wages/week	
William R. Edwards	11 September 1879	8 July 1902	Porter	16s	Resigned 28 August 1906
George Roberts	2 February 1855	10 June 1873	Porter	17s	Llanfechain 18 January 1901
John L. Williams	9 March 1890	28 November 1907	Porter	13s - 15s	Resigned 28 January 1913
Frank Humphreys	20 December 1895	31 January 1913	Porter	15s	Resigned 31 January 1914
D. Richard Jones	21 September 1893	2 February 1914	Porter	15s	Resigned 7 July 1914
Edward Foulkes	22 November 1895	7 October 1914	Porter	15s	Welshpool 9 August 1919
James Herbert Brown	12 April 1898	4 August 1919	Temporary porter	15s	Resigned 10 September 1919
Humphrey Tudor	10 June 1879	3 November 1919	Temporary porter	18s	Transferred to goods 29 December 1919
Joseph George Hughes	10 April 1905	2 February 1920	Porter	10s - £1 5s	Maximum pay was £1 14s on 2 February 1921
Albert James	25 May 1886	23 March 1903	Junior porter	9s - 10s	Newtown 27 November 1907
John L. Williams	9 March 1890	28 November 1907	Junior porter	10s	Porter 1 February 1909
William Pritchard	22 May 1892	1 February 1909	Junior porter	10s	Bettisfield 11 August 1910

Between 1940 and 1949 three standard gauge carriage bodies were installed at Llanfair to provide additional warehousing space. Used as living accommodation by volunteers in the 1960s, conditions in this former brake-composite carriage were described as 'insanitary' when the directors were being persuaded to invest in the Doncaster-built sleeping car which replaced it in October 1969. (Michael Bishop)

REVENUE 1960-2018

	1960	1961	1962	1963	1964	1965	1966	1967	1968	1969
Income			£1,191	£2,742	£3,788	£2,798		£2,844	£4,252	
Expenditure			£1,603	£3,042	£3,998	£3,059		£3,520	£3,763	
Net income			£412	£300	-£210	-£261		-£676	£489	
Carried forward										

1970	1971	1972	1973	1974	1975	1976	1977	1978	1979
£2,898	£2,604			£4,637	£4,155	£10,759	£4,418	£4,998	£17,888
£1,968	£2,207			£2,249	£3,131	£16,172	£4,513	£5,454	£12,221
£930	£397			£2,388	£1,024	-£5,413	£95	-£456	£5,667

1980	1981	1982	1983	1984	1985	1986	1987	1988	1989
£21,374	£26,425	£35,094	£79,953	£84,167	£88,058	£87,228	£83,370	£86,723	£108,841
£13,807	£13,874	£18,227	£77,804	£82,673	£86,405	£85,003	£78,569	£72,589	£90,680
£7,567	£12,551	£16,867	£2,149	£1,494	£1,653	£2,225	£4,801	£14,134	£21,244

1990	1991	1992	1993	1994	1995	1996	1997	1998	1999
£128,055	£327,926	£178,215	£190,572	£202,459	£149,162	£159,157	£273,659	£469,453	£377,442
£99,870	£139,495	£168,902	£184,145	£218,980	£159,901	£172,927	£167,115	£208,550	£220,540
£28,185	£188,431	£9,313	£6,427	-£16,521	-£10,739	-£13,770	£106,544	£260,903	£156,902
					£339,470	£466,705	£573,249	£834,152	£993,054

2000	2001	2002	2003	2004	2005	2006	2007	2008	2009
£280,140	£303,798	£451,209	£322,209	£400,289	£413,151	£977,411	£494,585	£504,059	£722,110
£228,324	£282,572	£325,789	£298,699	£438,928	£386,275	£361,934	£489,774	£477,577	£580,192
£51,816	£109,085	£125,420	£43,257	-£38,639	£26,876	£615,477	£4,811	£26,482	£141,918
£1,044,870	£1,146,955	£1,262,835	£1,309,612	£1,276,893	£1,319,269	£1,947,746	£1,952,157	£1,902,639	£2,053,557

2010	2011	2012	2013	2014	2015	2016	2017	2018
£512,527	£493,965	£476,162	£479,476	£511,193	£719,673	£588,148	£596,254	£1,113,732
£601,628	£573,858	£585,139	£596,160	£554,431	£526,741	£562,748	£741,532	£618,225
-£89,101	-£79,893	-£108,977	-£115,684	-£43,238	£201,932	£44,400	-£127,699	£444,474
£1,983,956	£1,895,063	£1,795,586	£1,700,902	£1,672,664	£1,874,596	£1,918,996	£1,791,297	£2,103,425

APPENDIX 13

GENERAL MANAGERS 1960-2020

D.T. Edwards	1960-1
David Crathorn	June 1962 – September 1962
Michael Polglaze	September 1962 – 31 October 1971
Major Michael Ilott	1 March – 31 August 1972
Ralph Russell	1 March 1973 – October 1988
Andy Carey	October 1988 – March 1999
Terry Turner	3 May 1999 – 31 October 2014
Charles Spencer	March 2015 –

APPENDIX 14

COMPANY CHAIRMEN 1960-2020

Sir Thomas Henry Salt	1960 – 1965
Sir David Williams	1965 – 1967
John C. Wilkins	1967 – 1970
Kenneth Charles Fenton	1970 – 2005
D. Alan Higgins	2005 – 2014
I. McLean	2014 – 2015
S.G Clews	2015 –

BIBLIOGRAPHY

Baxter, Bertram; *Stone Blocks and Iron Rails (Tramroads)*; David & Charles, 1966

Boyd, J.I.C.; *Narrow Gauge Railways in Mid-Wales*; Oakwood Press, 2nd edition, 1970

Calthrop, E.R.; Light Railway Construction; *RE Professional Papers* No IX, 1897

Cartwright, Ralph & Russell, R.T.; *The Welshpool & Llanfair Light Railway*; David & Charles, 1972, 1981, 1989

Cartwright, Ralph I.; *The Welshpool & Llanfair*; RailRomances, 2002

Cozens, Lewis; *The Welshpool & Llanfair Light Railway*; Author, 1951

Davies, A. Stanley; Early Railways of the Ellesmere and the Montgomeryshire Canals, 1794-1914; *Transactions of the Newcomen Society*, 1942/3

Gasquoine, C.P.; *The Story of the Cambrian – a biography of a railway*; Woodall, Minshall, Thomas & Co, 1922

Gratton, Robert; *The Leek & Manifold Valley Light Railway*; RCL Publications, 2005

Johnson, Peter; *The Cambrian Railways – a new history*; Oxford Publishing Co, 2013

Mawson, E.O; *Pioneer Irrigation*; Crosby Lockwood, 1904 (with additional chapters on light railways by E.R. Calthrop)

Oxley, J. Stewart; *Light Railways Procedure*; Jordan & Sons/W. Hay Fielding, 1901

Welshpool & Llanfair Light Railway; *Traveller's Guide*; Welshpool & Llanfair Light Railway, 2005

Williams, Glyn; *The Welshpool & Llanfair Light Railway*; Wild Swan, 2010

For many years the occupants of Cyfronydd Hall played a significant role in propoals to develop the railway between Welshpool and Llanfair, and then in its promotion, construction and operation. In 2015 the former Foreign Secretary Lord Hague of Richmond and his wife made it their home, becoming good friends of the railway and visiting regularly with family and friends. They were photographed during their visit to the 2015 gala.

INDEX

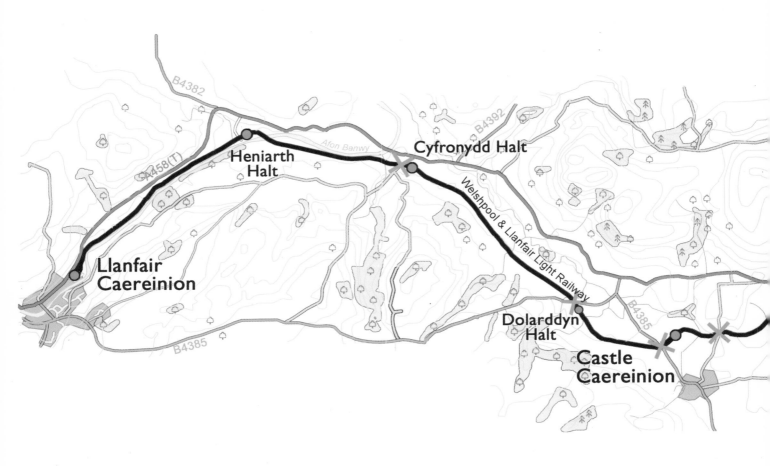

Heniarth
Halt

Cyfronydd Halt

Welshpool & Llanfair Light Railway

Llanfair
Caereinion

Dolarddyn
Halt

Castle
Caereinion

B4382

A458(T)

Afon Banwy

B4392

A458

B4385

B4385

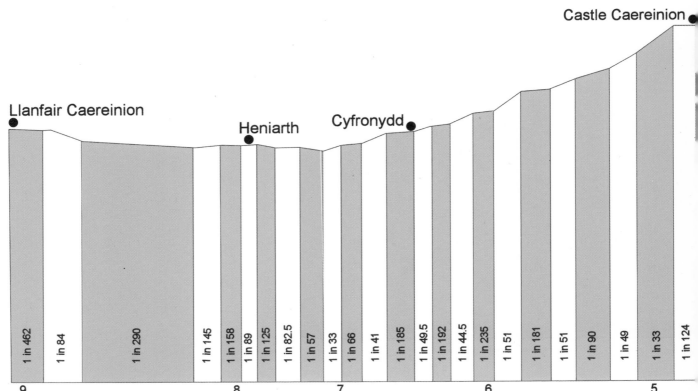

Castle Caereinion

Llanfair Caereinion

Heniarth

Cyfronydd

| 1 in 462 | 1 in 84 | 1 in 290 | 1 in 145 | 1 in 158 | 1 in 89 | 1 in 125 | 1 in 82.5 | 1 in 57 | 1 in 33 | 1 in 66 | 1 in 41 | 1 in 185 | 1 in 49.5 | 1 in 192 | 1 in 44.5 | 1 in 235 | 1 in 51 | 1 in 181 | 1 in 51 | 1 in 90 | 1 in 49 | 1 in 33 | 1 in 124 |

9   8   7   6   5